Terry and Howard.
Hollywood Couldn't Invent
a Love Story Like Theirs.

Dear Howard,

You were absolutely right when you told me I'd never find what we had together again. I have loved you consciously and unconsciously my whole life. My only regret is we've spent all these years apart.

The only marriage I've ever believed in is ours—and I know now I'd like to spend the rest of my life with you.

By now we both realize how short a lifetime really is, I'd like to share eternity with you.

Oh, Howard, I've had to fight it so hard alone. Romantics like us with a lot of imagination will always be called crazy. I've had my own flying boats through the years, but like you I swear I'll get it off the ground.

I always knew it would be my love that would outlast everyone else's.

All my love,
Terry

The Beauty and the Billionaire

Terry Moore

PUBLISHED BY POCKET BOOKS NEW YORK

Distributed In Canada by PaperJacks Ltd., a Licensee
of the trademarks of Simon & Schuster, Inc.

Another *Original* publication of POCKET BOOKS

POCKET BOOKS, a division of Simon & Schuster, Inc.
1230 Avenue of the Americas, New York, N.Y. 10020
In Canada distributed by PaperJacks Ltd.,
330 Steelcase Road, Markham, Ontario

ISBN: 0-671-50080-5

First Pocket Books printing May, 1984

10 9 8 7 6 5 4 3 2 1

I dedicate this book to my mother . . .
the greatest friend I ever had,
and my sons,
Stuart Warren Cramer and
Grant Lamar Cramer.

Acknowledgments

This book was made possible through the love and devotion of Jerry Rivers, who believed in my talent when no one else did.

My heartfelt thanks to William Brian Lowry, who blocked and researched this book while I was busily writing it, and to authors Jess Stearn and Bob Slatzer.

I wish to acknowledge the dearest friends in the world: Angelo and Carmen Mariani, Jim Keenan, Randy Shields, Hap Houseman, Brad Larsen of Lowry and Larsen Entertainment, and my beloved brother, Wallace Koford.

Special thanks to L'Ermitage Hotel in Beverly Hills, The Dunes Hotel in Las Vegas, the Hilton Riviera in Palm Springs, and to Richard Tovar.

And last to Poppa, whose spirit was always with me.

My Preface

I AM THE FIRST WOMAN TO WRITE ABOUT HER LIFE WITH Howard Hughes. We were together from 1948 to 1956, and he is still in my thoughts every day of my life. There have been dozens of books written by men: men who never laid eyes on him, men who worked for him, though never an intimate friend. No woman has ever written about Howard, yet he spent most of his life with women; he much preferred the company of women to that of men.

People all over the world all ask the same question, "What was Howard Hughes really like?" This book cannot be read without having an insight into this wonderful man: his aspirations, his dreams, the women he loved and who loved him, and the tragedy that befell him.

He was my lover, my adversary, my father, and my husband. From the moment we first met, an eternity ago, my life has been inextricably wound around his like the spirals of a double helix. It was useless to marry again when I was so tied to the man. I would lie in another's arms, but in the moment of supreme passion call out his name.

When we finally parted, his life began a rapid descent. I was too young then, too selfish. I should have stayed by his side regardless of the consequences, for he was my living soul.

If I had stayed, the world today would probably still have Howard Robard Hughes. It would have had the real man for the past twenty years, instead of the emaciated recluse, and the great wealth and power he accumulated would have gone toward the betterment of mankind.

Howard was one of history's greatest visionaries. He dreamed of world peace and a cure for cancer. He dreamed not of better wheelchairs, but of seeing the crippled walk again.

He made every personal sacrifice as a reminder of his personal debt to humanity. He lived like a pauper, asking for nothing except peace and privacy to work on his inventions.

There are people who go back to his beginnings, who worked side by side with him, flew with him, shared laughter and tears with him, and—most important—loved him. These are the people who have never written a book or talked to the press. These are the people who have come to me and asked that the real truth be told about "The Man."

Prologue

WHAT WAS IT THAT EVERYBODY WANTED TO KNOW ABOUT Howard Hughes? What was it that everybody envied? What was it that all the women and all the men, even those who supposedly had everything, wanted to know about Howard Hughes? They all wanted to know about *Howard and his women*.

But before I tell you about Howard's women, let me tell you a little about Howard the man.

Howard Robard Hughes was a creative, daring, charming, caring, secretive, powerful, manipulative, warm, eccentric, patriotic, sympathetic man, a genius, an adventurer, a billionaire playboy, and a great lover.

He was born December 24, 1905, in Houston, Texas. He

was the only child of a well-to-do father and a mother who was obsessed with her child's well-being the way an auto mechanic monitors the performance of a race car. She was constantly concerned with his physical, mental, and social abilities and was phobic regarding sickness; she scrutinized his diet, hygiene, weight, skin color, and even his bowel movements.

Howard's childhood wasn't a very happy one. He spent much of his youth away from home at camps and private schools but was quite the loner and made no close friends. Howard said he possessed a great craving for love and physical affection, but the only time he got the much-needed attention was when he was ill. As he neared his teens, he was considered sickly and spent most of his hours in isolation. At age thirteen, Howard mysteriously lost the use of his legs and was confined to a wheel-chair. His parents were frantic, and their exhibition of care and concern put him back on his feet in a few months.

When he was completely recovered, he was sent back east to school. During this semester Howard took his first airplane ride and loved it. After the school term, his parents placed him in Thatcher, a private school in California, where he spent most of his free time alone, riding his horse in the hills.

In the spring of 1922, when Howard was sixteen, he was suddenly called back to Houston. His beautiful, seemingly healthy mother had died. His father, Howard, Senior, was devastated and began traveling so as not to face the painful memories. He finally settled in California and pulled Howard out of school so he could spend some time with his son. They also spent some time with his father's brother, Rupert, who was a screenwriter. It was the beginning of Howard's lifelong love of the world of make-believe and movies.

Since Howard hadn't graduated from school, his father bought his way into college, first the California Institute of Technology in Pasadena, California, near Howard,

Senior, and then the Rice Institute in Houston. Howard returned to Houston alone; his father still couldn't face going back.

In January of 1924, Howard, Senior, did go home and, shockingly, suffered a fatal heart attack. Howard was crushed. In less than two years, he'd lost both his parents. He was nineteen.

He cut himself off from the families of his deceased parents and their attempts to gain control of his inheritance. He refused a guardian and refused to go back to school deciding that he would operate his father's tool company; it manufactured a unique drill bit, used for oil exploration the world over. There was considerable opposition from the family, but he was legally declared by the court to be of age. He took charge of the business and immediately bought out any family members who owned a piece of the company, giving himself one hundred percent control.

In May of 1925, the nineteen-year-old Howard Hughes executed a will leaving almost everything he had to medical research. It was a mature man's dream for humanity and a tribute to his late father.

Later that year, he married Ella Rice, a Houston society girl, and moved off to California.

Howard's fascination with flying grew into a passion. He received his pilot's license in 1928. In the same year, while producing *Hell's Angels,* a flying film in Hollywood, he had his first plane crash. He was knocked unconscious and underwent surgery for a crushed cheekbone. Four months later he separated from his wife; they divorced in December, 1929.

In 1932, Howard founded Hughes Aircraft Corporation in California for the manufacture of airplanes.

In 1935, he set the new land speed record in an airplane.

In 1936 and 1937, he went on to set two new transcontinental speed records.

In 1938, Howard established a new record for flying around the world.

3

In 1942, he became involved in the war effort; designing and manufacturing planes for the United States government.

In 1943, Howard had his second crash. The plane plunged into Lake Mead; the two men with him died, but Howard escaped with minor head injuries.

Howard disappeared in 1944. Some believe that he suffered a nervous breakdown during this time; others hold that he was secretly involved in the war effort. It *is* known that he was arrested for vagrancy in Louisiana and spent some time in Florida. I'm certain about his Florida sojourn because he often spoke so fondly of a waitress he met there. It seems she took pity on the woebegone wanderer who often sat in the diner where she worked. Howard never lost that little-boy look; there was such a gentle kindness and trust about him that you wanted to put your arms around him and protect him from the cruel world. And that's exactly what that lovely lady did, never dreaming that the tall stranger was Howard Hughes.

I write this story hoping she's still alive and able to read this, because I'd like her to know that Howard never forgot her. He was so thrilled that this lady, who never knew his true identity, befriended him, gave him money and took care of him. It made him feel special, and loved. If through her life a rainbow always appeared when she needed it most, I'm sure that tall, lanky stranger had something to do with it. It was his way: he gave the most when no one suspected.

It was during this period that I believe that Howard was involved in the war effort, and in a power play in the West Indies that also involved Sir Harry Oakes, a multimillionaire whose murder in 1943 was never solved.

In 1946, Howard crashed again, this time in Beverly Hills on a test flight of the XF-11. He suffered a severe blow and lacerations to the head, broken ribs on both sides of his chest, and a collapsed lung, and the left side of his body was badly burned and bruised. He was in critical condition

4

for several days and spent many weeks recovering. This crash, in addition to the ones in 1928 and 1943, caused tremendous physical damage that resulted in a lifetime of suffering; yet Howard Hughes went on to build the largest private business empire in the free world. In addition to factories that built airplanes and made drill bits, he owned a brewery and a beanery. He was sole stockholder of RKO Studios and held controlling stock in Trans World Airlines.

Howard's companies built advanced electronic communications and spy satellite systems. They created the largest amphibious aircraft ever built and the spacecraft that made the first soft landing on the moon. A division of Hughes Aircraft created the first operating laser and went on to create innovative laser weaponry.

Recovering from the 1946 crash, Howard invented a more sophisticated hospital bed and a submarine. He even invented a new bedpan.

He acquired newspapers, television and radio stations, and Theta Cable.

He influenced the politicians who would eventually rule the free world.

He owned land and mines and Las Vegas hotels and casinos such as the Desert Inn, the Silver Slipper, the Sands, and the Frontier.

Howard's empire was intricately involved with the United States government and the Central Intelligence Agency. For example, in 1939 Howard's companies were working on experimental military aircraft. In 1942, he was awarded an eighteen-million-dollar government contract to build what were known as the flying boats. Many of the men who held positions of power and responsibility in the Hughes organization were involved at one time or another with the CIA.

On top of this, he was a fun-loving flyboy and a fabulous lover.

Now that I've told you a little about Howard the man, let me tell you about Howard and his women.

Howard's achievements as a lover were as impressive as his achievements in the world of business and finance. He loved to talk to me about the other women in his life. At the beginning of our relationship we would talk on the telephone until the wee hours of the morning. Like any teenager, I was interested in all the movie stars, past and present, and I loved to hear his stories as much as he liked to tell them. Howard had a great need to talk; perhaps I became the childhood buddy he never had.

Howard was first and foremost a Texan. He might not have been the two-fisted, drinking, brawling Texan, but he was definitely the two-fisted, lover-type Texan. He felt that his father's image overshadowed him most of his life. Howard, Senior, from all reports, was a ladies' man. Howard's mother fell in love and married one of the roughest of the Texas wildcatters, but she raised little Howard with all the gentility of a southerner. She nearly made a sissy out of little Sonny, as she called him; she most certainly made a hypochondriac out of him.

Howard's first wife, Ella Rice, was the most sought-after debutante in all of Houston; and her conquest was a challenge. Howard was also impressed with her social background—she was a Rice family, as in Rice Institute. After their divorce, he never dated a debutante unless she was also a star.

Howard's move to California, the land of movie stars and beautiful women, marked the true beginning of his romantic conquests. He became a connoisseur of female perfection.

Most of what's been written about Howard states that the two biggest loves of his life were Billie Dove and Jean Peters. According to Howard, that was not true. Billie was older than Howard and was his first movie star. He was just out of his teens and completely smitten; nothing could cool his ardor until she had a romance with his golf pro. After he

6

discovered her betrayal, you couldn't have revived that romance with the promise of everlasting life.

Jean Peters and Howard met in 1946, but the fact that she saw other men at same time prevented a serious romance. Their relationship turned into a friendship that lasted Howard's entire life.

In 1957, he learned that there were people trying to take over his financial empire. Because he either owned or controlled everything, Howard figured that these men would try to have him declared mentally incompetent and have him committed to an asylum.

Howard was determined to beat them at their own game. He knew that, according to California law, if he had a wife, she, as his next of kin, would have to sign any commitment papers.

Enter, Jean Peters.

According to sources in the Hughes' circle, she was guaranteed seventy-five thousand dollars for the next twenty years from Hughes Tool, in return for never signing any commitment papers of any kind, never giving any private or public statements to the media, never writing a book, and *never contesting* a will.

After Howard's death, I was offered a similar arrangement.

Now that Howard had ensured himself against having his empire taken from him by his closest associates, to complete his plan he had to insure himself against Jean. They applied for a marriage license in Tonopah, Nevada, using assumed names: G. A. Johnson and Marian Evans. As you can see from the photostatic copy of the application, Howard never signed his pseudo-name. If he ever actually had to prove his marriage, he *could* sign it. On the other hand, if he wanted at a later date to prove he *wasn't* married to Jean Peters, he could leave it unsigned as it still stands today.

Affidavit of Application for Marriage License

STATE OF NEVADA,   } ss.
COUNTY OF NYE.

Being duly sworn, says:

My Name is _G. W. Johnson_

I am _46_ years of age, Date of birth _June 8, 1916_

I reside in the City of _Las Vegas_

County of _Clark_

State of _Nevada_

Previously married _Yes_   Wife deceased _No_

Divorced _Yes_   When _1929_

Where _Tipo_

On what grounds _Mental Cruelty_

I desire a license to authorize my marriage with:

Marian Evans

whose age is _29_ years, Date of birth _Oct 15, 1927_

and resides in the City of _Los Angeles_

County of _L.A._

State of _California_

Previously married _Yes_   Husband deceased _No_

Divorced _Yes_   When _Dec. 1955_

Where _Los Angeles Cal_

On what grounds _Mental Cruelty_

I know of no legal objection to our marriage.

I hereby certify that the foregoing answers as given by me are true to the best of my knowledge and belief.

Marian Evans

Sworn and subscribed before me this _12_
day of _January_ A.D. 1957.

Gudrun V. Murphy County Clerk

By _____ Deputy Clerk

License issued _12_ day of _January_ A.D. 1957.

STATE OF NEVADA,   } ss.
COUNTY OF NYE.

being duly sworn, deposes and says that_____ is the
_____ and legal guardian of
named in the within application for a Marriage License, and hereby consents to said Marriage, and the issuance of a License authorizing the same.

Sworn and subscribed to before me this_____ day of
_____ A.D. 19____.

_____ County Clerk

By_____ Deputy Clerk

A pretty clever plan for a man who everyone thought was not competent enough to run his own companies, and cheap at seventy-five thousand a year to keep control of his billion-dollar empire.

Howard told me that he had loved just three women in his life—Katharine Hepburn, Ginger Rogers, and, years later, me.

Miss Hepburn's influence remained with him his whole life.

Katie was the ultimate, the movie star and socialite, all wrapped up in one. After Katie, who is famous for her unconventional style of dress, Howard no longer played the role of the dandy from Texas. He lost all interest in being the well-dressed, dapper young tycoon and gave little attention to his personal appearance.

The only other woman who embodied this rare combination of beauty and glamour for him was Grace Kelly. A friend had taken him to a small gathering which Grace was to attend. Howard was ecstatic. Later, on the way home, Howard dejectedly said, "Well, she didn't show up."

"Who?"

"Grace Kelly."

"Who the hell do you think that was who served you lunch, dummy?"

Howard let out a moan. "That was Grace Kelly in the glasses? Why didn't you tell me? I really flubbed that one."

Howard was too embarrassed to go back.

While still the much-sought-after bachelor of Hollywood, Howard fell head over heels in love with Ginger Rogers. He started dating her while he was still with Katharine, and the sparks began to fly. Katie never spoke to him again after they broke up, but he never stopped sending her four dozen long-stemmed roses every Christmas until his flight from reality.

Howard delighted in telling the story of how Katie called Ginger Titmouse, for obvious reasons. One day when Ginger was walking down the narrow RKO lot, Katie

9

dumped a bucket of water on her from a second-story window.

After Miss Hepburn became the smash of Broadway in *Philadelphia Story,* Howard bought the motion picture rights for her to star in. He had no intention of making the picture himself; he just wanted to ensure that no one else did her part.

L. B. Mayer wanted to make the movie in the worst way, but he said he'd never use Katharine Hepburn because she was box-office poison. Howard told him in no uncertain terms, "No Hepburn, no picture." It was a Mexican standoff for over a year until Mayer finally conceded.

Howard was never in love with Gene Tierney, but he always spoke of her with respect and affection. According to Howard, their relationship was never a physical one. He was impressed with the fact that she had been schooled in Switzerland and had a genteel background, like Katharine Hepburn. There was still a little left over of his fascination with the debutante. That Gene was one of the most beautiful women in the world didn't hurt, either.

Both Katie and Gene were in his life at the time he was preparing his round-the-world flight in 1936. Katie even attempted to stow away on the plane. Gene said that when he spoke of flying his eyes glowed and and his language was almost sensual. There was a soft, boyish, clear-eyed quality about him; Gene remembered him as sweet and almost aesthetic-looking before his accidents changed his appearance.

Gene's mother kept insisting that all Howard needed was to be loved. She said that for all his millions, she was touched by some emptiness in him. The lack of it would eventually kill him.

Actress Linda Darnell held Howard's attention for at least six months. He was mesmerized by her flawless beauty and porcelain complexion. He told me that in person she was one of the most beautiful women he had ever beheld; but once she agreed to divorce her husband (who demanded a settlement from Howard) Howard was off and running into the arms of Ann Miller, Linda's best friend. They dated only once, on the pretext that Howard wanted Ann's help in making Linda understand that he was not marriage-minded. He never dated Annie again, because he found his feelings for her were more those of a buddy. She was a fellow Texan, and Texas girls were too capable and strong for Howard's blood.

Another woman who frightened Howard was Joan Crawford. She was simply too strong and domineering.

Bette Davis claims that Howard was impotent; but since she was the only woman he was impotent with, you'll have to draw your own conclusions.

During the time I was married to Glenn Davis, Howard told me he had taken up with Kathryn Grayson. Kathryn was one of the biggest stars at MGM at the time, and Howard was so proud that he even offered to let me listen in on a telephone conversation with her when she called. I declined—not because I was so nice but because I was too much in love with him.

Howard always put Ava Gardner and Lana Turner in the same category, though he remained friends with Ava all his life and quickly forgot Lana after his last plane crash. He told me Lana was demanding marriage but Ava didn't care. Howard realized that neither lady ever loved him; he told me that Lana and Ava both had to get drunk before they could go to bed with him. In *Ava* by Charles Higham, I read that she said Howard was strong and masculine and an expert lover, but she wasn't satisfied because she wasn't in love with him. She also said that Howard just thought of her as a big pair of boobies and a good lay. I know that's not true; Howard adored Ava and always talked about her with real fondness. If she had loved him he might have even married her.

He had met exotic Faith Domergue, the star of his picture *Vendetta,* when she was only fifteen years old; she was his protégée for ten years.

Howard was always extremely fond of Faith and tried to make her a star. She was definitely star material, but the

11

picture he chose for her would have stopped a career as lustrous as Elizabeth Taylor's. Howard spent almost as much time on *Vendetta* as he did on his flying boat; but, unlike his boat, he never got the movie off the ground. I thought Faith was one of the most stunningly beautiful women I'd ever seen. Her eyelashes were so long that the makeup man had to curl them on a pencil.

A story Howard loved telling was about Olivia de Havilland and her sister, Joan Fontaine. Howard had been dating Olivia fairly steadily and had a huge crush on her. He said she had one of the purest reputations in Hollywood, and no man could ever lay a hand on her; she was almost a professional virgin. One afternoon when he was at her home, who should come in but her younger sister, Joan, as vibrant and coquettish as any girl could be. Every time he looked Joan's way, she gave him the eye—both of them. He said that the sisters were equally beautiful, but Joan was a flirt and a minx.

When he left later that night, Joan was waiting for him in his car. She threw her arms around him and told him she'd been watching him for days and she simply couldn't stand it any longer; she wanted to see him alone. How about lunch tomorrow at the star-populated Lucy's restaurant across the street from RKO? Howard readily agreed, for that moment forgetting all about Olivia.

Howard was at Lucy's ten minutes early, all spiffed up in one of his finest suits. He couldn't help but gasp when Joan swept in, a vision in white. Everyone noticed that she was heading straight for him; he was absolutely intoxicated at being the most envied man in the room.

Joan came straight at him with her arms outstretched as if she couldn't wait to get them around him. She scooted her chair in as close as she could to him, took both his hands in her own, and looked lovingly up into his face with her large baby blues. At that moment, Olivia walked in and went right to their table. Joan looked up and said, "I told you what a bastard he was. Now will you believe me?"

The two sisters stormed out of Lucy's arm in arm while everyone in the place snickered behind their napkins.

You'd think Howard would have learned something from that lesson, but he never did.

Twenty years later, when Joan Fontaine was married to movie mogul William Dozier (who was later to become the head of RKO after Howard sold it), Howard started wooing her again. He turned on the Hughes charm full force, and soon after the Doziers were divorced. Howard told me he had promised to marry Joan, but as soon as the lady was free, he was off like a big bird, promising the same idyllic situation to Susan Hayward. She, luckily, recovered from an overdose of barbiturates that she took when she, too, found out his intentions were strictly dishonorable.

Poor Joan! Poor Susan! I really believe Howard was sincere for the moment, but when he finally had what he desired, he was looking for his next conquest. He was like the little boy with his hands and mouth full of cookies. He had to drop some to grab for more.

He was terribly impressed by movie stars, a fact that amazed me when he knew he could "create" them himself, as he had done with Jean Harlow and Jane Russell.

Howard was an enigma. On the one hand, he was so jealous he couldn't stand another man's eyes to touch me; yet he enjoyed my having dated others so he could take me away from men like Nicky Hilton, James Dean, Greg Bautzer, Bob Wagner, Robert Evans, Tyrone Power, and Rock Hudson. What better proof of love than the most desired women in the world desiring him to the extent of giving up the most desired men of the times? I did it happily.

Howard also had an extensive stable of starlets stashed around town. Most of them were very young, sweet, innocent girls, about eighteen years old. He would bring the girl and her family to Los Angeles, and later get rid of the family. Howard was very fatherly and would tell them he would find a place for their daughter to live and see that she had servants and care. He would assure them she would be perfectly safe.

Howard had agents, such as Walter Kane, who were always looking for potential young starlets. He never stopped looking for a new Jean Harlow, or so he often said. The girls were selected from photographs made especially for Howard. He insisted that all their makeup be removed and that closeups be done from every angle.

Howard would often forget about girls he had around town. Each girl had a driver-bodyguard whose main function was to report back to Howard. One of the girls for whom he made such arrangements was Gina Lollobrigida. She was brought here and set up in the Hughes pattern; she felt she was a prisoner who never saw her captor. Gina convinced her guard to take her to the airport. In fact, she had him feeling so sorry for her that he allowed her to escape.

When I learned of these girls, I figured he was sleeping with all of them. I have found out since that he was innocent in most cases. Morally, he was pretty straight and true to me, but he was a collector—of beautiful girls.

Howard would have had to have a fantastic libido to have taken care of all these females sexually. And, though he was a great lover, I do not believe any man could have been capable of maintaining that extensive a harem. He needed to collect these beautiful women the way others collect art.

Some of the women Howard pursued included Ida Lupino, Carol Lombard, Patti Paige, Yvonne DeCarlo, Hedy Lamarr, Ingrid Bergman, Shelley Winters, Jane Russell, Judy Garland, Janet Leigh, and many, many others. And he had stories about each of them.

So how did I enter into the plans of this man of the world? I was a child star and twenty-four years younger than he; I was a baby-faced girl-next-door type, in complete contrast to these glamour queens of the silver screen; I was a naive, idealistic Mormon kid from Glendale, California. So why did Howard choose me and promise me eternal connubial bliss? Why did he desire me over so much beauty?

14

I started out fearing Howard Hughes. I soon grew to like him and then to love and need him with a deep dependency. I knew very little about life, love, and death, and I refused to believe him when he repeated over and over how much he loved me and told me he was dependent on my love and devotion. Like most young girls in love, I was too worried about other women to see the truth.

When I suspected Howard of cheating, I always believed the worst. As our relationship moved through time, I hardened myself, built an invincible wall to protect my heart, and failed to listen to his side of things.

I allowed my own insecurities and rebellious spirit to take me away from him when he needed me most. I made a decision that I've regretted ever since. When I was convinced his love was genuine and I was his one true wife and soul mate, it was too late. The lines of communication had been closed off.

As time went on, Howard and his women were forgotten. As time went on, Howard was forgotten. Forgotten by all his women . . . *all* his women, except me.

This is my story.

Chapter 1

THE DAY WAS ELECTRIC, ONE OF THOSE CRYSTAL-CLEAR days that happen only in Beverly Hills.

The whole world was exciting, especially when seen through the eyes of a teenage actress who had just starred in her first grown-up role.

Jerome Courtland (the boy who gave Shirley Temple her first kiss in *Kiss and Tell*) and I were weaving our way out of the Beverly Hills Tennis Club after the championship matches when we were recognized by a group of teenagers. They began passing us an assortment of autograph books as countless flashbulbs went off in our direction.

Jerome (or Cojo, as we called him) whispered as he pressed me closer to him, "Well, do you feel like a star?"

I did, I did, I did, for the very first time!

Little did I know that this was the same afternoon I was to meet Howard Hughes.

It was November 1948 and I was under contract to Columbia Pictures, which was owned and reigned over by Harry Cohn. King Cohn, as he was called, had changed my name from Helen Koford, my given Swedish name, to Terry Moore, my present Irish one. He had starred me opposite Glenn Ford in a movie called *The Return of October*.

Up to that time I had only played the roles of children on the screen and radio, but after my braces were removed, I blossomed into a full-fledged cover girl. In one year I appeared on dozens of billboards and forty national magazine covers.

Those were the years when every studio had their contract stars and starlets and a schoolroom where we studied and palled around together. When I worked at MGM Studios, I went to school with Elizabeth Taylor and Margaret O'Brien. Twentieth Century-Fox had Roddy McDowall and Mitzi Gaynor on its roster. At Columbia there were Cojo, the kids from the *Blondie* movies, and me.

We soon formed our own clique: Jane Powell, Elizabeth Taylor, Cojo, Marshall Thompson, Richard Long, Ann Blyth, Debbie Reynolds, and Roddy McDowall. We would meet Saturday afternoons at Roddy's or Jane's home because they had swimming pools. I remember Roddy tossing Liz in the pool one afternoon, and when she dried off, her black hair fell into curls around a face that looked like an artist's sculpture. Words cannot describe Elizabeth's beauty at fifteen years of age, nor have photographs ever truly captured it.

Those were the days when the Hollywood kids were very close. On Monday nights we'd gather at the local ice rink or go bowling together. At many of these outings, we were followed by photographers from the various fan magazines. Those were the happy, carefree days when Elizabeth Taylor and I were still escorted to evening premieres and parties by our mothers.

The Return of October had, perhaps, the choicest girl's role of the decade, and one that every teenaged actress coveted. Harry Cohn had owned the script for years but hadn't found an actress with enough innocence and naiveté to play the part.

The story was about a girl named Terry Ramsey who lived with her Uncle Willie, a racetrack enthusiast. Uncle

Willie had often said, "Honey, when I die, if I ever come back again, I swear I'll come back as a horse." After he dies, Terry finds a horse with all of her uncle's characteristics. She thinks this is surely Uncle Willie who has come back to life to win the Kentucky Derby; the thing he wanted the most while he was living.

Well, there aren't too many girls who look naive enough to believe a racehorse could be their uncle. This was the quality Howard saw and fell in love with.

A long time before this day his plans to meet me had been made. I didn't know it then, but Howard Hughes had seen the film and wanted to be introduced to its teenage star; he even had people on his payroll planted at functions I attended, to observe me. The tennis match was one of those functions, and an observer was in the crowd to bridge my way to Howard. Cojo and I were blindly being led over that bridge.

Of all the celebrities at the tennis match that day, Cojo and I seemed the most celebrated. We were swamped by people and made little progress toward Cojo's car. As we signed our autographs, Cojo looked so proud as the young fans oohed and aahed over my handknit turquoise sweater with the matching accordion-pleated skirt of raw silk and high heels of the same fabric. I always felt confident when I had a new outfit that I knew I looked well in. Sweaters and skirts were my look. I wore very little makeup and kept a tan the year round.

I looked up and smiled for another camera; I could always sense when someone was taking my picture.

We saw a pair of arms waving at us from the crowd. It was Johnny Machio, a motion picture agent. He was yelling at us as he pushed his way through the crowd. "Wait up, I've been looking all over for you. No excuses this time; you're going to have a drink with me at the Beverly Wilshire Hotel."

Every place we'd been lately, we'd run into Johnny inviting us to meet him somewhere. The idea didn't appeal to me at all. The hotel scene was too staid; I liked the zippier places where the kids hung out.

Cojo must have sensed my feelings, because he said, "Look, we can't make an excuse again. He's just trying to be nice. After all, he's a friend of Mother's."

Without giving me a chance to answer, this six-foot-five, Nordically handsome boy with the impish grin swung all five-foot-two, one hundred pounds of me up to his shoulder. We walked to the car with me perched on his shoulder that way, amid the screams of delight from the fans and the clicking of shutters. The photographers loved it. They followed us all the way to Cojo's silver convertible while I madly checked my skirt to ensure all was covered; then I pointed my toes and placed my legs in a photogenic pose and threw kisses as I was lowered awkwardly into the car.

Cojo sang along with the radio those few short blocks to the hotel. He had a singing voice that would send chills down any girl's spine; even Elizabeth Taylor's. He was her first schoolgirl crush. She had played his records over and over for me the year before.

We pulled into the valet entrance of the Beverly Wilshire Hotel. Johnny was already impatiently waiting for us at the huge wrought-iron gates. Why do Hollywood agents always have that exasperated, "You're late!" look?

We followed Johnny into the dining room where the maître d' flashed a big smile. "Oh, yes, Mr. Machio, come right this way. Your table's ready."

We were royally escorted to a choice table in the center of the magnificent dining room. The crystal sparkled in the sunlight and so did those emerald cut diamonds that adorned many of the ladies. It was so elegant that my whole posture changed as I entered and my effervescent behavior became queenly.

Johnny scanned the room with an agent's eye and, lo and behold, spotted a tall, slender man sitting alone against the wall. (I wouldn't learn until years later that this meeting, which seemed so accidental, had been set up and deliberate-

19

ly staged. After you came to know Howard, you realized that nothing was left to chance.) Johnny delightedly exclaimed with just the proper amount of disbelief, "There's Howard Hughes! Howard, come join us. I have friends I'd like you to meet."

Howard awkwardly slid out and unfolded all six-feet-three-and-one-half inches from behind his table and ambled over to ours. I rapidly tried to recall all I'd heard about this man. In those days, it was easy to confuse the three H's: Howard Hawks, Howard Hughes, and John Huston. All were tall, lanky motion-picture directors; in fact, both Hughes and Hawks had directed portions of *The Outlaw*.

Let's see . . . Hughes . . . Harlow? . . . oh, yes, he discovered Harlow . . . *Hell*'s *Angels* . . . oh, sure, airplanes . . . he set the around-the-world record in a single-engine plane . . . oh, and Jane Russell . . . bosoms . . . *The Outlaw*. He's the one who crashed the plane in Beverly Hills and almost died. . . . Lana Turner, Rita Hayworth and all those stars were crying in the anteroom. . . . He made *The Front Page* and *Scarface* . . . they're classics, I loved those . . . isn't he the one? . . . likes young girls? Aha! Howard had recently acquired RKO Pictures and, with it, my then-unreleased film, *Mighty Joe Young!*

As he slipped into the chair directly across from me, I stared at his face. He's the one who was always photographed in the old felt hat. It was the same kind of felt hat that my Uncle Willie, reincarnated as a horse, wore in *The Return of October*.

It was strange I would meet Howard right after making this movie because that is the one film script that I can still remember every single line of, especially when I talk to the horse named October.

TERRY

October . . . I don't know if these things really happen. If you really *are* my Uncle Willie . . . or if you aren't. But I hope you don't mind if I pretend

20

for just a little while that you *are.* Anyway, no one will ever know . . . it'll be our little secret . . . Uncle Willie . . .

(quickly)

I hope you don't mind my calling you Uncle Willie?

Johnny started the introductions before poor Howard had even reached our table; he practically shouted, "Meet the infamous Howard Hughes." If every eye in the room wasn't already watching, they were by then. Howard's legs were so long that he had reached the table in three steps. I giggled. All I could picture was a giant jackrabbit.

Johnny continued, "And this is Terry Moore, 'Terrible Terry,' the terror of Columbia."

Howard laughed. "You don't look terrible to me."

I looked up to see if he was serious and I found myself staring into the most piercing, intense eyes I had ever seen.

From the moment Johnny made the introduction, Howard never took his eyes off me. No matter who was speaking, his eyes never left my face. He directed all his questions to me: Where was I born? Did I like to fly? How long had I been an actress?

I found him utterly repulsive; I wanted to escape those eyes. Cojo must have sensed my discomfort because he put his hand firmly on my arm so I couldn't move.

Howard told me how much he had enjoyed my pictures. He seemed to know a great deal about my life in Glendale. In spite of my discomfort, I couldn't hide my enthusiasm for aviation. I told him about my lifelong dream to fly.

"You have no fear of flying?"

All the time he talked, he devoured me with his eyes. Those deep brown, penetrating, unescapable eyes. His eyes would analyze a person from head to toe, inside and out. They seemed to reach inside me. I was growing more and more nervous. From an expressionless face, I felt his eyes undressing me. I felt fifteen years old again and naked in my chair.

I could have been imagining it all. I was still a virgin and

21

the type of girl who displayed a wide-eyed innocence; men had always wanted to protect me. Even kids at school would not tell me dirty jokes. I was often asked how I grew up in the movie industry yet did not hear or see vulgarity, obscenity, or pornography. My associates referred to me as the bishop's daughter, and many were careful about using profanity in my presence.

Sex was not discussed even in the closeness of my family, who were careful how they worded anything pertaining to love, marriage, or lust. I remember once my saying the word *pregnant* in reference to someone we knew, and my grandmother, Grandma Bickmore, flushed and left the room. You referred to such a state as "being in the family way" or said someone was "that way."

"Heavens no! When all the other kids were drawing houses and people in elementary school, I drew the cockpits of planes and made model airplanes, the kind with struts that were put together with airplane glue and covered with paper. They flew, too. I've always known I'd never be killed in a plane, so I've always felt safe . . . sort of like being in a giant womb."

Everybody laughed, and I felt my whole body grow hot with embarrassment. Howard didn't laugh, but I didn't dare look at him; nor did I care what he thought.

"I have to fly to Palm Springs tomorrow to see Darryl. . . ." (Darryl? I assumed he meant Mr. Zanuck.) "Would you and your friend like to accompany me?"

Just as I began to make an excuse why we couldn't, Cojo said, "Yes, we'd love to," giving me a swift kick under the table.

Cojo was also a pilot and an avid follower of Howard Hughes's career. Despite that, I was angry, very angry. Cojo was committing me to something I wouldn't think of doing. Had he lost his mind? It must have been obvious that I couldn't stand Howard. The sight of him at this moment practically made me ill.

After setting a date and time he would take us flying, Howard said his farewells and departed. I felt like I wanted to take a bath and rub myself witth disinfectant. I lashed out at Cojo. "Why did you say we'd go flying with him? I never want to lay eyes on him again."

Cojo just opened his eyes wide and said, "Don't you realize that he's a living legend? I'd love to do his life story. Terry, this will give me an opportunity to observe him."

Legend or no legend, I had to find a way out of this rendezvous.

Chapter 2

EVERY RING OF THE PHONE JARRED MY UNCONSCIOUS MIND back to reality. This was the night Cojo and I were supposed to go flying with Howard Hughes, and I had chosen sleep as my escape; it was only seven-thirty in the evening.

Why wasn't anyone answering? The whole family— Mom, Dad and my brother Wally—was home, and the whole famaily revolved around me. I was the commodity; we had all sacrificed and worked hard for my career. My mother made everyone tiptoe around and always answered the phone on the first ring if I was resting; maybe if I ignored it it would go away.

If no one's answering, then maybe no one's home, I thought. Maybe there's a fire or an emergency and they're trying to warn me. Somehow I managed to wake up enough to answer.

"Hello . . . Cojo. Of course it's me. Who did you think it was? Where is everybody?"

Our flying date was for 9:00 P.M. Cojo and my mother had decided to let me sleep to the last moment; it was time for me to get ready.

Then I remembered whom we would be flying with.

"Did you hear me?" he was asking.

"Yes, I heard you. Have a good time," I said and hung up.

I buried my head under the pillow. The phone started ringing again. This time my mother answered it.

"Yes, she'll be there . . . I'm sure because I'll drive her. I know exactly where the Glendale airport is. My needlers' group meets near there. You're sure it's safe? . . . I know he's a test pilot but don't forget about his crashes. . . . What should she wear? . . . Oh, no—not jeans!"

From under the covers I piped, "Ha! You should see what *he* wears!"

Mom hung up and started pulling open the blackout curtains. "Wake up, Merry Sunshine," she sang. This was the cue for the wrecking crew to enter. Mother and two of our neighbors were rushing about the room, and my dog was climbing all over me on the bed. Several large white boxes with white satin ribbons had arrived that morning and my room was full of beautiful fresh flowers.

Mother pushed me into the shower while Harriet and Carolyn, the two neighbor ladies, decided what I should wear. They knew my wardrobe better than I did. Whenever there was an exciting premiere or grand opening, Mother and the girls put their heads together and made my clothes. I was the best-dressed girl in Hollywood in those days, and everything I wore was an original creation. Harriet knitted all the sweaters—strapless, off the shoulder, you name it—that I was becoming so famous for.

That day I stepped out of the shower into powder blue pedal pushers with a matching scoopneck sweater with felt hearts around the neck. It sounds terrible, but it didn't look too bad, especially when your hundred pounds are all in the right places. I wonder what Howard thought. I think he was amused by whatever I did or wore. He only got upset over big things like sticky hands.

I don't remember anything about the trip to the airport. I only remember that when I got there, Howard was sitting in

25

the cockpit with the plane all warmed up and ready to go. It was as if he didn't want to give me time to change my mind.

We drove right to the steps that pull up into the plane. Cojo helped me in and we waved good-bye to the disappointed neighbors and Mom, who hadn't even gotten a peek at the elusive Mr. Hughes.

The most beautiful sight in the whole world is Los Angeles at night when the lights cover the darkness like millions of flashing, colored Christmas bulbs. "Look down there," Howard said, "because you'll never see anything else like it. All the jewels in the world can't compare to this—and I've flown all around the world."

I couldn't even enjoy it. Cojo was somewhere in the cockpit. I hadn't seen him since takeoff.

Howard had an engineer aboard. Howard never spoke to him; he just pointed and the engineer seemed to know that he meant: Hand me a carton of milk (or a map).

Howard sensed my uneasiness. It wasn't difficult; I sat bolt upright and stared straight ahead. I yearned to become smaller and smaller and disappear. I still thought he was repulsive with his scraggly mustache, frayed collar, and worn-looking clothes. He always wore a white shirt, smooth beige wool slacks, socks, brown orthopedic-looking leather shoes. He *never* wore tennis shoes. He always carried a blue sports jacket with a rumpled tie in the pocket, which he would wear only if absolutely necessary.

The engine was so loud in that old DC4 that I had to strain to hear him.

"Nope, I've never seen anything to compare with it, the prettiest sight in the whole world . . . especially when you're lost or out of fuel." He laughed really loud at that, as if he'd made a tremendous joke.

He turned that penetrating look on me again. "You don't talk much, do you?"

"Where's Cojo?" I sputtered.

"Are you cold?" he asked, ignoring the question.

I was freezing. To my utter amazement, he just got up

26

and walked to the back of the plane. I didn't know where the engineer had disappeared, either.

I sat there frozen for what seemed an eternity. Howard came back carrying two of the most delapidated army blankets I'd ever seen; Cojo was right behind him. The two of them tucked the blankets all around me, completely oblivious to the fact that the plane was flying around by itself.

The rest of the trip I sat there stoically while Cojo and Howard chatted about the airplane.

Howard kept asking if I needed anything, but, remembering the blanket episode, I said no to everything. He poured on the charm and southern hospitality. He seemed more concerned for my comfort than how he flew the plane. I was still saying no when we landed about two hours later.

I went along on several of these flights, clutching Cojo and doing my best to stay as far away from Howard as possible.

Life was never boring with Howard. He was continuously managing other people's lives and interfering with their relationships.

Howard knew I wouldn't see him without Cojo, so one day he called Cojo and told him to meet us at the Glendale airport. Then he called and asked me to meet them at the Burbank airport. After Howard talked with me, he kept his end of the telephone line off the hook to make sure Cojo couldn't call me and learn about the change of plans.

I arrived on time. There was Howard, in the company of Johnny Machio; Johnny's wife, Connie Moore; and her sister. I sensed a slightly patronizing attitude on the part of Howard's other guests, who were all older and more sophisticated. "Another one of Howard's girls," their raised eyebrows seemed to be saying.

I was extremly sensitive about the difference in age between myself and this "wild man" called Hughes. The rumors I had heard about him did not help matters any.

Cojo was nowhere in sight. For fifteen minutes or so

27

Howard stormed around the airport, putting on a convincing display of annoyance and chagrin at being kept waiting. I was furious at his behavior, which was rude and upsetting. At the same time, I was confused and worried. Where was Cojo? Why would he stand up his idol? Surely he'd show up soon.

Howard grew more and more impatient, and finally we flew to the desert home of Darryl Zanuck in Palm Springs. Clifton Webb and Louis Jourdan were there, along with many other glamorous people. I felt intimidated. Moreover, I was embarrassed because Zanuck was wearing the most revealing pair of knit bikini bathing trunks that I had ever seen. He was my host, but I was too shy to look in his direction.

Howard sensed my awkwardness and asked, "Would you like to leave?"

"Yes. Now, please!"

Howard took me by the hand and we went to the Doll House, an adorable restaurant built just like a doll house. It was the most popular place in the Springs with its calypso combo that everyone loved dancing to. Rumbas, sambas, and morengos were the popular dances.

We had just settled down when an extremely handsome young man came up to our table and said politely to Howard, "May I introduce myself? My name is Dale Robertson, and I would like to dance with your daughter."

Howard said, "I'm Joe Blow. Now beat it."

"How do you do, Mr. Blow. I don't mean to be offensive. My intentions are honorable. I would like to dance with your daughter."

Howard nearly choked.

This was to happen to us many times.

After the Palm Springs episode, Howard really started pestering me. He wanted me to go places with him, do things with him. Luckily, I had to leave town on an extensive publicity tour to advertise *The Return of October*.

This was a great relief to me. My tour would take me to twenty-two states and twenty-six cities. I would be rid of Mr. Hughes, and then some other unfortunate starlet, more easily accessible, could gladly become the object of his persistent attentions.

Things were going quite well for me on the tour. I missed Cojo, but with the hundreds of people I was meeting I didn't have a minute to be lonely. I had all but forgotten Howard Hughes. Then, as Mother and I were about to board a plane after our stay in Indianapolis, there he was at the airport, watching me from a distance. I didn't say a thing to Mother but just kept on walking as if I hadn't seen him. He made no attempt to approach us but just stared at me with a smug grin on his face.

Later, I dismissed the idea that I had seen him there. I was sure that my long hours and traveling had my imagination working overtime, until I saw him again when we were in Minneapolis/St. Paul. This time I let him know I saw him by giving him a jaunty wave and then I disappeared into the crowd.

After that, I couldn't get him off my mind. What did he want? What was wrong with him? Couldn't he tell I didn't like him? Why wouldn't he leave me alone?

Everywhere I went I looked over my shoulder to see if he was following. I scanned every crowd for his face. It was a face that haunted me, day and night. It didn't frighten me at all; it was warm, patient, and good-humored, but I didn't like it.

When the tour took us to the East Coast, I was positive he wouldn't follow me. I was looking forward to seeing Cojo again. Howard Hughes's face entered my mind less and less, until one bitter-cold day in Buffalo, New York, when I looked up and found myself staring into his deep, dark eyes.

"Fancy meeting you here, Miss Moore," he said. He was dressed for sunny southern California and looked ridiculous.

"Go away, Mr. Hughes!" I blurted. "Get back in your plane and fly away and leave me alone!"

I felt I wouldn't see him for the rest of my tour; I was right.

When I returned home, the house was full of flowers and I received daily invitations from him. I didn't want to accept them, but I was running out of excuses why I couldn't. I mentioned it to my studio schoolteacher, Lillian Barkley.

"Why not invite him to your home?" she suggested. "Let him see what a fine family you have and what kind of a girl you are. Maybe he'll leave you alone."

It seemed like sound advice; my mother agreed.

"Poor thing," she said. "Nothing but restaurant food for months on end. Well, he'll get a real home-cooked meal from me."

My family looked forward to "the coming of Howard." Mother, being a feline Leo lady, dressed up in her red flannel wedding dress with its black patent leather belt. Dad, the typical Taurus, wore what was most comfortable. No one impressed my father; to be taken away from his books meant a wasted evening as far as he was concerned. "If you want to waste your time, that's up to you, but leave me out of it." Daddy didn't need people to clutter up his life.

Howard arrived exactly at the stroke of eight.

I answered the door wearing the least revealing thing I could find in my closet: a pleated plaid skirt, a navy-blue slopppy joe sweater, bobby sox with Joyce Alert white shoes. The uniform for girls of that day. The only thing missing was my Glendale High pom-poms.

My sheep dog scooted ahead of me and bounded all over Howard.

"Hi, he likes you. His name is Stormy. He's part collie and part German shepherd—hey, he really likes you! Mom, Dad!" I shouted. "Come quick—Stormy's got his front paws on Mr. Hughes's shoulders and he's licking his face. You sure have a way with dogs, Mr. Hughes. . . . Oh, this

30

is my mom. We call her Mama Blue. That's southern, so you can call her that too. You've already met Stormy. I don't know where my brother Wally is. He couldn't wait; he ate earlier. . . . Oh, I'm sorry, this is my father. Daddy, what do you want Mr. Hughes to call you?''

Daddy, who was always in a vile mood when he was hungry, replied, ''Let's decide at dinner.'' He turned to Howard. ''You're late. You were supposed to be here at seven. Don't blame Luella if your meat's overdone.''

We all filed into the dining room while Mother fluttered into the kitchen. Funny, I'd never seen her flutter before.

Now I realized Howard was the perfect age for . . . Mother. She had been born in 1909 and Howard in 1905. Daddy had been born in 1897. As far as he was concerned, Howard was one of those young whippersnappers who think they know it all.

At the table, Daddy announced, ''We're having Luella's company dinner: Swiss steak, smothered in onions, baked stuffed tomatoes, and potatoes.

''Try one of the biscuits while they're hot . . . made right from the beginning. Help yourself to some more salad. You'd better like garlic!''

Howard paled at the mere mention of garlic and onions. He believed they oozed out of your pores for weeks after.

As Mama Blue was serving the food, Daddy said, ''Now, don't you girls have any more company this week. I've *had* Swiss steak!''

That was the cue that Howard had been waiting for. ''Then I want you to be my guests for dinner tomorrow night. I have a little place that serves the best steaks and wines in Los Angeles. Or we can go somewhere else since you don't drink—''

Daddy quickly interrupted. ''We'll go there. The girls don't drink, so I have to drink for them. Just don't do it in my own home.''

Inwardly I moaned.

That night, Howard wolfed down his food. Looking

back, I realize he probably swallowed it whole so as not to taste it. But he laughed and joked all during dinner. He seemed delighted when I asked, "Do you prefer to wash or dry the dishes?"

Ever the southern gentleman, he washed so I could keep my manicure.

After dinner, we retired to the living room. Howard sat on the gold sofa in front of the bay window by himself as we proceeded to cross-examine him.

He loved being center stage and told us delightful stories about building his first "steam" car and airplane right in our backyard—Glendale! This revelation almost made him family.

To my surprise, he was adorable when he laughed.

He came right to the point. "I know you're concerned over my interest in your daughter, Hel— Do you mind if I call you Helen? I notice your family does. And please, no more Mr. Hughes. Call me Howard."

"You may call her Helen, Howard," Daddy interjected impatiently.

Howard continued. "You've done a beautiful job raising your daughter, and if I were ever blessed with a daughter, I'd want her to be just like Helen. I realize I'm out of my league, but there's no reason we can't all be friends. I can run movies you like and fly you anywhere you'd like to go."

I was surprised to hear my brother's voice . "Gee, we'd love that Mr. . . ."

"Howard! You must be Wally."

Howard soon knew it was time to leave as Daddy was on his third yawn and this one wasn't silent and a stretch had been added.

Stormy, our dog, and the whole fan-damily followed Mr. Hu . . . Howard to the door.

(I questioned Mama Blue while writing these pages. "What was your first impression of Howard?"

(Her answer? "He was kind, considerate, and boyish."

(Daddy interjected, "What did he do that was kind and considerate? I thought he was a bore.")

Later that night the phone rang. It was Howard. He sounded lonely. I felt a lump in my stomach. It was the first time he'd called me direct.

"This is Howard . . . Helen."

The lump grew bigger.

"I'm back at the hotel." There was a long pause. I swear it sounded as if he were eating. "I've just ordered some movies I think your family would enjoy."

Howard liked my family but never felt comfortable with my father. I don't think Howard ever dated anyone before without giving a job to some member of the family. Later he offered my father all his insurance business, but Dad turned it down. He would have been many times a millionaire, but he believed that nothing was free in this world, and he only wanted what he had earned. He was the only incorruptible man I've ever known.

Howard loved my mother because she was fair; if I was wrong she took his side, and he felt he had an ally. They also compared ailments. Mother treated us both like her children. She loved to be Earth Mother, and Howard lapped that up.

I was dating Cojo and other boys my age, but I had to be home by midnight. Howard knew this, and he would telephone every night from his bungalow at the Beverly Hills Hotel. He said he wanted to be the last person I talked to at the end of the day. Sometimes we would talk until four or five o'clock in the morning. And it was fascinating! He knew about everything and made the whole world sound exciting and stimulating.

We talked like two high-school kids. He wanted to know every detail about the boys I dated. He loved to tease me about my teenage romances and asked how many times I had been in love. At this point in my life, I lived and breathed for acting; that is all I loved, so that is what we discussed: the parts I would most like to play, the actresses

I'd like to emulate. He not only knew all my favorites, he had dated them all. He actually lived in my world of make-believe.

Soon I was rushing home from my dates. I couldn't wait to get home to talk to him.

I told Cojo about my feelings, and he said, "I think you're falling in love. Why don't you go out with him?"

I was shocked. I would have expected any reaction from Cojo except that.

It had never occurred to me that I would ever go out with Howard Hughes alone. After all, he was four years older than my mother! But . . . well, why not? Maybe just once. But I'd keep it a secret. I didn't want the other kids to know.

Finally I agreed to go out to dinner with him. As the time grew near I grew more and more excited. He was so totally different from anyone I'd ever known.

Our first date was full of surprises. First, he picked me up on time, and we drove off in one of his postwar Chevrolets. He'd even had it washed! I noticed as we drove off that the whole neighborhood was watering their lawns . . . their front lawns.

My mother had treated him like any other date, insisting he have me home early. "Remember, you have that screen test tomorrow with John Derek. You want to look your best."

"Yes, mother." I was embarrassed, but Howard looked delighted. He was living a part of life he'd missed.

We cruised down Hollywood's famous Sunset Strip till we came to a restaurant called the Somerset House. Howard parked his own car because he was afraid the parking lot attendant would lose his keys.

My second surprise was to find we were the only customers in the place. He had hired the whole restaurant, complete with waiters and violins.

Everything that happened that night struck both of us as hilarious. The waiters were trying so hard to please that

34

they kept bumping into one another, spilling and knocking over everything. When the dessert cart was wheeled in, the wine steward backed into it and the whole table came crashing down, with him smack-dab in the middle of the desserts. Howard pointed at him and said, "I'll have one of those." That really cracked us up. We laughed until we cried.

Howard had a wonderful feeling for the ridiculous. I think his happiest moment was on the way home when he realized that, during all the chaos, they'd forgotten to give him the check.

That night as we were driving home, he took my hand and kissed it. *Zing!* Fire seemed to spread through my body, and I thought I knew what love was all about. He had awakened feelings inside of me that were different from anything I had ever known. I wanted to hold on and stay as close to him as I possibly could; I didn't want to let go for a minute. I needed to be near enough to breathe and touch and feel him. Howard realized the spark in me had been kindled and did everything he could to keep it glowing. Poor baby, he had so much to overcome: my girlish timidity and my strict upbringing and, not least, Glendale!

He walked me to the door. I wanted so much to shock him, to show him I was grown-up and sophisticated, that I grabbed him and kissed him with all my might—then ran into the house, slamming the door right in his face.

The moment I was inside, I snuck to the window and peeked out to see his reaction. He was laughing. Why, he laughed all the way to the car!

"Good night, Mr. Hughes," I whispered breathlessly as I saw his car disappear into the night.

I slipped into the soft security of my bed with my mind full of Howard. I couldn't sleep. My body still tingled from that magic moment when Howard took my hand. I still felt all warm and wet. I'd been kissed by boys before, even soul kissed a couple of times, but I'd never been sexually aroused before. Somehow Howard did this to me with a simple kiss on the hand. I wondered what it would be like if he were with me, what he'd do and say. What would it feel like to have him lying next to me, to go to sleep in his arms and wake up with him there?

I was the princess in a fairy tale, impatiently anticipating the next page.

Chapter 3

A FEW DAYS LATER, I RAN INTO COJO. I DIDN'T HAVE THE nerve to tell him he had been right; for the first time in my life I was hopelessly in love. Why is it that when you've never been happier, something has to come along to mar it?

Even though Cojo had suggested I date Howard Hughes, he never in his wildest imaginings thought anything would ever come of it. He thought it was an amusing schoolgirl crush that would soon fade away.

Cojo and I had dated each other for over a year; we were inseparable. He had followed me on my statewide personal-appearance tour for *The Return of October;* we had missed each other so much that he'd ridden a bus all the way from Los Angeles to New York just to be with me. All our friends assumed we would be married; Jane Powell and Elizabeth Taylor were already engaged.

Cojo loved me enough to never take advantage of me. He'd always said, "If any man ever gets you before I do, I'll never forgive myself." I'm sure I really made it difficult, because I loved to neck up a storm in the car, never realizing I was straining his will to the nth degree. I loved to kiss because it felt good, like a back rub. I hadn't connected it with sexual urges. When Howard kissed my hand he opened a Pandora's box that would take me to the ends of the earth with him.

Cojo cared; even if I didn't love him, he had to save me from Howard. He had never once taken advantage of me, and, by damn, neither would Howard Hughes!

I sat in stunned silence while Cojo named all the women he knew Howard was keeping. He couldn't miss seeing the tears that flowed beneath my heavy dark glasses—or the heavier heart I drove back to Glendale with that day.

When I walked in the door, Mother was calling.

"Pick up the phone! It's lover boy; he's been calling all day. Be nice! He's been worried sick about you."

"Where did you say I was, Mom?"

"I told him the truth—at the studio. He called the studio and you weren't there, now he thinks you've been with Cojo."

It was my second shock of the day: Howard Hughes was having me followed. No one had known Cojo and I were together. I had run into him by accident as I was leaving the cleaner's.

My voice was unusually low and shaky when I answered the phone.

"How did you know I was with Cojo?" I asked.

He replied in his twangy Texas accent. It only twanged when he was annoyed. "Someone saw you two together."

Then I blurted, "Well, someone saw you with ———," and I named all the girls' names I could remember. All the tears I had been holding back came rushing out.

"I hate you, Howard Hughes."

Then he spent forty-five minutes telling me how he was misunderstood:

"These are poor girls, who have no parents, who have come out here to have a career. There are other girls who have come from all over the world and their parents have entrusted them to me. Do you think I'd break that trust? *Never!*" He went on: "Won't you ever learn that people in this town are envious? They would like to destroy what we

38

have, because they can't have it. Are we going to let them? Are you going to let them?"

"No, Howard. I felt so terrible, and now I feel so good. I just love you. But, Howard, there's something else. Everyone talks about you and Jean Peters."

"Any talk you hear about a romance is pure rumor. Jean's a friend. She was there at the hospital after my XF-11 crash in Beverly Hills."

"I wish I'd been there to take care of you, baby."

"I wasn't a pretty sight. Hell, everyone gave me up for dead. The whole left side of my body was nearly destroyed. My heart was even pushed out of place. I had such a low pain tolerance that Verne (Verne Mason, Howard's physician) had me to the limit on morphine."

"Oh, Howard, the suffering must have been awful. I think you still hurt a lot."

"I'm fine," he mumbled. There was suddenly a sense of pride in his voice. "I walked away from the crash. The papers said a marine pulled me from the wreckage. Not true. I forced open the cockpit. The whole goddamn plane was on fire, and so was my clothing. Christ, I was a human torch! The marine rolled me in the grass and put out the fire. He saved my life."

"And what about you and Jean?" I asked. "Did you fall in love with her?"

"I think I did for a while, the way a patient falls in love with his nurse. Jean is a real Florence Nightingale."

I was puzzled and Howard went on to explain. "Everyone rushed to the hospital after the accident: Lana Turner, Rita Hayworth, Jane Russell. They were all there, but they soon became bored and stopped coming. Jean stayed on long after I was able to go home. Anyway, I've always looked after her. Hell, I couldn't even think about being romantic with Jean. She's a friend."

I nodded my head in agreement. "I know—just like Cojo."

"Now wait a minute. I don't see the similarity at all. Cojo obviously has ulterior motives because he's in love with you. When will you start believing me that all those boys want is to get up your skirt? That's all they've got on their minds.''

And what about you, Howard? I thought to myself. I wanted to ask him how he knew I had been with Cojo, but I didn't want to feel any more hurt now. Hadn't he said he loved me? Three times. I counted, and . . . *"Mother,"* I yelled as I hung up. "He wants to marry me."

Mother stopped what she was doing. "Wait a minute. Do you want to marry him?''

I flippantly replied, "Of course not. What would the kids think?''

That night he was in a wonderful mood when he picked me up. He walked into the kitchen, sniffed a few times, peeked under the lids of a few pans, gave Mama Blue a squeeze, and slapped my father on the back and congratulated him for raising such a wonderful daughter. "I'm sure you deserve the credit.'' He winked at Mother. My father gave her his He-must-want-something look.

He did. Me.

He wouldn't tell me where we were going, but he had given me strict instructions to wear slacks. That was after the secretaries at his Romaine Street office had already called me three times. When we pulled up at the La Cienega bowling alley, it all made sense. *Movieland* magazine had just hit the stands with a layout of Jerome Courtland and me bowling. Howard, bless his heart, wanted to demonstrate his prowess on the lanes.

After that, we went there frequently; bowling became one of Howard's favorite sports until one day we stopped, just as abruptly as we'd started.

He'd never call ahead to reserve an alley. He preferred just walking in, changing into rented bowling shoes, and waiting our turn. We'd watch a game already in progress and make small bets; a Coke or a hot dog. (Howard would always say, "A hot dog tastes better in a bowling alley than it does at home.'') Howard won most of the time; he had an uncanny ability to pick winners. Good thing I usually lost,

40

because at least I had the money in my purse to pay; Howard never carried any money with him.

I was always worried about people or fans coming up and bothering us; Howard just laughed. "First of all," he told me, "people aren't going to recognize either of us, especially at a bowling alley."

Before I had a chance to answer, he took me by the hand, led me into the bathroom and washed off all my lipstick.

"There," he said. "The only time people notice you is if you dress for it."

When it came our turn to take an alley, Howard walked right up to the lane, tried on several balls, and finally chose one. It was fun to watch; he was a perfectionist in everything he did. Howard held the ball, stood as poised as a good pointer, took careful aim, and sent the first ball down the lane. He would hit strike after strike, and he rarely missed a lone pin.

True to his prophecy, we were never recognized. Howard, dressed in his white shirt with the rolled-up sleeves and unpressed trousers, and I with no makeup and bobby sox, pulling up in one of Howard's old Chevrolets, were certainly not going to attract any attention.

There was only one occasion at the bowling alley when Howard became upset—the night that a handsome young man of my own age walked over when we were between games.

"I was admiring your daughter, sir," the boy began in a gentlemanly manner. "Could I have an introduction?"

"No, you can't," Howard fired back, turning away. The boy looked at me and shrugged as he left.

Howard looked around and caught me grinning.

"So you find that funny, do you?"

I couldn't hold my laughter back. Then we both laughed and he held me in his arms.

The following day I drove straight to the schoolroom at Columbia Pictures, where I was still putting in three hours of school a day. I couldn't wait to tell Lillian Barkley about my date with Howard.

Lillian Barkley was one of the outstanding people in my life. She had five doctorates in education and was the niece of Alben W. Barkley, Truman's vice-president. On her mother's side she was a Lincoln. Lillian was everyone's confidante; she knew everything that went on in Hollywood. We were all Lillian's children, from Shirley Temple on, even after we grew up. I was sure she loved me more than the rest . . . but no doubt the others thought the same about themselves.

I was happy to find Lillian alone. Usually the room overflowed with her students and friends.

"Guess what? You were right about having me invite Howard Hughes over to the house. Now he's my best friend. He runs pictures nearly every night for the whole family at Goldwyn Studios. Do you believe," I said, in a very confidential tone, "that last night we went bowling? Yes, at just a regular old bowling alley and we had . . ." My voice faded; something was wrong. "What's the matter? Aren't you thrilled?"

"No," Lillian said, "and I don't want you to be so thrilled either. This man has a reputation—"

"Oh, I know all about that," I interrupted. "But that's just because people are jealous. He's not like that at all. Really, he's not. I told him all about you, and he wants to meet you."

"Terry," she cautioned, "I've met Mr. Hughes."

Now it was my turn to be surprised. "You have? When?"

She went on. "I had a long talk with Luella, and she thinks—"

"Louella Parsons! She knows?" I gasped.

"No, your mother. She told me he's mentioned marriage, and we don't want to see you get your hopes up."

"Just because he mentioned it doesn't mean I'd do it."

"Terry, listen to me. You're a special prize for any man. Remember, I didn't even feel that Cojo was good enough for you. I can't stand by and watch Howard take the bloom off the peach. There *are* other women in Howard's life. One in particular I know he promised marriage to. I'm breaking a confidence, which I've never done before, but Jean Peters hasn't dated a man other than Howard in three years.''

I felt all the blood drain from my face. I felt as if she'd hit me with a wet towel. Lillian loved me. She loved me as much as my own mother. When she said she knew, *she knew*.

"Oh, dear God, help me take away this pain!"

I had to talk to Howard.

I couldn't wait to call back Lillian later that day.

"Oh, Lillian, you don't have to worry about me anymore. I talked to Howard, and you were right, though, of course, he doesn't know it came from you. Can you imagine, Jean Peters *hasn't* dated anyone for three years! But, you see, she was dating Audie Murphy when he had just become the most decorated soldier in the United States, and she met Howard Hughes with Audie the night before his big airplane crash. Howard said she fell in love with him and continued visiting him at the hospital long after the others had stopped. Well—listen to this—Howard flew to Mexico when she was filming a movie called *Captain from Castile*. He surprised her—she didn't know he was coming —and when he got there, guess what? Poor Howard found out she was in love with another man, her assistant director, Stanley Hough. Well, he was brokenhearted. He told her they'd always be friends, but he could never trust her again. So she won't date anyone else because she's still trying to prove to Howard she can be trusted . . . but it's too late. Howard said he would never make love to her again. He begs her to go out with other men, but she refuses, and it's really hard on poor Howard.''

Dear Lillian took it all in. I'm sure if I could have seen her face, she would have been shaking her head as she always used to do and thinking *I'd* taken it all in.

The hook had been baited. There was nothing anyone could do now but wait. . . .

My trust in Howard was short-lived. Mother had become friendly with the various boys who worked for Howard.

Howard was so impressed by my strict Mormon upbringing, and by the fact that we don't smoke or drink, that he began hiring Mormons. Often when they were picking me up or dropping me off, Mother would offer them something to eat or drink. Sometimes Howard had them wait at our house until he called, which could be a couple of minutes or a couple of hours. She soon saw more of them than she did of me. Mother was the kind of person whom people trusted and confided in, especially since she was a Mormon, a bishop's daughter.

The Mormon boys got together and collectively decided to save one of their own. It seems that after Howard dropped me off at midnight, my curfew time, he would go to the homes of other women, where he would spend the remainder of the night. Some nights he went to Joan's or Sally's, Carla's or Colleen's, and every month or so he'd show up at Jean's house.

"But how did they know?" I cried.

"Because they picked him up or dropped him off there."

I had stubbornly refused to believe Howard was seeing other women till the boys told Mother. At that time, they were glorified messengers, a group of young men just out of school, hired to answer his calls, relay messages, and drive his girls. Later they were called the Palace Guard or the Mormon Mafia.

Right on time, the phone rang. It was midnight—it was Howard.

I was ready. I told him there was no use lying, that I knew about *all* the women in his life, and I *named* them one by one. I made up a clever story so he would never suspect the boys. He never did. I would have given my life before giving them away.

There was dead silence on the other end of the phone. It was perhaps the only time in his life he didn't have a ready answer.

I screamed, "Howard Hughes, you are not only the biggest liar I've ever met, but the most deceptive man on earth. What's the matter, don't you have an answer?"

I heard a meek, "I can explain."

"No, you can't explain. You can lie, but you can't explain."

Then he cried. Howard Hughes cried. He became the poor little boy who had no mother, who couldn't sleep alone. It was all my fault. If I'd sleep with him he'd never go near any of the others.

"All right," I said to Howard levelly. "I'm not going to continue seeing you unless you sleep on the sofa in our den. It's the only way I can keep tabs on you."

"What about the nights I have to work late at the factory? Surely you don't expect me to drive all the way to Glendale, do you?"

"You're damn well right I do," I screamed. "It's the only way I can trust you."

"But that's nearly fifty miles of driving," he moaned. "I'm too tall for your couch . . . besides, I once saw a cockroach scoot under one of the cushions."

"Why worry? That's probably the only thing you haven't slept with. I'll leave the key to the front door under the mat."

I finally cried myself to sleep, knowing I'd never see Howard Hughes again.

But I was awakened in the middle of the night. The front door had slammed shut, and as I lay there and listened I heard the springs of that old mattress squeak as Howard lowered himself onto that dilapidated couch.

Chapter 4

HOWARD MENTIONED MARRIAGE AND OUR FUTURE EVERY-day; he wanted to be married so we could get away and be alone together. I loved discussing marriage and dreaming of it, but the reality was still a long way off in my mind, something I'd do when I grew up. I had my career and I wanted to have fun; I hadn't even started living yet. I needed to know Howard was all mine, but I wasn't ready for marriage. As long as I heard that front door open every night and the springs in the old convertible couch, I was secure.

Once in the middle of the night I snuck into the den. I'd gone to sleep early after a long day at the studio, and wanted to make sure that Howard had come in. He had. It was such a funny sight the way his feet stuck out over the edge of the sofa.

I couldn't help surprising him and climbed in beside him. The danger of it was exciting. If my father had found me there, he would probably have killed Howard. But it felt good and natural being there next to him.

Howard told me that after I finished the film I was working on, he wanted to take me away to Harbor Island, a place that caters exclusively to the rich elite; it lies off the Balboa peninsula in southern California. We were both tired and needed a rest. At that time I was working on the movie *He's a Cockeyed Wonder*, with Mickey Rooney. My whole life centered on movies. I loved to be working and hated the time between pictures. It was always the same laborious routine: tours; publicity layouts; singing, dancing, and acting lessons. I worked hard while Howard fooled around talking to Louella Parsons, Bob Mitchum, and those two new Generals he'd just hired, General Eaker and General George. It seemed to me Howard wasn't working because he never went to an office or sat at a desk. He appeared to be on vacation, relaxed and easygoing. He was always tinkering with something, taking my camera, gadgets, and toys apart. It used to infuriate me, because he never put them back together. He would spend hours figuring out ways to emphasize the curve of a bosom on the ad art of his latest movie. He was the only person I ever knew who had the time to talk for hours with me on the phone. I thought of him as a playmate whom God had put on this earth to take care of me.

Several years later, when someone was threatening to sue me, Howard insisted that I record my phone conversations. Unbeknownst to him, I also recorded a number of *our* conversations! I still have his voice on tape saying, "Honey, why don't you decide you need someone to take care of you and why don't you let me have the job?"

My high-pitched baby voice cooed, "Oh, Howard, do you want it? You mean that, don't you? Oh, I love you. You can have the job."

As Howard had promised, he rented a beach house on Harbor Island for the month of June.

He gave Mama Blue detailed directions to the place several times and then had her repeat them back to him. He told me he'd have to leave from time to time to take care of business, but Frank, his cook, would be there, and after I was settled in I could have some of my girlfriends over.

Mother and I drove down together; my father and my

brother Wally followed us with the excess luggage. When Mama Blue and I arrived, Frank greeted us at the door. Frank had been the steward on Howard's boat *Southern Cross* which had been given to the war effort years before. The navy used Howard's classy old yacht of the thirties for submarine patrol and changed its name to *Crystal*. There was a secret sliding panel between the stateroom and the main guest room. The navy sure had fun with that.

Frank looked glum at the prospect of working again. He'd been in mothballs for years and looked it. (Howard kept his crew on the payroll for the duration, just in case he ever bought another boat. He never did.)

Mom and I followed Frank and my suitcase to the bedrooms. I couldn't believe my eyes. Howard stood at the top of the landing and playfully slid down the banister. He thanked my mother profusely for driving me down and he invited her to stay for lunch. Mother and I looked at each other, perplexed.

In the meantime, Wally and my father had arrived and came struggling through the doorway, weighted down with fishing poles, beach umbrellas, inner tubes, and more luggage. Now Howard was the one to look perplexed.

My father looked at Frank in his little white waistcoat and dropped everything on the spot. He tipped Frank a quarter, "Be extra careful with my fishing tackle," he warned. Then he turned to Howard. "Whatever's cooking sure smells good. I'm starved."

Howard was speechless as he backed away from Daddy's cigar. "You wanted to be part of our family," I reminded Howard.

The house and furnishings were in the Mediterranean style. It was so palatial that at first glance we thought it was a hotel; you could wander around all day and not run into anyone. The panoramic view of the bay with all the yachts and sailboats going by was breathtaking. Like the other homes on the island, it had a private beach and pier.

Anchored within view were two famous old sailing ships, the *Good Will*, which I believe belonged to Donald Douglas, of Douglas Aircraft, and the *Pioneer,* which belonged to the Vanderbilt family. Howard told me of the many parties he had attended on these old classic yachts with Errol Flynn, Charlie Chaplin, Humphrey Bogart, and other great stars of the past.

Howard often pointed out the magnificent house on the point which belonged to the violinist Jascha Heifetz. Howard was a big fan, and so fond of the violin that he always said "Jascha Heifetz" in a revered tone. Another reason for Howard's respect might have been that Heifetz defected from Russia to become an American citizen in 1925. (This was during the time that Howard was waging his big war against communism and firing confirmed *party members* from RKO Studios.) Howard never passed his house without hoping he might catch a glimpse of the famous violinist, or catch the melodic strains of his Stradivarius.

The atmosphere on our secluded island was relaxed and luxurious. Howard felt that our moonlight strolls on the seashore would dissolve my reserve and lead to my surrender. His talk of marriage became more frequent and more sincere. I still didn't want to be married, but I must admit it was becoming easier and easier to imagine.

Howard loved to stand on the pier and watch the boats sail by. He'd tell me sea stories of his past when he lived on Long Island, and about Sir Thomas Lipton, the famous tea merchant who made five attempts to win the America's Cup, and about all those wealthy friends who were building ten-meter boats for the big race. He talked about the exciting days of yesteryear, about Dan and Bob Topping. (Bob later marched Lana Turner down the aisle when she announced, "This is forever.") He told me about his good friend Sherman Fairchild of Fairchild Cameras, and the rich Prince Charming who married Sonja Henie. I sat wide-eyed as he related how the Long Island rich had lived. Their stables were larger than most of our houses, and a footman stood behind each chair while dinner was served. The homes had two or three dining rooms and, naturally, a

49

ballroom. Naturally. I could just see the young, handsome Howard Hughes with all those beautiful debutantes, bowing and filling out their dance cards. I relived every moment and was transported back to those days with him. I was enthralled.

He'd tell me about his yachting days in Florida and his boat, *Southern Cross,* which even had its own barber shop. He promised he'd build me the largest ship in the whole world and I'd have my own shopping center. I was thrilled by this man with the magic imagination. He found some meat-wrapping paper in the kitchen, spread it out on the dinette, and together we designed our wonderland ship. We'd sit and figure which harbors were large enough to accommodate us. I understand those plans are still at the Romaine Street office; I believe he fully expected to build our dream ship. To me, Howard was the only man in the world who could make fantasies into realities, and he usually did.

There were silent moments when he'd take me in his arms and just hold me tight. I loved the way he always pushed my hair out of my face and ran his finger down my turned-up nose. I laughed when he told me I had the most beautiful smile and teeth he'd ever seen.

"That's because you have a short upper lip," he said. "It makes it easier to smile."

"My lip is not short," I pouted. "Yours is just long." Never before in my life had anyone found me beautiful. He could just sit and look at me for hours, admiring the curve of my neck, my dainty ears or slender ankles. No one had ever paid me so much attention or given me so much confidence.

I loved the way he smelled. "You smell like Chinese laundry."

Howard looked as if he'd just been insulted. I hadn't realized I'd spoken out loud. "Chinese laundry?"

"Oh, Howard, that's my favorite smell in all the world. There isn't anything that smells so good. Chinese laundry is the highest, highest compliment, because it's the cleanest, freshest smell there is."

"Oh, is it, now?" he teased. "I remember what you told your friend Jerry Courtland about me on that first flight: 'Doesn't he know that cleanliness is next to godliness? He's dirty.'"

I was so embarrassed I couldn't look at him. "Oh, no! You heard that? I thought you were deaf. How could you hear me in that noisy airplane?"

"I hear better in an airplane. I have the kind of deafness where sound carries sound."

"I was so wrong. I thought just because you didn't shave and wore old clothes, you were dirty."

Howard laughed. "Ava Gardner always told me I'd be waterlogged, I took so many showers."

Howard was silent for the longest time. Then I heard him mumble, "Chinese laundry, huh? That's good, hmm. That's good."

I couldn't see his expression on that moonless night, but I could hear the warmth of his voice.

After a few days, I sensed Howard was feeling crowded by my family. Even though the house was large enough that he wouldn't have to see or hear any of us all day, it wasn't his nature to stick around and play the family game. Howard belonged to the sky. Up there was where he was the happiest and most comfortable. I was to understand and eventually share that splendor with him, above and beyond this world, where words or touches weren't needed for our souls to be one.

Being young and inherently possessive, I became annoyed and inconsolable as Howard began leaving the island more frequently and staying away longer. He would usually be gone before breakfast and return after we'd all finished our evening meal. Frank would have to mess up the kitchen all over again and prepare Howard's food. Even though that was what he was being paid for, he acted very put out. Sighs of exasperation punctuated his every effort.

Recognizing my dismay, Howard decided I should learn how to sail, and what better instructor than a full-fledged international sea captain? Captain Flynn had been the skipper of Howard's yacht and had unlimited master's papers to sail any ship in the world; he had papers for seven seas and five oceans. He was a corpulent but very dignified sixty-five; the nicest, sweetest captain there ever was.

The first sight of Captain Flynn was something no one could ever forget. He arrived on Harbor Island in full regalia to instruct a teenage girl in the piloting of a four-by-eight sailboat. Imagine him with his one-girl crew aboard that tiny, easily capsizable catboat in the Pacific Ocean. Every day we went out sailing, and every day I capsized the boat. I still see him so clearly in his full-dress uniform, upright in the bow, making the boat tilt forward. As powerboats and yachts passed us in the bay, he kept his chin high. When I would come about while heeling, he would be thrown overboard with great dignity. He even seemed to sink at attention into those chilling waters.

Every night when Howard arrived, he was devastated to see all our clothes hanging out to dry on the clothesline. Only a bathing suit and a terry-cloth jacket belonged to me, but the captain was bundled up in socks, garters, long johns, pants, shirt, tie, jacket, and captain's hat.

Howard was sympathetic and felt sorry for Captain Flynn, but he couldn't conceal his amusement when he passed that clothesline each night. "Poor Captain Flynn," Howard would moan to my mother. "That girl will be the death of both of us."

One day when the sea was especially turbulent and I made a maneuver that really gave the captain a toss, he contributed his false teeth to Davy Jones's locker. Later, Howard tried to act stern, but it was all he could do to remain straightfaced. The false teeth episode brought my sailing lessons to an abrupt halt, but Captain Flynn didn't hold a grudge.

We had the Harbor Island house for a month. As the month drew to a close, Father had to leave us and go back to work. The rest of us stayed on in a house Howard rented on Balboa for the month of July. It was nice but wasn't on the water. We saw very little of Howard, but now I wasn't bothered much by it. I didn't have to think about marriage or the responsibility of a relationship. I just played and horsed around with my little brother and had my girlfriends down to stay. I was bound and determined to enjoy at least one more month as a child.

It was a wonderful summer, unmatched to this day. But soon it was time for me to get back home and back to work.

One day a flower truck arrived at the house and the delivery boy brought in boxes and boxes of flowers. Since the day of that first flight, Howard always kept my parents' home full of fresh flowers. This new shipment wouldn't have been unusual, except for the fact that the whole house was already filled with fresh flowers. When Mama Blue saw the new arrivals, she thought there had been some kind of mistake and tried to send them back. But, as always, no card accompanied the boxes and there was no indication of what florist or nursery they came from, just gigantic white boxes with beautiful white satin ribbons. The steady flow of boxes was already popular with all our neighbors to store things in, but that day they got the flowers too.

Howard called me that afternoon to tell me to be ready to be picked up at a certain time that evening. He told me it was nothing fancy, but it was a special evening for us. He said he was busy, and if he wanted to keep our date he'd have to get off the phone. He hung up knowing he had accomplished what he had set out to accomplish. I was burning with curiosity all afternoon, wondering why that evening would be "special."

By the time Howard's boy arrived to pick me up, I had worked myself into a state of frenzied anticipation. I pumped the driver for information, but he didn't know a thing. He drove me to the corner of La Cienega and Holloway—that's just off the Hollywood Sunset Strip. We pulled up behind Howard's Chevy. Howard walked over and told the boy to take his car; he was out of gas. (Howard

53

was always losing cars, forgetting where he left them, or running out of gas. I often wonder if there aren't still cars around the world, rusting, that we lost.) I was full of anticipation as we drove down the Pacific Coast Highway. We pulled off onto a winding dirt road that went into the foothills. Back off the road was a small, rustic restaurant with sawdust on the floor and about three ice-cream tables and chairs.

We were greeted by a little old man in a white suit who had the twinkliest eyes I'd ever seen. I could see immediately that he was fond of Howard and knew him well. It turned out that he had owned an ice-cream parlor when Howard went to prep school at Thatcher in California, and Howard thought he could make the best hot-fudge sundaes he'd ever tasted. Wherever Howard moved, he'd set him up in business. The years have erased the memory of that dear man's name, but I'll never forget how proud I was when Howard introduced me as the next Mrs. Hughes.

"Terry Hughes," I mused out loud.

"No, Helen Hughes," he corrected.

I think that's one of the most thrilling experiences for a girl: when she hears her name joined for the first time with the name of the man she loves.

The only other thing I remember about the room are the hand-carved owls, hung all over the walls, that the man had made. For good luck, he gave me a small one. After that, Howard always bought me owls whenever he saw them, in memory of that night.

That was the only time Howard ever allowed me to have two hot fudge sundaes. I knew we were about to experience something special.

Howard was being so mysterious! I snuggled beside him while he drove the back roads. He loved to be behind the wheel of a plane or car; it was when he did most of his thinking. He was freer and his mind could fly.

"Why are you so quiet, little rabbit?" he asked. This was his Harvey period, so I was "little rabbit" or "little cottontail."

We'd been going around curves for fifteen minutes. "I'm carsick," I said.

"I suppose that's my fault. I shouldn't have let you have the second sundae, and now you'll probably break out and your mother's going to blame it on me. Hold on. We'll soon be there."

I scooted under the shift and laid my head in his lap. When I woke up, we were high on a hill looking out over all the city lights.

"Where are we?" I gasped. "Oh, it's beautiful." It was pitch black except for those faraway lights of the city.

"We're on top of Mulholland Drive," he said, "in the Hollywood hills. You're facing the valley; the other side is Hollywood. I come up here a lot because I feel a closeness to God and the universe. Weekends, it's full of kids. They call it Inspiration Point. Do you remember what you said, that only God could marry you?" Howard asked.

"I said only God could marry you forever, because man says, 'until death you do part.'"

"I believe that," he said. "And I want to marry you, Helen Koford, forever."

I took a deep breath. Howard extended his arms and I threw myself into them. I squeezed and squeezed and held on with all my might.

"Oh, Howard, I love you. I do, I do, I do."

"Then let's get married."

"When? How?" I cried.

"Here, now, above the lights and under the stars. Don't you believe God can marry us? Don't you believe what you just said?"

"Of course I believe it, with all my heart and soul I believe it . . . but how?"

"Oh, you nonbeliever." He laughed. Then he opened the door and I slipped out from his side after him. Hand in hand we walked out to the highest point and knelt down under the stars, said our vows together, and prayed that God would open up our hearts and join us in holy matrimony forever. Then Howard slipped a ring in the shape of an owl around my finger, picked me up off my knees, brushed off the jacket that we had knelt on, placed it around my shoulders, and sealed my lips with kisses.

Silently, we walked back to the car. "Oh, dear, we wrecked your jacket."

"Don't worry, it's not mine; it belongs to the driver."

Married forever, we drove down the hill. I still have and cherish that sapphire-ruby-diamond owl ring.

I couldn't take my eyes off Howard. I was so lost in him that I didn't even notice that we weren't heading back toward Glendale. When I finally looked to the road, we were on Sunset Boulevard and the Beverly Hills Hotel was coming up on the right.

"Where are we going, Howard?"

"Home to our bungalow," he said. "A wife's place is with her husband. That's the law of God."

"Oh, no, Howard. You're taking *me* back home to Glendale. We might be married spiritually, but not physically. Mormon law says we must follow the laws of the land, and the law of the land wouldn't consider us married. So, if a wife's place is with her husband, I know one husband who's sleeping on a couch in Glendale."

I laughed, then hugged and kissed Howard. He couldn't decide whether to be disgusted, disappointed, or amused. He finally shook his head and laughed as he wheeled the car around toward Glendale.

Years later, my friend Suzie Zanuck said, "That silly Jean Peters . . . Did you know that Howard Hughes took her to the top of Mulholland Drive and married her under the stars? Can you imagine anyone stupid enough to fall for that?"

Ouch!

Chapter 5

I ANSWERED THE TELEPHONE AND HEARD HOWARD'S voice.

"Get an overnight bag packed and be ready in an hour. We're taking a trip. I'll send a car for you and your mother."

It was several days before Thanksgiving in 1949.

I replied, "I have to do my nails and wash my hair and get my legs waxed, and then Mother's friend Sally is coming over to help us with the scrapbooks—and I told Carolyn and Harriet that they could come over, too. I can't just call them up and tell them not to come."

"This is more important," he said, dismissing my reasons.

I stood my ground. "I'm sorry, Howard, but it's just impossible for me to leave on such short notice. And for what?"

"Now, honey, why do you have to be so difficult? You make it so I can't even surprise you anymore."

My tone changed. "It's a surprise, Howard?"

"Well, it was supposed to be, but it's not anymore. If you have to know, I have it all arranged. We're getting married this afternoon. We're going to do it your way. Legally. Those long treks to Glendale every day are making an old man of me before my time. You're going to come and live with me.''

I was so thrilled I could barely breathe. I was afraid the excitement I was feeling would cause my asthma to flare up and I'd miss my own wedding.

Just a month before, I wouldn't have considered taking the big step. I liked the security and love I had at home, and my friends there in Glendale, and being part of the movie gang and one of Columbia's up-and-coming stars. I even liked the schoolroom, Lillian, and college. I was certain you couldn't be married and have fun. Now I was on cloud ten with the feeling that I'd just been given something I had craved for all my life.

Howard's recent devotion to me and the deep need he'd expressed had consumed me. As important as my career was to me, I think I would have even given that up for him if he asked me to. But he wasn't asking that. He just wanted me to be his wife, forever.

"I love you, Howard, and I'll be ready in *half an hour.*" I hung up the phone.

I felt like calling all my friends and telling them. I wished they could all be with me on this glorious day, but Howard had decided that a publicized wedding could be damaging to both of our careers, and for the present our marriage would have to remain secret. He said the publicity would hurt my virgin image. After all, I was the little girl in all the animal pictures. I'd worked with Lassie, October the horse, Mighty Joe Young the gorilla, and this year I'd costarred with a squirrel, the Great Rupert.

He also stressed that if I wanted to be a *big* star, I'd have to remain single in the public eye. I was the blossoming starlet coming of age and available for marriage. Howard was right. I received a countless number of engagement rings and marriage proposals in my fan mail. He didn't want what was happening to Ingrid Bergman on *Stromboli* to happen to me. Already married, Bergman got involved, while shooting in Italy, with Roberto Rossellini, who also was married. Bergman became pregnant by Rossellini, and there was a horrible scandal.

We had even decided to keep the wedding secret from Wally and my father. Daddy had a heart condition, and we were afraid the shock would be too much for him. Mother and I were bumping into each other and tripping over the telephone cords in our rush to be ready.

When the car arrived, half an hour later, I was wearing a sleeveless sheath of white linen, piped in powder blue. A cashmere cardigan in the same shade of blue was slung over my shoulders, and I carried the small, hand-carved owl that Howard's friend had given me as a talisman. Of course, I always wore my owl ring.

When we arrived at Howard's bungalow, he was waiting with his copilot, Earl Martyn. Howard took one look at my dress and sent me home to change.

That time my mother stood up for me. "Why, she looks lovely, Howard."

"No." He was insistent. "You wore that exact same outfit when we had our first quarrel, don't you remember? I'm not one to be superstitious, but there's no need to take any unnecessary risks on a day as important as this one. Earl, you drive Helen back to change. Luella, you wait here with me. No need to make a circus of it."

Imagine, here it was my wedding day and I got sent home. I changed into a navy blue off-the-shoulder sweater that Harriet had knit, and a beige linen skirt, embroidered with a tree of life in different shades of blue.

My second outfit passed inspection. When Earl and I returned to the Beverly Hills Hotel, Howard greeted me with a bouquet of lilies and a kiss of approval. We drove to Hughes Airport and were flown to San Diego and driven to a waiting boat.

The huge cabin cruiser was idling as we walked up the plank. I held on to mother's hand as we followed Howard to the main salon. Her hand was as cold as mine, but she reassured me with a tight squeeze, and some of my

59

nervousness subsided. I suddenly wished Daddy and Wally and Grandma Bickmore were here. I felt I was letting them down; but Howard had felt that the more people who knew, the harder the secret was to keep. It didn't really matter how you married, but who you married. I was leaving my little girl's world and entering the world of this tall stranger. I knew it would be lonely, but it would be ours.

The first person I saw as I was going below was dear Captain Flynn. What I didn't notice was that he was covered with bilge grease. Someone had left the bilge open and he'd fallen in, dress whites and all. I threw my arms around his neck and kissed his red Irish nose; he tried to stop me, but it was too late. Now we were both covered with bilge grease.

I heard Lillian's good-natured laugh. "Don't worry, child, it's good luck."

"Do you think Helen and the captain have a good lawsuit?" Howard asked his attorney, Will Wright.

"The suit's too dirty for me to handle. I'd suggest they take you to the cleaner's."

It was the first time I realized Howard had invited friends. I was so happy that I forgot my nervousness and joined their laughter.

Even Frank the steward was there, more sullen than ever. That was a good sign, too. If he ever smiled I'd know something was wrong. He popped a bottle of champagne that shot all over Howard and the shirt box he was holding with all his belongings (clean shirts and a toothbrush). Now I laughed so hard I cried.

Mother went below to a cabin. We hadn't left the pier and she was already seasick. She said that if we'd wake her up for the wedding, she'd be fine. I went below with her to get cleaned up.

That's where Howard found me later, fast asleep. After I'd cleaned up I felt a little queasy so I thought I'd lie down a minute and get my sea legs, and I never could stay awake on anything that moves or floats. I'd never tasted champagne before and I didn't realize it would add to my drowsiness. When I returned to the salon several hours later, I begged everyone's forgiveness and vowed never to partake of champagne again. My legs were still unseaworthy. Mom was still below, greener than I was.

When Howard led me topside, the boat was a vision to behold, banked deck to bulkhead with white gardenias and lit with white candles placed in large brandy snifters. It had grown dark while I'd been sleeping and we were far out to sea heading for Mexican waters. I refused more champagne and just drank in the stars. I wished on them all night.

Everyone was starved, and Howard announced he had had something special flown in from New York on his airline, TWA. We all waited in anticipation for some flaming shish kebob or duck à l'orange. Howard looked so pleased with himself when Frank served Nathan's hot dogs and french fries from Coney Island.

Everyone wolfed them down. Howard said they were very special and ate six of them. I thought they would be more special if they'd been left back in Coney Island. The fish devoured my french fries; Howard admitted they did taste better in Coney Island.

I remember Captain Flynn in the flickering candlelight as he held the Book of Common Prayer. The theme from "Meditation" drifted in. Howard held both my hands in his as we once again took our vows. I was back on top of our hill, so far above the city lights, so near to God.

The ceremony on the boat was like a dream while it was happening. Only Howard's voice seemed real when he said, "I do," and he whispered, "forever." Then his kiss brought me back, and around my neck he placed the very same string of valuable pearls his father had given his mother on their wedding night. I knew how another Mrs. Hughes once felt.

I cut the wedding cake, which was in the shape of Mighty Joe Young holding up a piano with a girl on it. The girl was me. Howard gave me a music box that played "Beautiful

Dreamer" in memory of the song I'd played in the movie. I still treasure it.

When we returned to San Diego and everyone had left the boat, I was the happiest I'd ever been in my life, and the most apprehensive. What happened next? How do we get our clothes off? Who takes them off first, or does it happen at the same time? I just knew I was going to do something wrong. I felt myself blushing as I wondered if Howard could read my thoughts with those sad brown eyes that penetrated my soul.

My parents had never told me anything. The word "sex" was never mentioned in our household. I had no preconceived idea and nothing to unlearn when I married Howard.

Howard could feel the tension emanating from me. He took my hand and led me to the bow of the boat, saying that he wanted to light me by moonlight. He turned my face in every direction until I was lit just right. He turned my chin up just a little. "There, that's perfect." Then he picked me up and kissed me and slowly slid me down against him to my feet. I slipped out of my shoes and scrambled barefoot back to the deck lounge. Howard followed.

We sat there in silence, listening to the waves slapping against the boat. After a few moments Howard spoke. "How can anyone be so tiny? Has anyone ever loved you as much as I do? Has anyone ever found you so beautiful?" He put my feet in his lap. "How can you possibly walk on these? They're so small. My hands are larger than your feet. What size shoe do you wear?"

"Four. Massage them, please, Howard. I just love that."

Howard started gently massaging my legs and feet, saying, "This little piggy goes to market. This little piggy stays home."

I broke into laughter. It sounded so ridiculous coming from Howard Robard Hughes. It would certainly have ended up on the cutting-room floor if one of his directors at RKO had put it on film.

"Howard, what's our life going to be like? Are you going to have time to spend with me?"

"Yep. I've got a dream, Helen. It will afford me a lot more time and you're part of that plan."

"I am?" I was excited. "Tell me the dream, Howard."

"Well, there are several things I have to finish up. You know marriage is a responsibility and something you have to work at to get the best out of. That requires time. I made a decision today. For a long time I've dreamed of endowing a medical-research foundation. I was going to leave everything I have so it could be set up after my death. Now I've decided to see it happen while I'm alive."

"That's wonderful, Howard," I responded.

"I want to build the finest medical-research facility in the world in memory of my father. It will attract and support every great mind in the world of medical science and provide them with the ideal environment and most sophisticated technology to accomplish the task of wiping out pain and suffering." Howard stopped massaging my feet and looked out at the water.

"Ohhh, that felt so good." He knew just how to massage my feet so I felt it in every part of my body.

"Go below and put on a robe," he said. "Bring back some lotion and I'll give you a Japanese massage. It'll relax you and you'll sleep better."

What a clever way to say, "Take off your clothes."

I went below to the master stateroom. As I undressed, I wondered what Howard expected. I didn't know what to take off or what to leave on, so I took it all off. I slipped into a flimsy silk wraparound robe that covered everything but was so light that it could be wadded up and held in one hand.

I started back to Howard, but I felt insecure and put my bra and panties back on. I felt much better and returned to my husband. "Husband" sounded so good to me.

Oh, damn! In my hurry I hadn't brought the lotion. I peeked my head out of a porthole and told Howard as if I were a dismal failure.

"Look in the medicine chest."

I went below again for the lotion and returned topside

with good old Jergens in hand. (Howard had taught me all the boat jargon. You don't go upstairs; you go topside.)

I slipped out of the robe.

"Lie on your stomach," he said. First came the white liquid, and then Howard's hands spreading it all around.

"Oh, it's cold. Umm, that's good." I had no idea my muscles were so tense and sore, but his touch soothed and his velvet fingers worked their way up and down my spine until I was gently purring and almost asleep. His hands were warm, so very slow and precise. They followed the tension and turned it into soothing pleasure. The pleasure seemed to be everywhere. Through the feeling and touching all my fears were vanishing. Howard made it so easy for me. It felt so holy.

"Don't move. Just fall asleep if you feel like it."

He was putting my body in restful tranquility, but at the same time I was waking. Things were happening inside me I'd never before experienced.

Howard's touch was so loving and sensuous I was afraid I would miss something. Each time he massaged up my legs, he was coming nearer to my center. I didn't dare breathe. Each time his hands moved closer, I wanted them away; each time they moved away, I wanted them back again. He was such a master of touch. He toyed and enticed me into such a heat I thought I was running a fever. At the time, I thought what was happening to me was dangerous, but I didn't care if it was fatal.

Howard planted occasional moist kisses, each at just the right second, in all the right places. I sometimes felt his tongue. He lay down beside me, pulled me close to him, and held me tight.

"A hug does wonders," he said, and he kissed me on the mouth. The hug did wonders, and the kiss . . . the kiss . . . I didn't want it to ever end. But Howard knew better. He raised me in his arms and carried me down to the stateroom, to our wedding bed.

Howard laid me gently on the bed and kissed my forehead, then my nose, then my lips. I was in another world. I was perfectly still as he undressed me. Articles of clothing made no sense to me anymore.

The lights went out, and then Howard was beside me. Nothing separated us. The first feeling of a naked body against mine was electric. I held him tight with the feeling that I wanted his bones to become my bones, his flesh my flesh. I squeezed him tighter. I really believed it could happen: no more separate features, no more separate thoughts or feelings. Our bodies fit so well together that I knew God had designed us for each other. Every line, curve, and dip on my body had its counterpart on Howard's.

Howard began kissing me and touching me, so slowly and so perfectly. He was everywhere at once, and he made me feel that I was everything that existed in the universe. I *was* the universe. He became the center of the universe, and we became one pure creation of God. His movements were like a majestic symphony, every one anticipated, every one applauded by my soul.

In my wildest imagination I had never believed that beauty could be so powerful. A series of explosions had been detonated inside me. They grew louder and louder, more and more intense. I was fragmenting in a million pieces, in a million different directions. From a thousand light years away I could hear myself screaming. My nails dug deeper and deeper into his flesh. I was terrified of leaving the world. I was gasping for air between my desperate cries for Howard to help. I thought I was dying. I was soaring through infinite space, through color and light. I was sure I was dying from pleasure and this was the journey to heaven.

"Hold me, Howard! Hold me! Don't let me die alone!"

He held me.

I was safe in his arms, and weak to the point of nearly fainting.

I hadn't died.

I didn't know what was happening or what had happened.

I was sobbing and clinging to Howard, but I was crying in joy, sheer, unadulterated joy. I was alive. I was in love. It was no longer me. It was us. I fell asleep in his arms.

A few hours later, I was wide awake. The events of the day had happened so quickly my head was swimming. Deep in my heart I felt I had done the right thing.

I watched Howard sleeping. I felt so much like a woman and so much like a wife. I wanted to share my joy with friends, but I had taken a sacred vow of secrecy with Howard. I understood his argument concerning the effect of marriage news on my career, but something was bothering me. He had said that a publicized wedding would be a detriment to *both* our careers. I couldn't, for the life of me, see what negative effect it might have on *his*. I was wondering how a known, rather than secret, wedding could possibly hinder the running of a tool company, a motion picture studio, or an aircraft corporation. I broke out in a cold sweat and wanted to be home in my own bed, with the knowledge that Mama Blue, Daddy, and brother Wally were there in the house too.

Did Howard mean his "career" of collecting the most beautiful women in the world?

Chapter 6

"I'M BORROWING YOU FROM COLUMBIA TO DO A PICTURE AT RKO," Howard said over his twelve kadota figs with half-and-half. He was still engrossed in his *Wall Street Journal*. He had said it so nonchalantly that, although I heard him, it didn't register.

Howard had his daily routine. He would go for months eating the exact same thing every day. One of his longest-running menus was this breakfast of figs. When he got hungry he would order room service. He would order my food too, and he was more strict about my diet than my parents were. He'd practically never let me have sweets anymore.

He rarely had meetings in the morning. Upon finishing his breakfast, he would go sit in a comfortable chair with a yellow legal pad and start making notes. Then he'd call in to the Romaine Street office for his messages and begin his calls. Whenever he was speaking to someone of great importance, he would excuse himself and set the receiver down, sometimes for five minutes at a time, and yawn and eat his figs and yawn some more. While His Royal Highness continued his yawn, the other party was waiting.

Usually, during the day, I was in some class and Howard stayed in the bungalow conducting business by phone. If we were both free, we'd usually just play. He'd take me flying or skeet shooting, or we'd drive around looking for houses.

In the evenings, we always had somewhere to go. We'd go bowling, flying, visiting Cary Grant, or driving around. But usually we went to the Goldwyn Studios screening room. We both loved movies. Howard's favorites at that time were mystery films.

Carl, our projectionist, was one of the few men who were unintimidated by Howard and took no guff from him. There was a genuine camaraderie between them. The three of us shared one another's company for years.

We were continually playing practical jokes on one another. When I teased Howard, Carl loved it and usually sided with me.

We always had contests, while watching the mysteries, to see who could guess the killer. Surprisingly, Howard wasn't very good, and I almost always won. That really irked him.

"Carl told you," Howard accused me.

"That's impossible. You've been right next to me the whole time."

"Then you've seen the film before."

"I have not; I wasn't even born when that movie came out."

There was hardly any television then, and no old reruns. We must have seen every old mystery film back to the thirties.

We had some definite favorites:

Charlie Chan series, starring Warner Oland
Bulldog Drummond, starring Arsène Lupin and
    Ronald Colman. (A later production came out
    with Lionel Barrymore.)
The Lone Wolf, with Warren Williams
The Thin Man, with William Powell and Myrna Loy

Ellery Queen, with William Gargan
Mr. Moto series, with Peter Lorre
Nick Carter series, starring Walter Pidgeon
Philo Vance, with William Powell
Mr. Wong series, with Boris Karloff

Howard's favorite mystery story was *Ten Little Indians* with Barry Fitzgerald, Walter Huston and Louis Hayward.

Howard didn't like horror movies; they frightened him so he couldn't sleep at night. I specifically remember one nightmare where an airplane had turned into a giant monster who was eating him alive.

I believed him.

Of course, the monster airplane he was talking about was what today is called the *Spruce Goose*. He always referred to it as the flying boat or the HK-11. He had sunk millions of his own dollars into its development. No one was allowed to call it the *Spruce Goose* around him; it would have been disrespectful.

We never saw any of Howard's old movies. Why? I didn't think to ask and I don't think it ever occurred to him to run *Scarface, Hell's Angels* or any of his other films.

Howard loved to take me into the men's room at Goldwyn before the movie began, when no one was there, and wash off all my lipstick. He'd wipe my mouth with rough paper towels until every trace of color was gone. Then he'd examine his handiwork closely and see if my complexion had any blemishes. If so, he'd find a needle in his office desk and burn the needle with a match and open the imperfection as skillfully as a surgeon. He had learned this method from a dermatologist. A special memo went to the Romaine Street boys: Keep needle in upper left-hand drawer at all times.

Then came the part he loved most: washing my hands. He adored this ten-minute procedure, turning them over and over and then just looking at them. He said I had hands like a baby because I still had dimples instead of knuckles, and he liked to admire and play with them. I would have to crane my head back to look up at him; he would always lift me onto the washbasin, give me a loving look, and tenderly kiss me.

"I hate mustaches because they poke up my nose."

Howard roared with laughter. "If your nose didn't turn up so much, you wouldn't have so many problems. Besides, it's crooked. It veers off to the left." Affectionately, he'd give it a shove to the right.

After our nights at the movies, I was usually starved because, by the time we were finished and ready for dinner, it was about 11:00 P.M. Usually we headed for the Beverly Hills Hotel, where our favorites, Bruno and Henry, took care of us.

Whenever I ordered dinner with Howard I found myself looking at the right side of the menu before making a selection. I always felt poor with him.

Howard ordered steak and hearts of lettuce, with Roquefort cheese dressing. Every single evening Bruno and Henry were directed:

"Cut the lettuce into one-inch square pieces. Make them bite size; don't let them fall apart. Use a sharp knife.

"New York–cut steaks must be charred on the outside, rare inside.

"The dressing must have the Roquefort crumbled in the bottom of the bowl. Pour in the oil and add one teaspoon French's mustard and Worcestershire sauce with a dash of salt and pepper, one teaspoon sugar and one tablespoon wine vinegar. Stir it well."

I can repeat that in my sleep.

He always left a ten percent tip. He added it over and over. Then he would just sit and stare at his signature and doodle with his pencil on it for at least five minutes. I couldn't understand why he became so mesmerized by his name on the check. For his own safety, he let it be known

70

that he never carried money or credit cards. The fact that he drove an old Chevrolet, shaved every three days, and dressed the way he did were just additional ways of not drawing attention to himself.

Howard has always been known as the Shy Billionaire, but he was not shy; he was very private. He was secretive. He didn't want people to get close to him. He built an image in front of himself and only let them know what he wanted them to know.

I was going over a scene for acting class when Howard looked up from his paper and said, "I'm borrowing you from that son of a bitch Cohn to do a picture for me at RKO."

I stopped what I was doing and ran to him, throwing my arms around his neck.

"Did I hear you right, Howard? Did I?"

He looked pleased as I rambled on. "Oh, Howard, what's it called? Do I have the lead? Who else is in it? Is it a big movie? Who's directing?" I hardly gave him a chance to answer.

"Yes, it's a big movie. It stars Victor Mature and you, with William Bendix. There are no animals, though I'm not too sure about Victor Mature. You take your mother with you. He may *be* an animal. Rita Hayworth told me a lot of stories about him."

"Really, Howard? Were they bad?"

"No, but I'm sure she was covering up for him. After all, she was in love with him." Then he looked annoyed. "How many times do I have to tell you all men are animals, baby? They just want to get into your pants."

"You too, Howard?" I asked sweetly.

"No, not me. That's not all I want. I'm different," he replied gruffly. "Ted Tetzlaff is the director. I understand he's good. You'll be happy, because it's a mystery–spy story. It's called *Gambling House*.

It was a dream come true. I had played Victor Mature's daughter years earlier, and now I was to be his leading lady.

71

He later teased me, "Yes, and the next picture we do together, you'll probably be playing my mother."

Howard's timing was perfect. I was really anxious to get back to work, especially in a film for him. At times like this, my fears of his being with other women were the furthest thing from my mind. There had been little opportunity for infidelity since the day of our wedding. We were together most of the hours of the day and night, and when we weren't I usually could reach him by phone. But there was always an element of secrecy that bothered me, and although I knew he was involved in government contracts, I couldn't help but feel, deep down inside, there were other women.

Over a month had passed since our marriage, and though we'd been busy, we had stayed pretty close to home, bungalow nineteen at the Beverly Hills Hotel. Our first night back at the bungalow from the boat is quite a memory.

Howard had to poke his nose into everything; he even had to know how regular I was. When I couldn't remember the last time I'd been to the bathroom, you'd think I just announced I had been bitten by a rabid dog.

It was well after midnight, but he rushed me into the car and we drove all the way to downtown Los Angeles before we found an all-night pharmacy. He bought a laxative, which he said was completely natural, and we drove home. He measured out two tablespoonfuls, but before I could swallow it, he handed me a full glass of water. He instructed me not to drink until I'd swallowed the laxative because it would swell up. He was right. I was rushed to the emergency room in Santa Monica with a throat full of expanding laxative that was slowly choking me to death.

Howard was a great influence on every part of my character; he's responsible for most of the good habits I have today. It's not that my parents didn't do their job; it's just I left home at a young age and Howard spent a lot of time communicating and explaining things in a way I could understand. These were the most impressionable years in my life. He was very sensitive and careful as he molded me into a woman. Everything he passed on to me was done with the complete understanding of what effect it would have on my psychological future. He was always thinking ahead.

It is still difficult for the young reader with the sexual freedom of today to understand the puritanical forties. Many of the boys my age were virgins too, and sex wasn't discussed. After every date, I'd come speeding into the house and right to the bathroom. I never even went to the ladies' room to comb my hair because my date might think I was doing something else.

Howard used to tease me because, even after we were married, I'd turn on the bathtub full blast so he wouldn't hear anything. I thought if I turned on the faucet in the washbowl, it could be mistaken for the real thing. Heaven forbid. Everyone *knows* that movie stars don't go to the bathroom.

It seemed to me that Howard knew everything about everything. It was as though I had graduated from Lillian Barkley's class and enrolled in the Howard Hughes College of Womanhood. I remember how he would discuss, in great detail, everything in my life, from menstruation to menopause.

Well, I'd had a six-week honeymoon, and now it was time to work on *Gambling House*. There was a story going around that when Howard bought RKO, he drove through the lot one time, late at night when no one was there, and said two words: "Paint it." Howard always denied this, but since he was never seen on the lot again, he was branded with the name Harvey, after the invisible six-foot-tall rabbit in the play that the Jimmy Stewart movie made so famous.

The day I walked onto the RKO lot I felt twenty feet tall. The idea that it all belonged to Howard stimulated a new confidence in me.

My first stop was the makeup department, where I ran into another one of Howard's former loves. She was breathtakingly, exotically beautiful. I was nineteen feet tall.

Next stop was hairdressing, where I saw Jane Russell, Janet Leigh, and Joan Fontaine. More of Howard's past. I shrank another foot.

Then on to wardrobe, where they tried desperately to make me glamorous and sophisticated. Impossible! Seventeen feet tall.

By the time I reached the producer's office and met with the director I was whittled back down to five-feet-two. Much to my surprise, I didn't feel welcome.

When production began and I came onto the set for the first time, I was to shrink to nothingness.

It was a total disaster. Lizbeth Scott, cool and exotic, had been the unanimous first choice and perfect for the part. She was mature, sophisticated elegance; I was bubbly bounce. She was everything I was not. Nobody wanted me. Not the director, not the producer, not even Victor Mature.

Next, Victor Mature wasn't large, he was *huge.* No wonder he was once chosen to play Samson. He dwarfed me.

I was supposed to verbally push him around all through the movie and tell him to get off his high horse. It used to cause the crew to laugh every time I said it. In order to do scenes with Victor Mature, they had to build a raised catwalk for me to walk on. I stood on apple boxes for all my close-ups.

Then Howard started meddling. He didn't like my wardrobe, so he sent buyers out for clothes that would make me look older. When they gave up, he had his top designer, Michael Wolfe, design special clothes and hats. The hats only emphasized my chipmunk cheeks. Michael was pulling his hair out. This was turning into a bigger fiasco than the special bra Howard had designed for Jane Russell.

Every day Michael Wolfe, his entourage of fitters, and I would trudge over to Howard's office at Goldwyn Studios and show him the latest attempt.

Once, even Howard burst out laughing. "She looks ridiculous."

I thought there was something wrong with me. I broke

down and cried. I cried and cried and cried, all the way back to RKO.

Later when the reviews came out, they all said that I looked like a little girl dressed up in her mommy's clothing.

Every girl on the RKO lot was rumored to be a Hughes girl except for me. I was the only one that no one suspected, so everyone spoke freely in front of me. "There's Carla—did you see that rock on her finger? Obviously a present from Hughes. She's under special contract to him."

They whispered, "Be careful what you say in front of Joan. She speaks to the boss every day, and one of his special cars delivers her to the studio."

In the makeup department, everyone thought Howard was in love with Mala Powers. She was a beautiful actress who had contracted aplastic anemia after being treated with chloromazine; Howard literally saved her life by having her treated by the top specialists of the day. The gossips were wrong about Howard and Mala, but I didn't know that, and I suffered all the pangs of hurt and jealousy.

Only my mother knew how it was tearing me apart. She began spending more time at the studio with me, giving me the will and strength to go on, and to fight. I tried desperately to put on a happy, nonchalant front; but there was always another rumor, another beautiful actress being signed to the long list of contract players. I felt I was competing with the whole world of women.

If the preparation for the picture was miserable, the shooting was pure agony.

I couldn't seem to do anything right. I *was* hopelessly miscast. The director knew I'd been forced on him. The cast and crew did everything to make things unpleasant. No one knew I couldn't be taken off the picture because Howard wanted me there. I talked to Howard and pleaded and begged to be replaced. He wouldn't give in.

Only Victor Mature was always pleasant to me. I remember he would eat junk food for breakfast. He was always offering me chili and hot dogs and a new drink he'd concocted, Coke mixed with root beer. He was so pleased

75

because it had the zip of Coke and the flavor of root beer. It was one of the few things I could keep down.

Mama Blue drove me home every night, and she usually had to stop the car while I threw up from tension and unhappiness. I vowed then I would never make another picture unless I was wanted by all concerned.

Rumors of Howard's other women were surfacing all around me. Everywhere I turned it was Howard this, Howard that. Harvey's new fling. Harvey's next glamour queen. I tried to close it out, but the message was too loud. I marked it off as gossip, which most of it was; but if you hear something often enough from enough different sources, it begins to sound true. Mother saw what it was doing to me and suggested I move back in with her and Daddy.

On top of all the other insinuations, more information surfaced to make Mother wary of the man I had just married.

Lillian Barkley called Mother in and, in absolute confidence, she posed the possibility that Howard might be on drugs in a serious way. Mother viewed the idea as conjecture on Lillian's part, but her unwavering respect for Lillian left her open to the suggestion. She also knew that Lillian was close to Venessa Brown, who was a confidante of Jean Peters. Lillian went on to say that Howard would visit a dentist in the seedy part of town and disappear for two days at a time. Lillian encouraged Mother to have me check Howard's arms for needle marks. Naturally, I thought the whole thing was ridiculous and was aghast at Lillian's allegation, but Mother made me promise to check Howard's arms.

I've always been naive concerning drugs. I wouldn't know a needle mark from a freckle. That time wasn't any different. When I next saw Howard shirtless, I lovingly examined his arms. They were covered with countless scars of burns and abrasions from his five plane crashes. I reported to Mother, and that's the last we ever thought about drugs connected with Howard for a long, long time.

All I knew was that my whole world was falling apart. I

was making a movie in which I was treated like a leper on the set and my own husband wouldn't let me off the picture. I was married but couldn't tell a soul, and now I had good reason to suspect my husband was cheating on me. Howard had become even busier lately, coming in late and leaving early. I was confused and miserable, so I decided to take Mother's suggestion and move back to Glendale, where I could more easily sort things out.

It wasn't going to be easy to face my father and explain why I was living with a man.

Chapter 7

MY MOTHER FIXED MY FATHER'S FAVORITE MEAL AND poured him a large Scotch before breaking the news of my new marital status to him.

He exploded. "What the hell do you mean, you were married at sea? Are you crazy?"

Mama Blue interjected, "It was a beautiful wedding by a real captain. Everything is legal."

"How can you be so stupid as to believe that crap? I bet you can't show me one shred of evidence to make it legal and binding on him."

"I don't need any evidence, Daddy. Howard and I love each other, and our marriage is recorded in the ship's log."

"Ship's log? What ship? Where is it now? Can either of you tell me?"

Mother and I were silent.

"You two should be locked up. How could you fall for such a thing? Why do you think Hughes didn't want me there? I'll tell you why. He knows I would've seen through the sham and never allowed you to go through with it."

"Howard thought it best kept a secret," I pleaded. "He was concerned about my career."

"He sure saw you coming," Daddy said sarcastically. "And to think your mother stood by and let that lecher wed and bed you. He probably pulls that stunt every week. People see those dollar signs and they lose all sense of reasoning."

I was angry at that, and crying because Father wouldn't believe us. "He loves me, Daddy. We're married forever. He said so. I believe it. I know it's real."

"I'll believe it when I see it. You can tell Howard that I want to see that ship's log, and until I do, young lady, you'll live right here at home."

I looked at Mother. She didn't dare do anything but agree with him.

"You've already made your bed, but you don't have to rush to lie in it."

I thought my moving back to Glendale would have a different effect on Howard than it did. I thought his first reaction would be to rush over with the proof for Daddy but Howard said the ship was on a cruise and wouldn't be back for quite a while. He said he would miss me a lot but agreed I should live at home part time in order for our marriage to remain secret.

When I stayed with Howard at the bungalow, we drove up a narrow dark street, no wider than an alley, and parked right near the entrance. Waldo, the guard, was usually around for surveillance. No one ever bothered us so security was minimal.

Our meals were ordered from room service and usually delivered by Rex, the captain, or someone else Howard trusted. If it was a new waiter, I remained in the bedroom until he'd left. Howard wasn't too concerned about appearances, but I was.

Back at my parents' home, I had little time to sit thinking about the problems of my not-so-normal marriage. *The Great Rupert*, and *He's a Cockeyed Wonder* were being released, and this demanded a lot of my time for publicity at Jerome Courtland's side. Cojo and I were Harry Cohn's new young hopefuls, so he was pushing our careers and pairing us up for the magazine layouts. This was becoming increasingly uncomfortable for both of us. Cojo was deeply hurt but covered it up. He wasn't buying my stories that Howard and my relationship was purely platonic, especially since I would only see him during the day. And there was no more "necking up a storm."

The publicity department worked overtime photographing me with Tab Hunter, Johnny Sands, Tony Curtis, Rock Hudson, and other young male stars who were popular at that time. Lillian and I sponsored Shirley Temple into Zeta Phi Eta, a drama fraternity. The press went wild. I was so nervous when I went to swear Shirley in that I completely lost my voice. She was such an idol of mine that I just stood there, dumb. Shirley came to my rescue; she was used to having this effect on people.

I continued going to parties at Jane Powell's and Roddy McDowall's, but I wasn't as comfortable as I had been. Jane and Geary Steffan were now engaged. Elizabeth had returned Glenn Davis's gold football. She had a new love, handsome Bill Pawley from Florida. His father was a former ambassador and had organized The Flying Tigers. Elizabeth and I were close friends, and she couldn't help notice things had changed between Cojo and me. He was beginning to stay away from the parties that I attended. I think Elizabeth's mother felt sorry for me. I was so faraway and quiet that she thought I was pining over Cojo. Sara Taylor called me a few times to fix me up with nice young boys, but when I refused, she didn't call anymore. I felt bad. It was such an uncomfortable position to be in, but I didn't know what to do. I'm sure the gang thought I was an oddball, but they always continued to be warm and friendly. I shared their happiness—engagements, weddings, and later, baby showers.

The busier I became, the more attention Howard gave me. It seemed that if he wasn't with me, he was either on the phone with me or trying to get hold of me. Wherever I went, he seemed to know where I was. No sooner would I arrive somewhere than the phone would ring. It was always Howard.

It was becoming embarrassing. I would go to lunch with Lillian or Mother, Jack Carson, Red Skelton, or whoever was working on the lot at the time. We'd walk into any restaurant—it didn't matter—and there'd be someone paging me to the phone. Red Skelton used to kid me that he knew I was having myself paged. "What are you trying to do, upstage me? Or have you got a secret lover who's having us followed?" he'd joke. If he'd looked at my face at that moment, he'd have known how close he'd come to the truth. But Red, being the professional he was, went into his comedy routine, "What-the-irate-lover-might-do-to-him." First, he hung himself on the coat rack; when that laugh died down, he tore the pockets out of his new suit. "I'll do anything to get a laugh," he quipped as he ripped off both his sleeves. I laughed, but he'd come too close for comfort.

The next time the phone rang, I screamed, "Howard Hughes, why are you having me followed? You must know by now I'm not doing anything wrong. I don't appreciate your mistrust. Is it because *you* can't be trusted?"

"Now, honey"—he sounded so hurt—"the way you and your mother run around, anything could happen. It's just not safe on the street anymore. What kind of a man would I be if I didn't look out for my baby girl?"

"Oh, Howard." I melted. "Do you really love me that much?"

"Do you think I enjoy breaking away from my business meetings all day and calling you? Why, I have sixty thousand stockholders all depending on me. I can't be worried about where you are and what you're doing all day long."

I thought, Here it comes again. I knew it would turn around and be all my fault . . . but Howard had a remedy. He wouldn't have to call me all day long if he knew where I was; if I took my acting lessons at Goldwyn Studios instead

81

of Columbia, he'd start using his office there and we could lunch together or have matinees in the afternoons. He gave me a list of drama coaches.

The very next day I was enrolled—alone—in Bob Paris's acting class. I had a whole studio almost to myself while things were bustling at Columbia and RKO. Bob Paris and I never dreamed that the drama room was bugged, or that the transcripts of our lessons went back to Howard.

After practicing what seemed to be every monologue written for an actress, I told Howard I had to have an actor to work with. For the next week, Howard had a different actor standing at the gate of Goldwyn Studios every hour. They were ordered to stare straight ahead, just like the soldiers at Buckingham Palace, while Howard would drive through and take a good look at their faces.

The young man finally selected was named Jay O'Hanyon. He had no idea why he had been asked to stand at the gate or that Howard Hughes had passed by and chosen him personally.

Jay was just out of college and had never worked before. I was just out of high school. Whatever transpired in the drama lessons was triple checked by Howard, through the tapes and by what Bob Paris and I told him. Howard wanted to make sure that no personal relationship was developing between Jay and me.

Bob Paris had us doing classics like *Elizabeth and Essex,* and *Mary, Queen of Scots.* It pains me to think how dreadful we must have been.

Later Jay changed his name to Touch Connors and then to Mike Connors and went on to *Mannix* fame. Howard always did have a good eye when it came to discovering stars.

Next, Howard took me away from Freddie Carger, who was teaching Marilyn Monroe and me to sing at Columbia Studios, and sent me away to Madame Nina Koshetz to study. Imagine me, who couldn't even carry a tune, studying with the former star of the Metropolitan Opera company. She had been the love of Rachmaninoff's life and owned all his unpublished works. When she gave up on me, Howard gave the great baritone John Charles Thomas a chance to teach me. Thomas told Howard he just couldn't take his money. Next came Tina Taylor Rone, teacher to the stars. She gave up. I was passed from one singing teacher to another. Danny Thomas once said the commissary walls at Twentieth Century-Fox weren't large enough to carry all the names of the singing teachers that Howard had sent me to.

When I was free, Howard wanted all of my time. Because of the importance of keeping our secret, we began spending less and less time in town. This was fine with me because it meant we were flying somewhere, and I sure loved that.

We would go to Catalina Island and scout it from one end to the other. It was owned by the Wrigley chewing gum family, but Howard wanted to buy it. We would often take friends with us and go dancing at night at the Pavillion. Johnny Meyers, Pat DiCicco, and their girlfriends were frequent guests. Howard liked Pat and Johnny around because they made him laugh.

Our most frequented place at this time was Palm Springs. We spent most of our evenings at the Chi Chi Club, which was owned by Irwin Schumann. We must have had over a hundred dinners there. Irwin later told me that Howard never paid for any of them but he liked him too much to send a bill. He also told me he'd never seen Howard as sweet and affectionate as he had been with me; he'd even wipe the ice cream off my face!

The Chi Chi was the only place where Howard ordered sparkling Burgundy, and we always had cherries jubilee for dessert. Howard always made a big production of it. He acted as if it were just for me, but in reality he was the one who loved his sweets.

After dinner, he and Irwin would have a cherry heering together. It seemed to be one of the few places where Howard laughed and joked with the waiters, and they loved him and looked forward to our visits.

Charell, the piano player, became a good friend and used to play the song "Again" for us. From the moment Howard heard it, it became our song. Howard saw to it that it was played wherever I went, especially if I was in another man's company. The orchestra would start to play the most plaintive rendition just as I started to look in some Lochinvar's eyes.

Even today when I walk into Gatby's restaurant in Brentwood, the pianist plays, ". . . Again, this couldn't happen again. This moment forever, but never, never again,"* . . . and the tears start rolling down my cheeks.

How many times I've repeated that last line and thought of Howard.

After dinner, we'd go into the showroom and watch the entertainment. Often we'd run into Desi Arnaz, Rosalind Russell, or John Wayne. They would join our table, and the party would continue to the wee hours of the morning.

Sometimes we'd fly to Las Vegas and see all the floor shows at the casinos. Howard could get money there, and if I was lucky he'd give me ten dollars to gamble with. He liked to go uptown where it would last longer.

One day when I was supposed to have some pictures taken with Tony Curtis, Howard said he had a surprise for me. Before I knew it, we were high above California flying eastward. Howard wouldn't tell me where we were going, and I was blindfolded during the last half hour of the flight. When he removed the blindfold, we were circling the Grand Canyon. We were both as excited as little kids over his surprise. When we landed at an airport in Arizona and went

---

*"Again," words by Dorcas Cochran, music by Lionel Newman. Copyright 1948, renewed 1976 by Twentieth Century Music Corporation. Rights assigned to CBS CATALOGUE PARTNERSHIP. All rights controlled and administered by CBS ROBBINS CATALOG, INC. All rights reserved. International copyright secured. Used by permission.

in to have lunch, we discovered we had only ninety-seven cents between us, so we shared a sandwich and a glass of milk. Howard went into the men's room, but he returned almost immediately to ask me if I had a dime. I reminded him that we had spent our last penny for lunch. The *very* next day all of the pay toilets were removed from TWA terminals all over the country.

Howard saw to it that the women at RKO who had bothered me so much became a concern of the past. Instead of running mystery films at night, he began running screen tests of all the beauties under contract to him, criticizing and making fun of them. We would roll on the floor in laughter. Howard believed he could make anyone a star, especially if she had a big bosom. Jane Russell turned out to be his prototype. Before she learned her profession, Howard would watch her dailies in the projection room and double up with laughter.

"Do you think I should give her dramatic lessons?"

He felt he had played a great hoax on Hollywood and Darryl Zanuck when Zanuck paid an enormous sum to borrow her for *Gentlemen Prefer Blondes*. The joke backfired. Jane stole the show and developed into a real talent. Jane was never a girlfriend of Howard's, but he never watched over any star so carefully.

Howard liked his women *au naturel*. He would never allow me to use any makeup. He wanted me just the way I was, which was in total contrast to the star image of the day. Hollywood loved its glamour queens: Rita Hayworth, Lana Turner, Ava Gardner, Marilyn Monroe, and Betty Grable. It was the day of bleached blondes and flaming redheads slinking around in bugle beads, sequins, and black satin dresses. You most likely went unnoticed unless you were all dolled up.

Howard sent out talent scouts like Walter Kane, Cubby Broccoli, and Johnny Machio looking for the next Jean Harlow. He had photos taken of girls from all angles without a drop of makeup. It was hard to pass his rigid test.

85

Girls like Marilyn Monroe were products of cosmetic beauty. Marilyn would never have passed Howard's scrutiny with her brown, kinky hair and freckled, thin skin. She could go unrecognized without makeup; a Star was born with "it."

Howard also insisted his ladies never shave their legs. When he gave me that ultimatum, I let the hair on my legs grow, but I cheated; and bleached it.

Then one day when Cojo and I were posing for pictures on the beach, he made fun of my hairy legs. I gritted my teeth and bore it until the next day, when I ran into Jean Peters at the studio. She too had hairy legs. I couldn't get home fast enough to shave. Howard be damned.

Clean-shaven and aloof, I was slated to do two pictures for Columbia. Howard wasn't too happy when I broke the news to him. I was to star in *The Barefoot Mailman* and *Sunny Side of the Street*, both opposite Cojo. Cojo and I had always dreamed of making movies together, but this wasn't going to be easy for Howard, Cojo, or me.

The first film, *The Barefoot Mailman,* was to be shot on location in Silver Springs, Florida, on Ross Allen's alligator farm. Another dream of Cojo's and mine was to go on location together. This distressed Howard even further. Here I was starring with my ex-boyfriend and live alligators three thousand miles away. Howard did his best to have me pulled from the movie but Harry Cohn was always conveniently not available.

There was one scene in which I had to fall out of a canoe into an alligator-infested river, then swim to shore in my long 1890s dress with all the petticoats. They used real gators, but their snouts were wired. When it came time to shoot this particular scene, they couldn't find a double to do it, so I offered to do it myself.

The most dangerous part of the alligator is its tail, which can break every bone in your body. If my swim to shore had been clocked, I'm sure I'd hold some kind of record. Tails were slicing the water from all directions, missing me by inches. The director was thrilled that the scene was so realistic, especially my bloodcurdling screams. In Hollywood the studio executives said our fake alligators looked terrific.

While I was in Florida, Howard was ringing the phones off the hook. Harry Cohn said he'd ban Howard from the set if he showed up, but there were no more scenes with alligators, so he didn't. His detectives in Florida were fired and a new batch hired who were told they'd be fed to the alligators if I went near the water.

I became fascinated with gators and read Ross Allen's book *The Sex Life of the Alligator*. Ross, who was the Frank Buck of the reptile world, taught me the alligator love call, and I have the distinction of having the only love call that could equal his. Even today I can stand at the edge of a swamp that might appear empty to you, let out my mating call, and alligators will miraculously appear from nowhere.

Howard was fascinated with the romance of the gator as I was. From the first time he heard my sensuous love call, he was hooked. I could never hang up a phone or say good night without giving my call of the wild. Howard practiced a lot, too, but his was never quite as good as mine. Anyone who happened to be around when I said good night to Howard on the phone looked a little more than startled when they heard that strange mooning sound coming out of the receiver. It was my alligator, Howard.

During the shooting of *Mailman,* I became a terrible prankster, picking that up from master Howard, too. For example, I learned how to handle a large indigo boa constrictor, and I didn't like the assistant director, who was giving us all a very bad time. He was terrified of snakes, and obviously knew little about them, because I convinced him that my snake, Midnight, was a dangerous cobra and the only reason I wasn't dead was that I milked out all the poison every morning. I cautioned that if he so much as raised his voice to me, the excitement would bring the poison back and the snake would strike. Howard was in on the prank by phone and had to be kept abreast of Midnight's every wiggle. He was having more fun than I was. He liked to help plot my next move. He suggested I paint red circles around Midnight's eyes, and that really made that snake look awesome. I airmailed Howard a color photo of that, and he was delighted. He loved to be in the know.

I was Midnight's mama, and my other co-star, Robert Cummings, who had top billing, was her papa for the duration of the movie.

Bob wound her around his body under his coat and brought her home for me on the airplane. The poor stewardess practically passed out when Midnight poked her ugly head out at her as she was serving coffee. The only reson we weren't sued was that we were flying TWA; Howard held 78.23% of the company's outstanding stock. Howard didn't find this incident humorous. He thought the snake should have flown Pan American.

Living in my movie world of fantasy, I had little awareness of Howard's huge holdings. Our two separate worlds were miles apart. My dream world was sometimes bigger than the real world of Howard, but the reality of his world seldom came through to me.

As I grew more aware of the great responsibilities this man had, and how many of his hours were consumed by me, I could hardly believe he had time left in the day to cheat on me.

But . . .

Chapter 8

ONE EVENING THE PHONE WOKE ME FROM A SOUND SLEEP. It was Howard, explaining that he was still at his factory in Santa Monica and he wanted to work straight through, so I mustn't worry. He'd be home sometime the next day.

Howard told me he was on the wooden flying boat and that they were having a terrible time getting the glue to work on the wood. He wouldn't be able to see me until they figured out a solution to the problem, and the engineers didn't know how long it would take.

At that time I was shooting the musical comedy *Sunny Side of the Street*, again costarring with Cojo. During a lull in production, I was back living at the bungalow with Howard.

Just before hanging up, he told me, "Well, I've got to go now; I have to get back to work." He added he would stay there working all week with them if necessary.

We said our usual I love you's, sounded kisses back and forth, and then he said, "Well?"

"Well, what?"

"You forgot," he pouted.

I opened my throat and gave him my sweetest, sexiest

alligator love call. In the dark, I missed the telephone cradle and automatically put the receiver back to my ear to blow him another kiss.

"Why haven't you hung up?" he questioned.

"I missed the cradle," I said, and I went through all the love sounds again . . . again in the dark I missed the cradle . . . repeat. When I realized he hadn't hung up yet, I became suspicious. I hit the receiver against the side of the phone so that it would sound like a disconnect. I quickly put it back to my ear just in time to hear the operator say, "Las Vegas, are you through?"

The Mormon boys still kept me posted as to Howard's whereabouts, but when I'd accuse him of anything, he'd always deny everything or make it out to be nothing. Still I wanted so to believe in him.

"If you still think it's true, catch me. Go on. Catch me," he'd say.

Here was my opportunity. Howard always talked such a good line, but there was always the possibility the boys could be wrong. I had to know, once and for all. I was desperate.

I drove frantically to my parents' home. How I managed to get there, I don't know; I couldn't see through the tears. I banged like a madwoman on the front door—even my father came running to see what all the commotion was about. I was sobbing so hard I could scarcely get the words out. "Howard lied to me. He lied. He called and said he was in Santa Monica working on the flying boat, but he lied; he's playing around in Las Vegas."

Mother said I kept repeating, "What can I do? What can I do?"

Father took charge. His normal calm broke as he said, "The son-of-a-bitch. I told you he was full of it. I never did believe there was a ship's log. I never believed you were married to him for one minute. He's never believed it for one minute either. If you catch him red-handed, will you give him up?"

90

"Oh *yes,*" I replied.

"Then I'll help," Daddy said.

My father contacted a friend, Lecky, who had been an agent for the FBI. He agreed to help us.

Lecky said that if Howard were in Las Vegas, he would find him. It was by now early morning, and our immediate concern was that it was Election Day; the banks were closed and we did not have enough cash on hand to get to Las Vegas.

Fortunately, our good neighbors Harriet and Carolyn came through again, and we were off to Las Vegas to catch Howard at play.

Lecky combed Las Vegas while my parents and I waited in a motel. When the phone finally rang, Lecky said, "I've located him at the Desert Inn. He'll be coming down for lunch in half an hour."

We waited in a car in front of Howard's hotel. Lecky was inside watching the action and would come out periodically and report to us. Once he reported that Howard had sent out for several toothbrushes.

Then Lecky told us that a deliveryman had brought the biggest box of red roses he had ever seen. This incensed me. Howard had given me two or three of these huge boxes of red roses each week since he started courting me. Since our marriage a dozen white gardenias had been added.

I was at the lunch table in the dining room of the Desert Inn ten minutes early, sitting next to the table Howard had reserved and holding a newspaper in front of my face.

Howard appeared with a blond girl around eighteen, her mother, and five others. In the group at Howard's table was Walter Kane, who knew us well. He didn't notice us, nor did anyone at the Hughes table. They were much too interested in what they were doing, and I'm sure Howard felt secure that I was home in Los Angeles and he had nothing to worry about.

Howard had purchased a number of bathing suits for his new find, and the entire party was oohing and aahing over his selections. The mother was cooing, "Oh, Mr. Hughes, the bathing suits you sent my daughter fit perfectly, but I never allow her to go near the sun because she freckles."

It's no wonder they didn't allow her to go near the sun. She had that white, puttylike skin that looked as if you pushed it, it would stay in. That girl never knew how close I was to finding out. To top it off, she had a thin, whiny voice. Howard may have thought her attractive, but looking back, I can be bitchy and say that she was a tall string bean with an unhealthy pallor.

Howard was playing Mr. Big. He had swaggered into the dining room as if he owned the place, as if he owned the world. We now know that at least, later he did own the Desert Inn, where he was later to live those lonely years on the ninth floor.

After the thanks were duly rendered for the bathing suits, I backed up in my chair and scooted it over, right between Howard and Miss Twinkletoes. I stuck out my hand as if for a handshake and cooed, "It's so gooooood to see you. I want to thank you for coming. How nice, your glue did dry after all."

Suddenly Mr. Big became Mr. Little. He seemed to shrink before my eyes. Howard did not know whether to include me in the party or whether to die on the spot.

I blithely gave the best and hardest performance of my life. I assured him, "No, no, I don't want to interrupt a thing. I'm very, very busy. In fact, I've been busy all night."

While I was giving this little speech, I was smiling, oh so sweetly, back and forth between Howard and his new light-of-life. No one knew what to say or do. The conversation went on, with the girl suddenly giving Howard thanks for the long-stemmed red roses—while I'm sitting there!

I chirped, "Red roses, how lovely."

The girl and her mother were totally unaware of the drama of the occasion, and they were proceeding to say all the wrong things. I was being the perfect bitch, and Howard was dying by inches.

With a final "I must go," I pushed myself up from the chair and departed in a great hurry.

Now a recap of that day reads humorously, but at that moment I was crying inside. There was a hurt that can't be put on paper, that is difficult even now to talk about.

Howard hated scenes, and his confusion during my speech and get-even performance was very evident. The people at the table who knew both of us were quite embarrassed for him. He loved crises and brinkmanship but would work hard to prevent its spilling over into outright war . . . or getting caught!

My parents and I beat a retreat to the adjacent showroom and found a table. We were sitting there when Howard came dashing through on his way out. He saw us.

There was confusion on his face and suffering played in his eyes; he did not know whether he dared to stop.

He kept going—out of my life.

The legs under me were walking toward the car in the warm fresh air. I was surprised it was still light, for in the past fifteen minutes I had stumbled through a lifetime.

"Where to?" asked a voice that sounded like that of my father.

"Glendale."

Thank God everyone had the good sense not to speak or sympathize, or I'd have disintegrated during the flight home. I felt the emptiness of betrayal, having to believe what I desperately wanted not to believe, and being too much in love and too young to judge it all proportionately.

Puppy love, my ass. Nothing in life that follows brings you to such a screeching halt. Hopefully, you never leave yourself completely open to that hurt again, but never again do you realize the complete ecstasy of loving.

The next morning I awoke feeling leaden and dispirited. It was a bright, shining day, the sky was clear, but all of the colors had faded away for me. I could never accept that a man could cheat after he was married.

Howard, *why?* Why did you destroy us? my mind

screamed—but my body lay inert. I'd marvel that others had the energy to dress themselves when for me it was an effort to breathe—to sleep . . . alone. We had been ripped apart like a torn photograph.

I recall the phone ringing, incessantly ringing. My mother held it to my ear . . . I heard Howard's voice, his alligator love call . . . my throat was too dry and scorched to answer.

There I lay. I'd imagined waking at my own funeral. I saw my room full of long-stemmed gardenias and roses. Howard's roses. Howard's gardenias.

You weren't very original. You send all the ladies red roses—the Mormon boys said I was the only one you sent the white gardenias with the long stems. It doesn't matter now. I'll never see you again.

Chapter 9

I INHERIT MY "BOUNCE-BACK" FROM MY GRANDFATHER ON my mother's side. Nothing could keep him down for long. Grandpa always said that it is better to wear out than to rust out. I was rusting. That night I dreamt I saw my grandfather's finger admonishing me. When I woke up I took a little nourishment.

Three weeks later I accepted my first date with Glenn Davis.

The phone rang.

"Howard?"

No. It was Glenn Davis.

Glenn was the all-American hero, the greatest football player of his time. He and Doc Blanchard had played for West Point during World War II and had run roughshod over all the other teams of the nation. They were nicknamed Mr. Inside and Mr. Outside, the best running halfbacks of our time. They were handsome and spectacular, and every girl drooled over them.

I had double-dated with Glenn and Elizabeth Taylor, so I had known him for some time. He was fun, glamorous and more intriguing than many of the young actors I knew, for he was in a different field of endeavor. Elizabeth used to tell us, in great detail, about her exciting dates with the football star. I had thought they would marry until Bill Pawley came along. I knew *they'd* never marry, because Sara Taylor never liked Bill, and Elizabeth still listened to her mother. She had recently married Nicky Hilton, and I'd been too sick with grief to go to her engagement party. She had just invited the girls whom she had wanted to be her brides-maids, and, thanks to Howard, I had missed out. She had chosen another girl in my absence. The old gang thought I wasn't interested in them. Howard had finally consented to let me go to her wedding with my good friend, Richard Long. I had to come straight home after the ceremony, and Richard went alone to the reception.

Glenn had asked me out before, but I hadn't accepted because Elizabeth was my friend and Howard my watch-dog. It had become embarrassing going to parties and places alone. I felt people were beginning to ask, "Why is she always by herself?"

By now, the old gang were all going in different directions and I was still suffering from the incident in Las Vegas. To hell with Howard Hughes!

Would I go to the Rose Bowl with Glenn Davis?

"Why, I would just love to, thank you."

The next five weeks were a whirl with hardly time to think. After New Year's, I was sent to Chicago for a big telethon for handicapped children. Howard would have made me refuse, but I had snapped the leash. My mother was to go with me, and I was told that I could take an escort. I invited Glenn.

We helped raise millions, and it was magnificent fun. We were the celebrity couple. The whole world loved the lovers, especially the photographers. Flashbulbs popped, crowds gawked, and I was the star again. It was a heady feeling being with the superstars of our day, and they were all happy to see me again. Where had I been?

Jane Russell was there, so I knew Howard would be

calling her to check on me. I posed for pictures with Gary Cooper, Burt Lancaster, and every star I was sure would make the newspapers so Howard would know I wasn't hurting. I even managed to smile.

Glenn and I went everywhere together, and photographers dogged our every step. Every picture seemed to say the same thing: "Look at me, Howard. Eat your heart out. You hurt me, and now I'm hurting you."

The telephone never stopped ringing. I could keep running as long as it rang. Oh, please don't stop. Thank God, it didn't.

"Howard Hughes, will you stop calling me? Have you no pride?"

"Now, Helen, I can explain if you'll just let me. This is one time I'm completely innocent. . . ."

"One time! . . . So you admit this isn't the first time."

"There you go, twisting everything your way. I told you, you should be a Philadelphia lawyer. Don't hang up. I'm putting Walter Kane on the phone—he'll bear out my story."

"Walter Kane would lie on his rosary for you." I hung up.

I tried to put Howard out of my mind. It was fun being with Glenn, eating hamburgers smothered with raw onions again, eating garlic, chili dogs, going to the movies and the beach, and seeing people my own age. All the things I hadn't realized I'd been missing.

I picked up the phone. It was Howard.

"Be strong," my mother cautioned. "Remember your promise to your father."

My hands still shook whenever I spoke to him. His voice had a debilitating effect on my whole body.

Mother held up Glenn's picture. "Look at him, Terry. You can be proud to take him anywhere, and you're back among the living."

"But Mom, I still love Howard. I can't help it, but I do."

"Nonsense. He has you brainwashed, but you'll get over

it. You have three unreleased movies. The studio's backing you all the way. Your father, family, and friends are all standing behind you. We're all praying you'll be strong.''

I slipped the phone back on the hook, but a tear slipped from my eye. I brushed it away before Mother could see my weakened resolve.

While in Chicago, I met Abe Saperstein, the owner of the Harlem Globetrotters. It was friendship at first sight. That darling man became my manager and remained so until his death. He approached Glenn with a fantastic idea: a basketball team comprised of superstars of sports other than basketball to play his Globetrotters on tour. Glenn loved the idea, and so did Johnny Lujack, Doak Walker, Herman Weidemeyer, and Luke Easter.

The teams were to tour the Hawaiian Islands, and Abe Saperstein invited Mother and me to go along. No one should go to the Islands unless they are prepared to fall in love; they were created just for that purpose. Everything is so beautiful and romantic. There were parties and games and music and laughter and all that beauty wherever I looked.

We went to the fabulous Don the Beachcomber's, where the famous Alfred Apaka, the most romantic of all the Hawaiian singers, sang just for us. He closed every show with the most requested "Hawaiian Wedding Song."

The room with the breezes softly blowing grew quiet with expectation . . . the music swelled and I heard Alfred's exquisite tones: "Again, this couldn't happen again . . .''

I blacked out . . . I must have. I don't remember another thing until Mother woke me the following morning. She was singing. "Good morning, Merry Sunshine. We're on our way to Maui, then the big island, Hawaii, tomorrow. Everyone wants to give you a party. I kept it quiet for you, but the phone has been ringing off the hook in the next room. The press is waiting downstairs for you; I've stalled them as long as I could. All your clothes are laid out, but we must hurry. . . ."

We did . . . from party to party, from island to island. Each one more beautiful than the last.

I was brought up onstage to dance with the fire dancers. Everyone was putting leis around my neck, kisses on my lips, and wrapping pareos around my hips.

I loved watching the Globetrotters play and sitting on the sidelines, rooting for Glenn. Goose Tatum and the Trotters put on one of the funniest shows I'd ever seen. Right in the middle of the basketball game, they'd start playing baseball or they'd run for a touchdown. They were hilarious. I became their mascot, and Abe always had me take a bow between halves.

Glenn was becoming impatient with all the phone calls. Even island-hopping didn't stop them. Mother had told Glenn it was the studio. He remarked that even Elizabeth Taylor had never been in such demand.

As long as Howard called, I could be angry and hurt and want to strike back at him. As long as he called me, I knew he was sorry and was paying for the wrong he'd done to me. As long as he called, I could go out, knowing he'd be on the phone with me afterward, crying to me about how much I was making *him* suffer. The score wasn't even yet, not by a long shot.

"Quit calling me, Howard! I mean it!" I lied. "This is harassment. It's illegal. And I never want to speak to you again," I continued. "You're a cheat and a liar and an adulterer. I never want to hear your voice again. I never want to see you again. Get out of my life. Leave me alone."

"How can you do this to me, Helen? You know how much I love you—"

I interrupted. "Glenn Davis loves me more than you ever did. He's asked me to marry him, and I know he'll be faithful."

"Are you crazy? You're married to me," he said.

"I don't know you. It never happened. It's all just a bad

dream. And besides that, I hate you, Howard Hughes.'' I hung up the phone and broke into tears. What if Howard never did call me again? What if I never did get to hear his voice or see him again? I felt sick all over, and there was no one to turn to. I still loved him but decided I would have to block him out of my mind.

What I told Howard on the phone was true. Glenn was falling in love with me, and I was enjoying his company more and more.

When we landed in Los Angeles, the press was waiting and began bombarding us with questions: ''Are you engaged? When do you plan to be married? Will you give up your career? Do you plan to have children?''

Glenn took over. He put his arm around me and pulled me closer to him. ''We're getting married before the Rams' spring training. We haven't set a date yet, but it will have to be soon if we're going to squeeze in a honeymoon.''

I couldn't believe what I had just heard. I don't know why I didn't speak up, perhaps because it took me by surprise. By the time I'd recovered, the reporters were gone, calling their papers with the story.

''I wanted to surprise you,'' Glenn was saying. ''But I didn't think you'd be speechless. Are you happy?''

I was speechless because we had landed and the phone wasn't ringing. My mind was screaming for Howard. Where are you? Don't desert me now.

Days passed by and the phone rang off the hook, but it was never Howard. Every newspaper carried the story of our pending marriage, and the whole world was calling to congratulate me. The studio called. Every fan magazine wanted pictures of us. Even Harry Cohn himself called to congratulate me. I was dumbstruck. Why didn't I tell them it was all a lie? I wasn't getting married to anyone. I was already married!

Since I couldn't say anything, I said nothing. I did nothing. My family, friends, and studio were all pushing Glenn Davis and me together. We had no control. It was just happening.

The only thing preserving my sanity was my going back to work on *Sunny Side of the Street*. I felt more at home on the set than I did anywhere else. This was where I belonged. The real world was too ridiculous, too unbelievable.

On one of the last days of shooting, Glenn visited the set. I was doing a love scene with Cojo when a phone call came in to me. It was Howard, but I couldn't talk. They were ready to shoot my close-up.

Upon completion of the production, Glenn's parents felt obliged to set a wedding date for us, and I found myself being led around in a flurry of preparation for a wedding I knew would never take place. No one else ever noticed, but wherever we went, one of Howard's cars was always in the background. They were never close enough for me to see if they were occupied by Howard, but I often felt his presence. I thought there might be a plan to kidnap me, but it was only wishful thinking.

Days went by; my life was rushing ahead without me. There were no calls from Howard. It was as if a fog had rolled in around me, cutting me off from the world. This feeling continued till the day before the wedding. Howard called.

"Helen, I've got to see you one last time."

"No, Howard, it'll be too hard. It's best we don't see each other."

Howard pleaded, "Helen, I've got to see you one last time. I have something for you. It's a surprise. Bill Gay will be there to pick you up at 2 P.M. Don't be late."

I couldn't resist. I decided to wear his favorite outfit; the one I'd worn on the yacht when we'd been married. I made excuses to everyone as to where I was going, because I knew they'd stop me. I was certain that Howard was going to whisk me away to some far-off land where we would live happily ever after.

Bill Gay delivered me to bungalow nineteen at the Beverly Hills Hotel at exactly 2:35 P.M. Old and trusted Waldo, who at sixty-odd years still talked of nothing but his

101

fraternity buddies and college days, stood guard outside. I had missed him.

Bill knocked loudly several times before Howard answered, dressed in his usual attire: beige pants, white dress shirt with rolled sleeves, and brown oxfords. I was wearing the appliquéd tree-of-life beige linen skirt with the off-the-shoulder sweater that looked as if it had been painted on me.

Howard's attitude was mysterious, and he was much more sedate than I'd ever seen him before. I followed him into the bungalow. We both just stood there, waiting for the other to say something.

"You're making a terrible mistake, Helen. I've told you before, you'll never find what we have with another man. You are my wife, and you can't marry Davis. You'll be a bigamist."

I had never had another man, and that in itself was exciting.

"Oh, come on, Howard, we've been over that a hundred times. If you start that again, I'm walking right out that door. Where's my surprise?"

My remark really tickled him. He burst out laughing when he had been trying so hard to be serious.

"How well I know you, Pork Chop, and that curiosity of yours. I knew the word 'surprise' would bring you. I'll have to show you in the bedroom."

"Oh, no you don't," I countermanded.

Howard gave his irreparably hurt-basset-hound look.

"It's not what you're thinking, Helen. Let me show you."

Meekly, I followed Howard into our bedroom, fully expecting him to beg my forgiveness, slip the largest diamond in the world on my finger, and announce to the world that I couldn't marry America's Sweetheart, heartthrob Glenn Davis, because I was already Mrs. Howard Robard Hughes—a fact that Howard would never let me forget the rest of my life.

There were three drugstore-type white paper bags gracing the bed. He meticulously opened each one and removed round plastic boxes and tubes of vaginal jelly.

"You can have your little fling, Helen, but you mustn't get pregnant. If you do, your nipples will get all brown instead of pretty pink and you'll get stretch marks, and then I could never take you back."

Dr. Hughes had gone out and bought dozens of diaphragms in all sizes and spent an entire afternoon fitting me.

How cold! How insensitive! I was outraged—first his taking for granted that I could never belong to another, then his thinking he could make me admit I was his by embarrassing me with gynecological details. I knew he'd go to any length to make me think he'd allow me to go through with the wedding.

That night, Glenn's parents threw a party for us. Everyone was offering toasts and having a marvelous time. Everyone but me. I was feeling so depressed that I slipped outside. After a while, Glenn followed.

"What's the matter?" he asked.

"Oh, Glenn, I can't marry you. I don't love you. I still love Howard."

"Don't worry," Glenn replied. "Once we're married, you'll fall in love."

"You mean like in 'they married and lived happily ever after'?"

"Exactly."

I believed him.

My night before the wedding was virtually sleepless. Every noise I heard was Howard, coming to take me in his arms and carry me away. Twice, I was up out of bed and into the den, imagining I'd heard the springs of that old couch. But the sun rose and there was no Howard.

The dreaded day had arrived. Old Howard was going to let me suffer to the last minute. Brinkmanship, huh? Well, two can play that game.

We planned a small wedding, just the immediate family

in a room at the Mormon church. Sure that there'd never be a reception, I'd arranged that to take place after we returned from our honeymoon. That way none of our friends would be disappointed. I had even given Glenn half the money for our honeymoon, and there wasn't going to be a honeymoon. . . .

The ceremony began. Howard was calling my bluff. Because of my religious beliefs, despite my stubbornness, he thought I wouldn't go through with the wedding. On the other hand, I was sure Howard needed me in his life. Still feeling the hurt from the Las Vegas incident, I was going to play it out to the end with a good poker face. I was calling *his* bluff. I knew he had to break down and *beg* me back. He'd *never* let me marry another man. I was his little girl, and I was also his security. He needed me to mother him and smother him with my affection (which I loved to do); he always said he couldn't live without it.

In support of my actions, Mother and Father were also forcing Howard's hand. Mother felt that if Howard truly loved me, and held our marriage at sea as sacred and real, he'd never allow me to go through with this wedding. She felt that it would take something this drastic for Howard to bring our marriage into the public eye. Father, still angry over the Las Vegas scene and never believing that Howard and I were really married, thought this would finally convince me. If our reunion were real, Howard would be showing up with that log under his arm.

It was time for the ceremony. I knew that Howard would never let me go through with it, but why was he making me wait so long? It had to be his sense of the theatrical. At the last minute, I thought, when the minister says, "If there is anyone . . . let him speak now or forever hold his peace," Howard would make a quietly dramatic appearance and say, "I do. This woman can't marry anyone; she's already married to me."

Everyone was there: my parents, my close friends, the press, the Glenn Davis clan. It felt as though the whole world had pushed me to the altar and was now watching this terrible farce. They all seemed to want me to marry Glenn, and I couldn't stand up to them alone. I needed Howard to stand up for me. With him there, I wouldn't be afraid to say or do anything.

As the vows were being said, I heard a plane buzzing overhead . . . Howard was up there . . . and I was down here.

Down! Howard had let me down . . . and I was too paralyzed to run. We had bluffed each other apart.

I was being pushed to a waiting car with Glenn Davis, and for the first time in my life I was terrified. Howard had abandoned me. I felt that my parents had betrayed me. Why hadn't they found a way to stop it? The reality of bigamy didn't even occur to me then. I had been so sure there would be no wedding that there was no reason to think about it. Now I felt like a helpless puppet. I vaguely remember a sea of faces and flashbulbs popping, but I was deaf to the clamor and detached from it all.

I married Glenn Davis on February 9, 1951, and I was off on a honeymoon with twenty-six diaphragms furnished and fitted by Howard Hughes.

Chapter 10

GLENN AND I SPENT ONE NIGHT AT THE SANTA YNEZ INN in Pacific Palisades before we were off on our honeymoon trip. One night, and I knew Howard was right; I didn't find what Howard and I had with another man. Howard was special, and I found out just how special he was.

We were invited to visit the plane's cockpit and immediately became friendly with the pilot, Sid Adger. Sid was a tall, handsome man from Houston, Texas . . . just like Howard. He knew Mexico well and offered to take us under his wing. Where were we staying in Acapulco? I looked questioningly at Glenn. He didn't know.

Sid looked surprised. "This is the heart of the season, and everything's booked solid. Don't worry, you'll stay with us. My friend Tom Cooper and I are staying at the nicest house in Acapulco. It belongs to the former vice-president of Mexico. It's magnificent, and there's plenty of room for all of us."

It was truly magnificent in every sense of the word, and it came with servants and cooks who prepared the best Mexican food I'd ever eaten. I thrived on it, as I always have on hot Mexican dishes, but Glenn became so ill with *turista* that he hardly left our room while we were there. I was concerned about him, but Sid and Tom told me not to worry; he would sleep for three or four days until the fever subsided, and after a few more days of bed rest he'd make a miraculous recovery.

"I've had it myself. He'll be happier if you make yourself scarce, because he'll be making rapid dashes to the john."

Sid was right on all counts, and I spent the largest part of my honeymoon with these two strapping, six-foot-four-inch Texans. They took good care of me; they knew where to shop and where all the best bargains were. They both spoke excellent Spanish, which helped. I felt comfortable with these men, especially with their Texas twangs.

"Damned if I don't feel we're being followed," Sid said.

"Do you really think so?" The pure delight had to be evident in my voice.

"Yep, I've been noticin' that little fruit in the porkpie hat trailin' us for three days now."

I smiled to myself and somehow felt safer—and more loved.

"Maybe he wants your autograph," Tom said.

"You're probably right. I'll go ask him. He looks like the shy type."

The boys waited while I walked over to the young man, who was no stranger to me.

"Quick, give me a paper and pen like I'm signing an autograph. How is he?" I asked.

"He's holed up in his office at Goldwyn and hasn't come out since your wedding. We've left food at the door, but he hasn't touched it."

I signed the paper with a flourish and returned to my paratroopers. "After we see how Glenn is, let's really celebrate tonight. I feel like having a great time."

I was happy, Howard was suffering . . . I was suffering, too. So was Glenn, but he was recovering. We visited Mexico City and Panama and then returned home.

Football season was just over, so we moved to Lubbock,

Texas, into a one-room apartment. The apartment was over a theater, and had a pulldown bed. Glenn was working in the oil business, off season, for a Dr. Clark, who was an oil supplier.

I didn't have a film to do, so I settled down to being the little old homemaker. I scrubbed and baked, hung curtains, and wondered if this would be it for the rest of my life. Somebody gave me a little portable oven. The only things I knew how to cook came from recipes in the cookbook that came with the oven. I'd bake bread, a cake, and pie all the same day. All my letters home were about baking.

Glenn's boss, Dr. Clark, had a son-in-law, Tom Welfelt, with whom Glenn decided to go into business.

"Terry, I'm going to make a lot of money. We've got it all figured out. Tom and I are forming a pipe and supply company."

"That's wonderful, Glenn. What made you think of that? You don't even smoke."

"No, not that kind of pipe. Oil pipe—the kind they drill oil wells with. All we need now is a supplier. That's where you come in."

"How?" I asked.

"Well, you were pretty buddy-buddy with Howard Hughes. If we could get tied in with the Hughes Tool Company, we'd have it made. . . . So we want you to call . . . sweet-talk him a little bit, you know how. . . ."

"No, I won't do it." I was adamant.

"Why, it's nothing to him, but it could be everything to us. Listen to me. . . . We need that distributorship. Do you have any idea how much money this could put into our pockets?"

"Glenn, do you have any idea what kind of position you're putting me in? You know how Howard and I once felt about each other. Go to some other tool company."

Glenn pouted. "Any other wife would be willing to do this for her husband."

Maybe he was right. I called, reluctantly.

The number was no longer in service. I felt the color

draining from my cheeks. Would I ever be able to reach him again? There had been no contact or incidents since Acapulco. All the thoughts I'd pushed deep inside came spilling out. Was he with other women? Worse, was he with another woman? Would she sleep all night in his arms?

I came out of my reverie and called Bill Gay. He promised to give Howard the message, but he didn't sound too friendly.

For the next three days, every time the phone rang I jumped. I'd break out in a cold sweat at the thought that he might never call.

Finally Howard called. He was silent while I gave my pitch. There was a long pause. I was terrified at what he might say, and to make matters worse, Glenn came over and put his ear to the phone too.

Howard spoke briskly but quietly. "Sounds like a good idea. I'll have the president of the tool company call you."

True to his word, the president of Hughes Tool Company called and had us flown from Lubbock to Houston to discuss the prospectus. We were shown every courtesy. Things looked good. He told us he would touch base with Howard and let us know.

Glenn was really thrilled. "He's really a nice man, that Hughes. Look what he's doing for me."

Soon after returning to Lubbock, Harry Cohn called and told me to report for work. RKO had borrowed me for a film titled *High Heels*.

So Howard was up to his old tricks again. How obvious it was. Howard still wanted me, and Glenn had given him the perfect opportunity. Howard had calculated that Glenn would allow me to return so as not to throw a wrench into the Hughes Tool Company deal, which hadn't yet been consummated.

I knew Glenn would never stand for that.

"Glenn, it's Harry Cohn on the phone. He wants me to come back to Los Angeles. RKO's borrowed me for a film." I put my hand over the mouthpiece. "I don't think I should go."

109

"Take it, take it. RKO, that's Hughes's company." He grabbed the phone from me. "Mr. Cohn, this is Glenn. When do you need Terry? . . . I'll put her on the next plane . . . Nice to talk to you, sir."

"Thanks for asking me," I said sarcastically, and thought, Schmuck, he's doing just what Howard knew he'd do.

"This is great—just what we needed to close the deal," Glenn went on. "Maybe you'll run into Hughes while you're there. No. Call him, make an appointment with him. You'll do much better in person. I can feel that money rolling in right now."

"Whatever you say, Glenn," I said dutifully.

When I arrived home in Glendale, Harriet and Carolyn came running over to welcome me home.

"You look awful," they told me. They never pulled any punches. "What have you done to your lovely, wavy hair? It's not attractive pulled straight back with that barrette."

"Glenn likes me to look collegiate," I said.

"Strictly World War II, and that dress has to go. You look like you've put on ten pounds. . . . Luella, call the studio and tell them Terry has the flu and needs a few days to recover. We can't let her go to RKO looking like a frump. Domesticity doesn't agree with her."

They were right. It didn't. I worked hard, and in three days the extra pounds were gone. I called Terry Hunt's gym in Beverly Hills and started my workouts again. I waved my hair back into the style that Howard liked. RKO, here I come.

I was sent to Mel Ferrer's office. An actor-director who later married Audrey Hepburn, he was wearing his director's hat for this film.

"Tell me about the picture, Mel. Do you like it?" I asked.

"After I rewrite it, I will. It's a story about taxi dancers called *High Heels*."

"I'm embarrassed, Mel, but I don't know what a taxi dancer is," I said.

"No reason to be. They're girls who work in dance halls and sell dances to lonely guys for ten cents a dance. They're not supposed to, but most of them hook on the side."

I was terrified. It sounded as if I were as miscast as in *Gambling House*.

Mel told me not to worry, he'd be there to guide me. "You start out a young, innocent girl, the way you are now, who takes a job at one of these taxi-dance joints. One of the older girls, a pro, takes you under her wing and teaches you the ropes. We watch the slow degradation of the girl you play. She hates it at first and finally comes to love it. It has the usual subplot, boy meets girl and saves her in the end. This gives you a chance to do a lot of emoting.

"And Howard's sparing no expense on this one. We're screen-testing all your scenes with wardrobe."

"Screen-testing?" I thought I had the part.

"You're solid—he probably wants to ogle your tits in those slinky dresses. I understand that's the way he gets his kicks in the projection room. Anyway, he wants to see how you and Bill Tallman play together. Tallman will be here tomorrow for you to rehearse with." Bill Tallman later costarred in the Ellery Queen TV series and "Mr. District Attorney."

Every day I reported to the studio and Bill and I rehearsed, with Mel directing. Mel sent word to Howard that we were ready to shoot the scenes.

Howard had designed the costume I was to slink around in himself. It was a Harlow-type gown of the thinnest black matte jersey, strapless except for a strip of rhinestones that rose from the deep décolletage and wrapped around the neck. It followed every line of the body and it felt as though I were wearing nothing but a veil of water after a skinny dip. Naturally, Howard had to give approval, so the wardrobe lady and I made our way to his office at Goldwyn Studios. It was amusing to hear all the cat whistles, and one man actually fell off his camera.

Howard seemed to stop breathing when he saw me; my impulse was to make a flying leap over that desk into his

111

arms. His presence sent chain reactions throughout my entire body. He was holding on to the desk to steady himself. He appeared as though he'd already been devoured by my thoughts.

The wardrobe woman excused herself to make a phone call.

The atmosphere was charged with emotion. We stared into each other's eyes. Neither of us could speak. At the same moment, Howard and I glanced at his old couch where we'd made love so many times; one night the janitor had surprised us. Howard reached out his hand and led me around the desk toward him. I wanted him and started to move toward the couch. He held me fast with one hand and slid his other hand beneath the thin material of the dress he had designed, encircling my breast, holding it firmly.

"They're still pink," I whispered.

Howard pulled me closer and kissed me deeply. With one smooth motion of his gentle hand, he peeled the dress off my body. This was the moment the dress was made for; it fell down around my ankles and I stood naked before him. I wondered how many times he had enacted this scene in his mind.

This was Howard's movie, and I was bound to stick to his script. He lifted me out of the dress and put me on his desk. I hungrily pulled him on top of me.

"Don't ever leave me again," he said.

We made love.

I don't know how that old desk, or the building for that matter held up through it all, but they did. I was sure that anybody passing by outside was either embarrassed or amused. I never did see that wardrobe lady again.

I was on top of Howard, my flesh bonded to his with our perspiration. Papers were strewn about the room, everything from the day's weather forecast for flying to top-secret government documents. Nothing took precedence over desire when we desired. I looked down into Howard's deep, dark, smiling eyes. We were both happy again.

"God, Howard, you are so good. I've gotta be honest

with you, I missed this about you and me more than anything."

Howard laughed. "Then what are you going to do about it? I need you here with me, and I need a lot of this."

"I'm going to stay here and do it some more, baby, lots and lots and lots more."

"Today?"

"Every day," I said. "In fact, I'm going to call Texas and ask Glenn for a divorce." Without getting off of Howard, I took the receiver and called Lubbock. "Hello, Glenn."

"There's a ball game on the radio. It just started. You usually call in the evening. What's up? Did you get together with Hughes?"

"Yes, I got together with him."

Howard moved inside me and caused me to giggle. I had to cup the mouthpiece of the phone so Glenn wouldn't hear.

"Well," Glenn asked, "what's the story? What about my pipe and supply?"

Again I cupped the mouthpiece. "He's asking about his pipe and supply."

Howard grinned devilishly. "Tell him you've got a pipe and supply right here that he wouldn't believe."

"I'm right on top of it, Glenn. I'm expecting more results very soon. I'll call you tomorrow."

Howard decided I needed some firsthand knowledge about taxi dancers. Several evenings he picked me up in Glendale and drove to some of the seedy sections of Los Angeles. He took me to old ballrooms, taxi-dance places, with names like Roseland and Dreamland. Even while we were there, it seemed mystical and unreal. Howard should have been an actor; he was enjoying himself more than I was.

Here he looked right at home. With a twinkle in his eye, he went to the cashier and bought a fistful of tickets with the money he'd just borrowed from me. He knew I got such a kick out of loaning him money. He came over—I can still

113

see him standing there, tall, erect, with his head bent completely downward. He was fourteen inches taller than I was. He liked to stand close and look straight down at me when he asked me for a dance.

"First, yer ticket, mister." I was getting into the role.

Howard's line was, "Show me you're worth it, baby" —real Bogie-like. He was hilarious. Really, it didn't fit; he was so bad I broke up.

"Stay in character," he reprimanded.

Then I realized he was serious.

"You men are all alike. You just have different faces so we can tell you apart."

He was pleased and happy now, and we played the whole scene out.

I couldn't believe he knew every line—then it hit me. He'd probably written them. Most of them were terrible. Mel Ferrer was going to play hell to get these lines changed.

I reached way up and hugged Howard's face to mine.

"Oh, Howard, you were wonderful. If only I could play this part with you, I'd win every award in the world. I mean, you are really good . . . not just good—you're fantastic!" I said it seriously with tongue firmly in cheek.

Then I saw his face in those cheap-colored-mirrored-balled lights. He was beaming, beaming from sheer pleasure. No wonder I loved that face and that man.

"Oh, Howard, I do love you!" I reached up to—

"Here, here, you can't do that. It's all wrong for your part. It's completely out of character."

I'd just created a monster. A genuine ham.

Other nights, we visited all the sleazy old burlesque houses for further research. I think he was searching for additional dialogue.

There was nothing sick or perverted about Howard. He just had a giant curiosity about everything, especially the poor and downtrodden. The poor are curious about the rich, and the rich curious about the poor. Howard lost all sense of self-consciousness in these deprived areas. He didn't stand

114

out and no one took any notice of him. His clothes and demeanor blended in well.

He loved the burlesque comedians. The more awful they were, the more he laughed. They seemed to be a remnant of a past he'd once known, and this was his attempt to catch their last fading light.

Those nights with Howard were fun beyond description. Howard realized the problems I was living with and those I was about to face. He wisely took me from the mundane world of Mrs. Glenn Davis and put me into the fantasy world of a script, a world where the problems aren't really real and the endings are always happy.

There was something fragile about the preparation of *High Heels*, but I didn't care. Howard put me in another world as another girl, and this time he stepped in with me.

If the world could have just left us alone, I'm sure Howard wouldn't have run out of dimes for dances for a long, long time.

Chapter 11

EARLY ONE MORNING, WHEN EVERYONE WAS STILL SLEEPing, I quietly picked up the phone, dialed Lubbock, and asked Glenn for a divorce.

Glenn didn't waste any time. He was packed, on a plane, and in California in a flash. His big business deal hinged solely on signing with Hughes Tool, and now his only in with Hughes wanted a divorce. Glenn didn't like that.

Once in town, Glenn went directly to my parents' home in Glendale, where he was welcomed with open arms. I hadn't told them anything yet. Divorce was something that happened to other families, not ours. I was in a very unique position: the wife of two men.

I was out researching my role with my employer, Howard. He dropped me off late that night. Mom, Dad, and Glenn were all waiting up. We could see them through the lighted bay window in the living room.

I panicked. "Glenn's here. I can't go in there."

Howard said, "I'll take you home with me."

"I can't do that, either. Oh, Howard, how can I be in such a mess? I don't know what to do. Please, I'm scared."
I started trembling all over and my lips were quivering. I

was shaking from head to toe. "Oh, now Mom and Dad and Wally know everything—oh, how could I do this to them!" I broke down sobbing.

Howard was as helpless as all men in these situations. He waited patiently for me to calm down. Nothing or no one could pacify me. It went beyond Howard or Glenn . . . it was human decency, my integrity, my family, my relationship with God. I had to do the right thing, and I didn't know what was right.

"I love you, Howard; I love you more than anything; I'll always love you. But *you* cheated on me. I can't take that. I can't!" All the emotions that I'd held back came bursting forth. "I hate you; I hate you for what you did, but I hate Glenn more. . . . Poor Mom, Dad—what are they thinking? Help me, Howard. Help me. I love you—please help me," I sobbed.

He put the car in gear and rolled farther down the street with the lights off. He stopped the car and gently held me until I was calm.

"Do you really love me this much? Are you willing to go through all this hell for me?"

"Yes, Howard, yes," I cried. "What do you think I've been doing? Don't you think I feel? . . . But you're tearing me apart. There won't be anything left of me for anyone— not anyone. . . . I want my mother . . . my daddy." I broke away from Howard, opened the car door, and blindly ran toward the house and around to the back entrance.

I didn't know where Howard was and I didn't care. I was hurting my parents. I hated men. I wanted to go back to the womb again. I wanted to sleep. I wanted to feel safe.

Quietly, I entered the back room and slipped into my bedroom. That's where Mother found me. She pulled the covers over me.

"Just go to sleep, Helen. We've talked Glenn into staying at a motel nearby tonight. Everything will seem brighter in the morning when the sun shines."

I loved her so much. Mother and Daddy understood; they loved me.

Half asleep, I heard the phone ring. I knew it was Howard. I heard my father saying, "No, she's not here. She's gone somewhere with her mother." Dad hung up before Howard could question him further.

Knowing Howard would be calling every five minutes, Mother took the phone off the hook before going to bed. When Howard kept getting a busy signal, he sent one of the boys over, in the middle of the night, to see if I was there. Mother answered the door. She said I was sound asleep and told to tell Howard that she'd come and talk to him tomorrow.

The next day while I was getting dressed, I could hear Glenn's whiny voice in the next room.

"Lamar, I even bought Terry a brand-new shotgun to go duck hunting with me. Top-of-the-line Browning twenty-gauge automatic. Cost me over two hundred dollars."

Ya-hoo, I thought bitterly, just what I always wanted. I was never invited to go duck shooting, but the gun went along.

"Why would you ever allow Helen to leave, knowing that the movie was for RKO?" my father reprimanded.

"Do you think I would have if I'd known? Not in a million years. I even wanted her to give up her career." That was the first I'd heard of that.

My father soon became as disillusioned with my second husband as I was.

Right after the wedding, my father had turned my whole life's savings over to Glenn; his mother turned a list of Glenn's assets over to me. He had my money; I had his list. That had begun to turn my parents sour.

Mother had thought things weren't right when I returned from Lubbock looking so worn down. She'd never seen me when I hadn't managed to look good.

Before Glenn arrived, Mother left to deal with Howard.

Howard was hurting, and Mama Blue was a good listener. He often said she was the mother he didn't have. Sometimes he put his head in her lap and cried like a little

118

boy. "I'm an orphan. I haven't got anyone. At least Helen has you."

He would frequently take Mother driving in order to complain about me. This time she was driving and Howard was complaining on my behalf. As Mama Blue remembers, he was too upset to drive.

"The girl's miserable. I've got to see her, Luella. Where is she?"

Mama Blue was trying to keep Howard and Glenn apart. "She's at our house talking with Glenn. You can't see her while he's there. Glenn is such an odd guy that he might just decide to take a pop at you."

Howard began looking for a pay phone. "Call up this Davis; I'm going over there. Helen's got to get out of this. I'll just tell him, man to man, that Helen and I made a mistake and that Helen belongs with me. She's over there crying, Luella. She's been crying ever since he showed up. I've got to get this Davis guy out of the picture."

"Glenn said they were happy in Texas."

"*He* said. What about her? She's my wife. He took her away from me."

"You should have thought of that before your Las Vegas fling."

"You don't hang a man till you know his side."

"It was pretty clear, Howard."

"Stop over there at the phone booth. I've got to talk to her."

I was sitting at the house with Glenn, my brother Wally, and my father. The atmosphere was tense. I told Glenn that nothing had changed, that I had tried to forget Howard, but it was impossible. He was too much a part of me, and I would never stop loving him. "I don't want to be one of the multitude of women who are married to one man and dreaming of another," I said.

At that awkward moment the phone rang, and I almost flew to it. "Hello."

It was mother on the other end. "I'm with Howard," she said. "He wants to come over there and talk with Glenn."

119

Howard took the receiver from Mother.

"Helen, are you all right? Why do you want to be around that guy?"

"I don't, Howard."

Glenn was on his feet and standing over me as soon as I said "Howard." "Ask him to come over. I'd like to have a talk with him."

I handed the receiver to Glenn. "Here, you ask him."

"Come on over, I want to talk to you. . . . You're too old for her. You're an old man. . . . I have my whole life ahead of me—yours is nearly over. . . . Come on over then—and you don't need to bring your bodyguards along. Don't worry, I won't hurt you."

As unhappy and apprehensive as I was, I couldn't help but be amused. Glenn thought he was frightening Howard. Howard wasn't afraid of anything or anyone.

Over the next thirty minutes of nervous anticipation, Glenn's tough-guy attitude began disintegrating. By the time Mother arrived with Howard, Glenn was shaking.

Howard walked in and I started to introduce them, but before I could even finish, Glenn began pleading with Howard. "Don't take her away from me, don't take her away." It was one of those moments when everyone was just too embarrassed to even look at one another. Glenn wasn't a bad actor himself, but he soon realized he'd lost his audience.

Howard, in deference to Glenn's feelings, had walked to the other end of the room, near the entrance to the dining room. He didn't say a word, just stared down at his brown shoes. Meanwhile, Glenn had worked himself back into the state of outraged husband. He walked over to Howard as if he were going to shake hands. Howard put out his hand; Glenn lunged forward and shoved his hand backward. Howard tried to step back to gain his balance and fell over a small ottoman that was right behind him, crashing into the dining-room door and falling on the floor. Glenn was in hot pursuit. Mama Blue, who always liked to get in the middle of everything, realized Glenn's intentions and threw her body over Howard.

Daddy and I were grabbing Glenn, trying to pull him off. I remember my brother Wally just stood there crying his heart out. Howard was his hero. With my father's help, we somehow managed to pull Glenn off. With that, Glenn ran out of the house.

I can still see Glenn standing at the end of the yard and hear myself crying, "You brute, you animal, you're the one who asked Howard to come here, and now look what you've done! Aren't you ashamed?"

Glenn apologized, "I'm sorry, I didn't mean it. Forgive me," as I ran back into the house.

I looked around. Everyone was shaken up. Mother ushered Howard out the door and into the car. She drove him back in the direction of Beverly Hills. Down on Brand Boulevard, not far from my parents' home, Howard saw a bus coming. "Stop here, let me out," he said. "I'll take the bus back."

"I'll take you," Mother offered.

"No, you get back to the house and be with Helen. And get her out of there immediately. I don't want her anywhere near that lunatic. You can't trust what he might do."

Mother gave Howard the bus fare, put him on the bus, and then rushed back home. She had us both packed and out of the house before anyone knew. She didn't even tell my father we were leaving.

For days we hopped around from motel to motel in the Los Angeles area. As per Howard's instructions, we did this under assumed names. He told us to contact no one but him, informing us that Wally and Glenn were out every day, knocking on doors and looking for us. Wally was keeping his eye on Glenn and keeping Howard advised.

The mounting tension was becoming too much. I had been crying almost constantly since we left the house, and Mother's ulcer was beginning to bleed.

Glenn wouldn't give me a divorce and said he was going

to fight it to the end. My father turned his back on Glenn forever.

Howard was still the only one who knew our whereabouts. Surprisingly, Daddy put up no resistance to his control over the situation. It wasn't until 1978, when my Father was on his deathbed, that he told me why Howard had visited him when I was hiding out from Glenn. He had finally shown Daddy the ship's log that proved we had truly been married in 1949.

Howard called late one night. "Listen baby, listen carefully. Something big has come up, and you and I have to fly out of town."

"Howard, what is it? Mother's too sick to travel," I cried.

"Now don't you start worrying. I'm watching out for Luella. She should be in the hospital where Dr. Mason can take care of her. I'm making the arrangements right now."

"I can't leave my mother if she's sick."

"Your mother agrees with me that this is the best solution and she'll be better off in the hospital. She'll feel better when you're out of town. We'll come back when this mess has blown over. I've got a call in to your stand-in, Mary Jane Carey. I'll get her to come along with you."

"Why do we have to leave?" I persisted.

"Well, if you have to know, Davis has got the whole goddamn Rams football team tearin' the town apart looking for you. They're looking for me too."

Chapter 12

"KEEP DOWN," MY MOTHER CAUTIONED. I WAS CROUCHED down in the backseat of her car. We were in Hollywood, circling Mary Jane's block for the thirty-second time. On orders from Howard, we were to continue circling until a signal came from Charlie, Mary Jane's fiancé, who stood outside her house. If we stopped and waited for Mary Jane to get ready, the car might be spotted. Howard thought the house was probably under surveillance.

Howard had had great difficulty in persuading Marjane (as he called her) to accompany me on my great escape. For a couple of days he had his secretaries trying to chase her down by phone. It wasn't easy, because she was a popular young lady and very active.

She had been my stand-in for some time. (A stand-in is someone who stands in the actor's position while the lights and camera are being readied for the shot. Mary Jane was known as one of the best.) During the torment of making *Gambling House,* I confided in her that I was seeing Howard, and she'd been a friend ever since.

When Howard's people finally reached her, she didn't want to go anywhere. This wouldn't satisfy Howard, though, and everyplace she went there was either a phone call or a message from Howard. She was bound and determined not to change her plans to suit his whims. Howard tried almost everything to convince her to go, but she held her ground and refused. Even her mother was encouraging her to go.

Finally, The Man himself called her. He used my condition as leverage, telling her that if she were any kind of friend to me, she would go, that I really needed her. She was truly concerned about me, but she had a young son, a boyfriend, and a life of her own to lead. She couldn't go off traipsing after Howard, for God knows how long, and leave it all behind her.

Howard knew I wouldn't go without Mother or Mary Jane, so he pulled a fast one. Several of Mary Jane's relatives worked at RKO. One in particular, Cliff Broughton, was one of RKO's top executives. Howard had Cliff call Mary Jane and tell her that if she didn't go along, his job was on the line. That did it. Mary Jane wasn't about to let her family suffer on her account.

Mary Jane had arrived at home that night shortly before we began circling the block. Her mother was excited about her opportunity to go off with the mysterious Mr. Hughes and had her things all packed. When Mary Jane was ready, the porch lights were put out. Charlie signaled us to stop, scurried her into our car, and we were off.

In the next phase of the operation, Mother was directed to a certain dimly lit street in Hollywood where one of Howard's cars was waiting with a driver. Mary Jane and I got into it. I gave Mother a prolonged hug and squeeze of the hand.

"I'm praying for you, Mom."

We were off again. As soon as Mother was out of sight I burst into tears. I had tried to be strong for her sake, but I couldn't hold back the tears any longer.

The driver of the car wasn't one of Howard's usual drivers, but a large, armed bodyguard. He drove us, in a roundabout way, to a dark street behind Bekins Storage in

Hollywood. There, one of the usual Chevrolets and a Mormon boy were waiting. We changed cars again and were taken somewhere near Sunset and La Cienega to meet Howard. When we arrived, Howard was waiting in a dark phone booth (he always found a phone booth that wasn't lit). We pulled to the curb; Howard approached the car and leaned in the window. He instructed the driver to take us directly to Hughes Airport.

The driver took us down a dark road and over a rickety old wooden bridge to find Howard's private landing strip. The brilliant lights turned night into day and brought out scores of cottontails to play on the green field. Howard loved those little rabbits and was always fearful we might hit one on landing or takeoff. One time, driving over the pasture to our waiting plane, he nearly killed us both, trying to miss running over one of them. He often affectionately called me his little rabbit, which always made me laugh, since at RKO he was still known as Harvey, the invisible rabbit. He started adding jewelry in the shape of bunnies to my growing collection of owls.

We were driven to a dark part of the field where an idling plane waited. It was Howard's latest test plane, and his test pilot, Colonel (later General) Shoup, took us aboard. The sight of the craft was enough to make anyone skeptical about flying. It was made of wood and had been gutted for speed. The lightweight construction was all exposed on the inside. We sat on barrels. Shoupy, as Howard referred to the Colonel, didn't act too enthusiastic about piloting us. Howard had probably called him away from something important that night.

There was no insulation. The flight was freezing cold and noisy beyond belief.

In only forty-seven minutes (fast for 1951) we landed in Las Vegas. Another old Chevrolet was waiting when we climbed down out of the plane.

There we were, two young girls being driven off into the dark Nevada wasteland by a stranger. Our destination was kept from us. I'm surprised we weren't blindfolded.

125

Just like secret agents on a dangerous mission, we were given new identities. From then on, I was to be Barbara Malone and Mary Jane was to be Betty Fredericks. We were told that we would be unable to contact anyone for any reason, that no cameras were allowed, and that Howard (alias Mr. Grimes) would arrive the following day.

In about an hour, we arrived at a ranch and were driven up to two bungalows. There was one for each of us, but I preferred staying with Mary Jane. The last thing I wanted was to be alone, nor did Mary Jane want me to be alone. I was still in a daze from all that was happening. I virtually had to be led around, and I'd just been led to I didn't know where.

The next morning, when Mary Jane and I awakened, we were starved. Howard always arranged everything else to the minutest detail, but he never remembered that people eat. Mary Jane and I were up bright and early at 8:00 A.M., only to discover that we were on a working ranch. Breakfast was at five, dinner at eleven, and supper at five. So we had to wait until eleven. Later, it was arranged for our meals to be sent in to us on our schedule.

There were cooks and maids at the main house, but no one seemed to be in charge. A cook told "Betty" and me that Cliff, the owner-foreman, was out with the cowboys working the ranch, and his wife was in town shopping. We were to make ourselves at home and "enjoy."

Enjoy? The place was empty. But outside our bungalow was the largest swimming pool we'd ever seen. It seemed to stretch halfway across Nevada. Along the pool was a beautiful row of weeping eucalyptus trees, and beyond that only desert. The golden glow of desert sands in the early morning dotted with spring wildflowers and distant mountains was glorious. The whole desert was in bloom.

Mary Jane and I hurried back to the bungalow and put on our briefest bikinis. (Mine was yellow polka-dot, as in the song.) We couldn't wait to test the waters. I ran so fast I accidentally slid into the pool. To my horror, the water was so cold that I became numb. The pool was filled with the natural well waters from the ranch and obviously not heated.

"How is it?" called Mary Jane.

"It's perfect," I lied. "Try it."

She was only halfway in when she started screaming, "Terry . . . Helen . . . Barbara Malone . . . whatever the hell your name is . . . you lied! . . . Even fish couldn't survive in this!" But we both loved to swim and soon became almost accustomed to the icy well water. The blistering desert sun was always there to warm us up quickly.

We both changed into our jeans for lunch. As we walked toward the main house and dining room, a cowboy came riding up at full gallop on a gray-speckled cutting horse. He was grinning broadly, and we could see his handsome, olive-complexioned face and dark, curly hair under his beige summer Stetson.

With great exaggeration he tipped his hat. "Howdy, ma'am." Then he threw his head back with laughter. "How's that for an opening line?"

I threw back, "At least it's original." I already felt at home with this cheerful stranger.

"You must be . . ." All three of us said it simultaneously; thank God he said Betty and Barbara first, because I couldn't remember who I was at that moment.

He was Cliff Devaney, the lord of Tulley Springs Ranch. (Today the ranch is part of the Floyd Lamb State Park.) I don't know to this day if they ever knew or discovered who we were, but Cliff and his wife Pat were lovely, pleasant people who made us feel we belonged.

Cliff said, "If you'd like to eat, I'd make a beeline for the dining room. Food doesn't last long around a bunch of cowhands."

In a matter of seconds, we were in the chow line. I don't know if that food was really sensational or if we were so starved everything tasted fabulous.

Then I heard the most glorious sound in the world: a plane circling overhead. I ran outside, waving my arms like crazy. Howard swooped down low and tipped his wings. I was more excited than any child at Christmas. To me that was the most romantic gesture in the whole world. Ohhh—I felt such great warmth and pride, knowing he was up there flying that enormous plane—alone.

I raced back to the bungalow to check my makeup and slip into a sexier blouse. He loved me in jeans, but I had to change my flimsy lace bra to a sturdier, heavier one. Howard would throw a fit if I ever bounced the least little bit. He said every shake would break my breasts down a little at a time and soon nothing would raise them up but plastic surgery. He always chided me that they were glands, not muscles, and no exercise in the world would lift them once they'd fallen.

Mary Jane was the first one to see the cloud of dust rolling over the dirt road. Mr. Grimes had arrived in an old gray Chevy.

I ran to meet him, all smiles.

"Careful," he said. "How many times do I have to tell you? You can't run like that, baby, not if you expect to keep them firm."

I didn't care if he was critical, I was so happy to see him.

Almost as soon as Howard arrived, he took me driving through the desert. He wanted to bring me up to date on my situation with Glenn.

As much as I wanted to, I couldn't publicly acknowledge my marriage to Howard, as it would put us in a legal hotbox and could even place me behind bars for bigamy.

Howard was trying to take care of things. Through our attorney, Lloyd Wright, we had first requested an annulment. We felt an annulment would be the lesser evil and would put me back where I started. Howard brought the news that Glenn flatly refused it. I was so disappointed. I wanted him to say that my problems were over and I'd never have to think about them again. I burst into tears and clung to Howard desperately. "What am I going to do? What am I going to do? How did this ever happen?"

Howard tried to comfort me. "Here now, baby, it's not all that bad. We're going to try to get you a Nevada divorce. That's only a six-week wait."

"Six more weeks!" I sobbed louder.

"It'll be all right. We're going to spend it on the ranch, together."

I continued sobbing. Nothing was going right for me.

"You'll have fun," he said. "I'm even going to teach you how to fly a plane."

I looked up at him with a sniffle. "Really, Howard?"

"That's what I said." He kissed me gently. "And you're going to be the best damn female pilot in the world."

Howard was my whole world. I felt like Joan of Arc, a martyr, giving up my career for the man I loved. Howard realized the risk I was taking. Even though I had four unreleased movies, I was sure that any unfavorable publicity regarding the divorce would be so damaging that no one would ever want to hire me again.

Both Mary Jane and I were eager to be home and living normal lives again. But if six weeks was what it had to be, then six weeks it was. We decided to try and make the best of it.

Sometimes Mary Jane and I would rise with the cowboys, eat a huge country breakfast, and then round up horses with them. I had made many westerns, but this was real and I loved it. There is nothing as exhilarating as the sight, scent, and feel of daybreak from the saddle of a horse. Everything smells better in the desert, and the aroma from the dew on the sagebrush is almost intoxicating.

The cattle were lowing and roaming around.

"Tighten your reins. . . . Your mount spins around on a dime, gives you nine cents change, and you're off."

What a feeling, being astride such a powerful living thing as it races through the wild, with the wind blowing its mane. I felt the wildness and the freedom of the horse as my own hair flowed and rippled back in the breeze of speed.

Later we returned to the stables, wet with sweat and

caked with dust. We splashed our faces with water and drank from the cool, cool well. Our mouths were almost too dry and parched to swallow.

Oh, dear God, I get breathless remembering those days.

Eleven A.M. and the dinner bell rang. We all made a hungry beeline for the dining room. I was saddle-sore and stiff and still felt the horse under me.

Dinner, oh, sweet, sweet dinner, served in chafing dishes on picnic tables. First come, first served, but there's plenty for everyone. It's all homegrown and homemade, including the hot biscuits, pickles, and preserves. Oh, glory be, I can still taste those biscuits with honey and the piping-hot apple pie à la mode.

After lunch we would go for a swim and sunbathe, or Howard would show up and take me for a flying lesson. He was usually gone mornings taking care of his business.

When Howard wasn't with us, he was usually testing airplanes. He would fly to Los Angeles during the day, returning to Las Vegas at night. He'd practice landings for government tests. Sometimes there were more than a hundred eighty landings in a session. Often he would take me to keep him company.

Flying over the city at night was something Howard loved to do. He would bank the plane until I felt I would slide off into all those lights below.

One night it was getting very late and Howard hadn't returned from the day's test-flying. He wasn't able to take me because some Defense Department people were going along to evaluate a new design.

I was worried and frightened when bedtime came and he hadn't even called. Mary Jane stayed up late to comfort me. She was usually asleep by this time and I would usually sneak out to spend most of the night sleeping with Howard.

In the middle of the night, there was a knock at the door. I ran to it, thinking it was Howard. It was Cliff at the door; Mr. Grimes had called and said he was tied up with the air force for a couple of days and would keep in touch by phone.

It was a long and lonely three days. I slept as much as I could, and Mary Jane did her best to cheer me in my waking hours. I was in a foul mood when Howard called on the third day.

An hour on the phone with him and he had me happy again. He was bringing me the biggest surprise of my life.

I spent the morning readying myself for Howard's return. He arrived about noon and whisked me away in his car.

"Where's my big surprise?" When we took our next turn and headed for the landing strip, I saw it. I couldn't miss it. It was the *Constellation*, the largest plane flying the skies at this time, with four engines and a split tail like a P-38.

"Is that for me, Howard? Is that the surprise?"

He drove up to the monster. We got out and walked under it. It was as large as a building.

"This is only part of your surprise," Howard said. "Come on, you're going to fly it."

"Oh, Howard, this is the biggest, greatest surprise in the whole world!"

"And there's more to come," Howard chuckled.

It was a day I'll never forget, and one I still dream about. Of all the colorful experiences that make up my life, this has to be the most unpredictable and dangerous and exciting.

Alone together, Howard and I went up in this huge plane on what I thought, at the time, was just another beautiful flight. It would prove to be the most beautiful of all.

He had been teaching me all the basics of flying, but I hadn't done the actual piloting yet.

Once we were up in the air, Howard explained the differences between the *Constellation* and the other planes, and then let me take over the wheel. It was choppy flying at first, but I soon caught on. I was a fast learner and Howard was a fast teacher.

We hadn't made love for days. All day long my teacher had been looking at me with a certain sex-starved look he had. I'll never forget the intensity of that look. "I want you," he said.

131

"I'm here, Howard. You have me."

That made him laugh, and oh, what a laugh it was.

He took over as pilot and abruptly pulled the nose of the plane up and began a powerful ascent. He climbed to an altitude I'd never before been anywhere near. It was far above what any commercial plane would ever attempt. I remember that the pressure in my head was constantly increasing and I repeatedly was clearing my ears.

Howard had a wild and happy sparkle in his eyes as he leveled the craft off, made some further adjustments, and put it on automatic pilot.

"I want you now," he said. He climbed from his seat and took me up out of my seat into his arms. He was so tall and lanky, and his arms were so very, very strong. He kissed me passionately, but tenderly, and carried me back through the plane to the aft cabin. There was no one at the controls. I was speechless.

There was nothing spontaneous about it; Howard had planned it all. I'm sure he had choreographed it over and over in his mind, every sensuous, beautiful detail. He laid me down on a bed of the finest mink and lowered himself on top of me. Between our kisses, movements, and embraces, we undressed each other, piece by piece, layer by layer. The inside of the plane was icy cold, but we were on fire. The mink was soft and slippery against our naked flesh.

My fears of the plane colliding or falling or exploding only heightened the mounting ecstasy I was feeling. Howard was thriving on it. My submission was the fuel for the magic he was giving me.

He was mine, all mine, the most exciting man of the century. This was Howard at his best, better than the best. He was in his own private domain . . . the sky, his supreme gift to me.

He was loving me wildly, deeply, while the engines roared like a thousand hungry caged tigers. The hot friction on mink soared to the point that our bodies became one with the pilotless plane, soaring, climbing, racing through time and space, until we spun out, nose-diving. . . . My entire body erupted and the universe disappeared.

When I revived I was powerless, spent, with nothing existing but Howard's warmth, the deep soft mink, and the promise of a new beginning. I was his wife again, completely.

At that moment, I felt like the most beautiful girl alive.

Chapter 13

It took Mary Jane only a day or two to gain Cliff's trust and get at the phone. Nothing came between her and her family. They were very close, and she knew I felt the same way about my family. I was extremely worried about Mother, so she would get me in to call too. Howard was keeping us informed about what was going on back home, but this was how we got the facts. We reversed all the charges so when Howard looked over the phone bills Cliff wouldn't catch hell.

My biggest concern was my mother's being in the hospital. I had never left her like this before. Even after my marriage to Howard, we were always together. Howard never allowed me to travel on my picture locations without her, and I loved having her with me. It would have taken three people to do all she did for me. She was my personal hairstylist, secretary, clothes designer, and my best friend. Her ulcer was still bad when I spoke to her. Glenn was driving her up the walls. He would come to the hospital every day, crying and complaining about me, ignoring the No Visitors sign.

In one of Mary Jane's secret calls home, her mother was

bubbling over with excitement. Glenn had paid her a visit in the company of half the Rams football team. Glenn had inquired where Mary Jane was, and her mother made up a story about her visiting a sister. She kept Glenn and his football squad on the other side of the door during the entire conversation. She said a couple of the linebackers filled up her entire porch.

Most of our evenings were spent on the ranch. It was Howard, me, and Mary Jane. Mary Jane was extremely fond of Howard, and although she was away from her loved ones, her memories of our days together are treasured.

Many hours we sat beneath the star-filled desert sky, watching meteorites and exchanging jokes and stories. Howard was more at home than I had ever seen him, and he was thoroughly enjoying himself, laughing uproariously at his own jokes. You could always tell when he was about to say something funny, because he'd first get that twinkle in his eye and then that little sheepish grin would start to break at the corners of his mouth. He looked like a big kid.

He was like a Will Rogers spinning his yarns and telling stories about a Hollywood of the past. He had so many stories from the days he ran around with Cary Grant, Pat DeCicco, and the movie director Nickey Neilan.

Evenings when Howard and I weren't around, Mary Jane would often go to the main house and visit Cliff and Pat. Mary Jane was Irish and needed her evening cocktail, and, like all good Irish girls, she enjoyed company. The only problem was I was always off with Howard, and didn't drink anyway, and the Johnsons didn't even know what a Tom Collins was. Perfect. They didn't know what they had missed, and Mary Jane was going to show them. She had a bottle of vodka smuggled in and combined it with sweet fresh limeade, and the Johnsons loved it. It tasted so good that you couldn't even tell the alcohol was there. Soon it became an every night ritual for Cliff, Pat, and Mary Jane to have their Tom Collinses. They would sit in the kitchen for hours talking and enjoying one another's company.

The daytime ranch life and nighttime chats were enough

for a while, but poor Mary Jane hadn't been anywhere since the night we arrived and she was beginning to suffer from ranch fever. We began needling Howard to take us both out for some fun.

Howard could only hold off so long; he finally gave in. He decided an all-day trip to the top of Mount Charleston by car would be fun. At the outset, so did we. Before lunch was served at the ranch we were off. Partway up the mountain, Mary Jane and I were feeling the pangs of hunger, and we didn't hold back our complaints about missing lunch or about Howard's kamikaze driving in both lanes up the blindly winding road.

In most situations, we could talk in a normal voice around Howard and not be heard by him. That day Mary Jane learned that Howard could hear sound carried by vibration. Mary Jane asked Howard if the story was true that he had quit going to parties because of his hearing. He confirmed it.

Howard was a legend, even as a young man. He enjoyed parties like any normal male. He was young and handsome and had lots of money and lots of invitations. One time he went to a party in Pasadena. When *the* Howard Hughes entered the large room full of people, everyone stopped talking at once and stared at him. Howard went completely deaf without the noise and clamor of the party. He just turned around and walked right out. That was his last party.

Despite our griping and name-calling, Howard drove right on by the mountain's only restaurant. He hadn't had the place cased, so we couldn't stop there. We did stop when we got to the top of the mountain, and he even let us get out and stretch. It was beautiful and picturesque, but we were too hungry to enjoy it.

On the way down the mountain, Howard's old car got too hot and the engine seized up, never to start again. We managed to coast to the bottom. Now we were stranded in the desert, miles from civilization.

Howard walked off down the road, alone, to find help.

His luck held and he ran into someone who promised to get word to Vegas. Several hours later we were back at the ranch much the worse for wear. It became Home, Sweet Home, and the pool never felt cold again.

Howard was determined to make up for the ordeal on the mountain. We didn't let him forget the hot hours we'd suffered on the desert without food or water.

"Just you wait till Mary Jane gets back to RKO and tells everyone you tried to starve us. We'll tell them that Harvey Hughes passes out invisible food. Remind me to give that one to Louella," I teased.

Howard gave us that knowing grin of his. "I have something planned that's going to knock the socks off you. And before you complain, I've brought box lunches so you won't starve."

"Aach." Mary Jane and I made a face. In the movie business, when you go on locations you are often served box lunches. They're the dregs. Usually they consist of a hard-boiled egg, a piece of dried fried chicken, and an orange.

Howard continued to look super-pleased with himself all the way to Lake Mead, where he had a boat waiting for us. In fact, he had two boats. James Bond Hughes had hired two identical forty-foot twin-screw boats, one for us and the other one to confuse whoever might try to follow us. Mary Jane and I giggled over the stratagem, but still it made everything dangerously exciting.

I slept for over half the journey. I always sleep at the beginning of a boat trip; it gives my stomach time to adjust and I don't get seasick. While I was below, Mary Jane started questioning Howard about all the myths that circulated about him. He laughed and thoroughly enjoyed hearing each and every story. Usually he set the record straight. Mary Jane found it hard to believe that she was on Lake Mead, sailing down the Colorado River, with Howard, the legend. I saw it in her face when I joined them. Nothing she had ever heard about him, none of the folklore correlated with what we shared on that cruise. His warmth and laughter were unforgettable. We sat there spellbound as he unwound story after story.

"Tell me," Mary Jane asked, "when you set the record for flying around the world . . . I read a story, which was later denied, that you used a piece of string to stay awake."

"That's true," Howard said. "I had an engineer but not a copilot. We could never count on our not falling asleep at the same time, so I tied a piece of string around my big toe and tied the other end to the stick. If we banked, climbed, or lost altitude, that toe woke me up real fast.

"However," he went on, "the most interesting thing that happened on the whole flight, I've never told anyone till now—didn't dare to. People think I'm crazy as it is, but my engineer will bear me out. I think maybe you all could understand." He paused for what seemed an eternity. "No, no . . ." He shook his head.

We could see he was about to change his mind, but we weren't about to let him. We wouldn't let up until he told us the whole story.

He told us that when he left India and flew over the Himalayas into Tibet, he landed in pouring-down rain just outside the city of Lhasa. "This was many years before the Chinese takeover," he said, "and Tibet was still as ancient as Shangri-la. It was such a mystical country with its lamas, monks, and nomads. They had absolutely no contact with the outside world, but thousands of people had been coming out of the mountains for weeks to greet the great white bird that would drop out of the sky. They came in caravans, on yaks and on foot. How they knew when and where I'd be arriving was as mystical as the Magi's arrival at the birth of Christ . . . but they knew."

"Go on, go on. What happened?" we both squealed in unison.

"Well, I got out, they watched me refuel, and I left."

Howard had a way about him in a situation like that. It wasn't humility; it was simplicity.

It reminded me of another spring-lit day, when Howard walked into an airplane hangar where Charles Lindbergh was examining a plane. Everyone waited with bated breath and a crowd gathered around to see what would happen when these two great men of courage and destiny met for the first time.

Lindbergh looked up, and when he saw Howard, he said, "Hello."

Howard glanced over his shoulder. "Hi."

That was it. That was all they ever said to each other.

Howard told Mary Jane that he was uncomfortable with older women, as if to explain why he was attracted to my youth. It was as if he were subconsciously relating these older women to his mother, who had died and left him alone. None of the older women in his family came to mother him after her death. After his father died, the women in his family came, not to give him love, but to take money. He never forgave and he never forgot.

While the hot desert breezes were blowing, Howard stopped the boat to go for a swim. I had gone below to rest. Howard had no false modesty or self-consciousness about nudity. Completely oblivious to the world about him, he stripped and made a beautiful dive into the warm Colorado River. He swam about and had a wonderful time, all by himself.

He had asked Mary Jane to go, but she had said, "I can't go."

"Why not?" he asked, a little surprised.

"Because I'm having my period," she told him.

They were still sitting on the boat. Howard turned and looked at her and he almost cried, "Oh, you poor thing." He patted her on the shoulder and asked if he could get her a blanket.

Mary Jane looked at him like he'd gone out of his mind. It was 110 degrees. Her inclination was to laugh, but she knew how sensitive he was. His deep concern for her was so sincere; the poor little thing is bleeding, he thought.

139

We were far up the river, heading toward the Grand Canyon, when I woke up hungry. Even the box lunch Howard had mentioned sounded good to me.

Howard announced that he was going to serve dinner. He put on a chef's hat and jacket and started prancing about the boat, delighted with himself. Mary Jane and I went into fits of laughter. Then he brought out huge boxes of food; he had had one of the Las Vegas hotels pack all the finest epicurean delights. There were lobsters, cracked crabs, caviar, steaks, and all kinds of delicacies. There was even a bottle of wine with Mary Jane's name on it. We squealed with excitement and gorged ourselves on all the goodies, especially the little French pastries and petits fours. It was truly a feast for the gods.

While the Nevada sky grew dark, the air became fresh and invigorating as we laughed and exchanged stories far into the night.

Howard went to check with the captain and was told we had to turn back. We were heading into dangerous waters and we were low on fuel.

It was a high-speed boat, but we were scarcely crawling. It was one of the few times I've been frightened, and I clung tightly to Howard. Now Mary Jane's stomach was uncertain and she had gone below. The night had grown so dark that the moon and stars barely lit the sky and the waters were becoming steadily rougher.

The captain reported every mishap: the radio had gone out, a big storm was coming in, he didn't think we had enough fuel. Howard calmly listened to all his complaints.

"I'll take over whenever you feel you can't handle it," he said.

Howard thoroughly checked the boat from stem to stern and came back confident that we had enough fuel and that the boat was seaworthy. He *didn't* tell us that there was no lifesaving equipment or flares on board. They were all on the decoy, our sister ship.

The trip back seemed endless.

Howard and I were standing on the ship's bow when we caught sight of huge searchlights sweeping the water. When they came closer, we saw it was the decoy boat out looking for us. When it pulled alongside, we found out that two doctors, a nurse, a stretcher, and other hospital equipment were on board for us.

We'd stayed out twelve hours longer than anticipated, and when we'd lost radio contact they Maydayed the troops. It was three o'clock in the morning when the search boat led us in to the dock. A crowd of people were gathered in front of the boathouse. We had been reported lost about six hours earlier, and Hughes's people from Vegas and others who had flown in from Los Angeles had sent out boats and planes. They were just about to launch a massive search when we appeared. Howard wasn't too happy about the situation and quickly scooted us ahead to the car before approaching the crowd.

"You sure made a circus out of this," he said. "It seems a person should be able to go on a little boat ride without half the damn nation showing up."

Howard borrowed some money from an employee and made a phone call before we left. The group of strangers at the dock seemed a bit disappointed that they hadn't gotten to go on a search.

Although we had mentioned it a few times while docking, we thought Howard might forget, so we reminded him how hungry we were. He told us he would stop at an all-night diner that was about halfway back to the ranch. Mary Jane and I were content. Not only were we going to eat, but what a nice change of pace it would be to eat in a restaurant with people.

We drove for quite a while, seeing no sign of civilization. Then out in the middle of nowhere we saw a speck of light. As we drew closer to the light, we could see it was coming from inside the second story of a two-story lopsided old wooden box of a building. This was Howard's all-night diner. We pulled into the lot. Our car was the only car there.

"Don't tell me, Howard," I teased. "I bet somebody made you a good greasy hamburger when you were in college, so you set them up in business in this great location to make you greasy hamburgers when you happen by."

Howard chuckled. "This area will be developed someday."

"Make a good cemetery," Mary Jane quipped. "I think it's closed."

We got out of the car and followed Howard up an outside stairway.

"Are you sure the food's safe?" I asked.

"Maybe we should just wait until we're back at the ranch," Mary Jane added skeptically.

"You two have been complaining for hours, and now that I go to the trouble to find a restaurant and stop, neither of you wants to eat." He opened the door and nudged us through. "See, it's open."

I remember I remarked about the air-conditioning. Even at this time of night, the air outside was hot and dry.

It was a real greasy spoon, consisting of about ten tables with chairs and a counter with a cash register. That was it, except for two waitresses, a cook, and a busboy/dishwasher. They were all standing stiff and wide-eyed when we entered. It was like walking into a wax museum. Then the cook and the busboy vanished through a door and the waitresses became as nervous as a June bride in a featherbed.

They seated us and set our table. As soon as the table was set, Howard got up and moved to another. He said the air-conditioning was right on his back. We sat down at another table. The two waitresses rushed nervously around, trying to get the next table quickly set. The busboy brought us water, but Howard was up on his feet again. He said the air-conditioning was right on him again. He walked all around the restaurant trying to find a place where the air wouldn't bother him. He sat down at another table. We followed and so did the table settings and water.

The food at the restaurant turned out to be surprisingly good, although we didn't get to enjoy it much, as we were table-hopping throughout the entire meal. It drove the poor waitresses crazy; they constantly were dropping and spilling things and running into each other. Mary Jane and I could barely eat for laughing. Overall, the service we received was above and beyond the call of duty.

When we finished our meal, Howard called everyone over. He pulled sixty or more dollars from his pocket and handsomely tipped everyone down the line. I'd never seen him with so much money. Then I remembered the employee back at the dock. When it came time for the check, Howard was penniless and turned to me. I hadn't brought any money, so he turned to Mary Jane. She coughed up her last twelve dollars and fifty cents. Howard never paid her back.

Toward the end of our stay at the ranch, Cliff finally recognized Mr. Grimes as Howard Hughes and eagerly wanted the privilege of meeting him. For days Cliff hounded Mary Jane to make an introduction. He said he and Pat were so excited that Howard Hughes was on their ranch that they could hardly sleep at night. Knowing that Howard didn't want anyone to learn his true identity, Mary Jane held out as long as possible, but it meant so much to Cliff that she finally approached Howard.

Cliff had praised Howard so highly to Mary Jane that Howard couldn't disappoint them. Cliff and Pat were thrilled when Mary Jane told them that Howard would stop by after supper for a kitchen chat.

The more time that went by, the more nervous Cliff became anticipating Howard's arrival. To build false courage, Cliff had been hitting Mary Jane's vodka, and after a few drinks he had to go out for some air.

Shortly after Cliff went out, Howard arrived at the kitchen door. He introduced himself to Pat, sat with her, and had a short, pleasant chat. She apologized for her husband, saying she didn't know where he'd gone off to.

Pat was shy anyway, but she became agonizingly tongue-tied with Howard. And where was her darling, extroverted husband, Cliff?

Finally Howard, not knowing how to make an exit, said, "I'll take a look around for Cliff on my way out."

Howard couldn't have been gone two minutes before he was back.

"Is Cliff dressed all in white with white boots?" Howard inquired.

"Oh, yes. You found him." Myra was relieved. "Where is he, Mr. Hughes?"

"Passed out! Dead drunk. In the bushes." Howard walked out.

After that incident, Howard wondered what den of iniquity he had us in and considered moving us elsewhere. But before we had a chance to do anything, our attorney called. He told us to forget the six-week waiting period, that we were just wasting our time. He said there was no way Davis was going to give me the quickie divorce. Glenn was still out for blood, and he was also out for a lot of money. Lloyd told us to come on home and we'd try to work out a new strategy.

The time on the ranch and the fun I'd had was being clouded once again by hopelessness, and the pain and sadness I thought was far behind waited for me back home.

Chapter 14

IT WAS LATE IN THE EVENING WHEN WE FINALLY SAID OUR good-byes and left the ranch. There were actually tears in the eyes of some of those ranch hands. To this day, I don't know if any of them knew who we were. I'm sure they would be quite surprised to learn that the "regular guy" spinning his captivating yarns and eating like a horse was Howard Hughes. I think it was one of the best times of Howard's life. He laughed more often and more deeply than I'd ever heard him laugh, and he knew without a doubt that these people loved him for himself. Here he had dared to let his guard down and be who he truly was. It was probably the last time in his life he ever would.

Our flight back to Los Angeles was fantastic, better than any amusement-park ride. We flew over the highway only twelve feet off the ground, skimmed treetops, dipped sharply into and steeply out of the canyons. I had teased, "Where's the daredevil, Hughes, the test pilot, the guy who made the number-one flying movie of all times, *Hell's Angels*? I think you're a phony, the result of your own publicity department."

All he said was, "See if Mary Jane's seat belt is on."

Then he personally checked mine and pulled it so tight I couldn't even wiggle.

Howard checked the tower. He had number-one clearance priority at any airport in the world. He didn't have to fly by the rules, and that night he broke them all. These were the days before radar and modern runway lights. They used to shoot great beams of light all over the sky to direct you in. Howard started playing hide-and-seek games with the lights.

"I take it all back—uncle!" I screamed before Howard pulled up off the highway we were about to land on. He had given us a ride the Blue Angels couldn't have duplicated.

Howard sent me back to check on Mary Jane. I reported she was in good shape but her ears were hurting.

"Ears," was the magic word. Howard was the most solicitous person in the whole world when it came to hurts, and he was the last word when it came to clogged-up ears. He soon had her yawning, holding her nose, and blowing and wagging her jaw.

When Mary Jane and I descended from the plane, we knelt down and kissed the ground. That really tickled Howard, but the waiting driver in Howard's car thought we were bananas. We had no idea where he was taking us, and neither of us wanted to ask. I didn't care as long as there was food. No one could possibly have a weight problem around Howard. Mary Jane had already slimmed down five pounds, and she didn't need it.

Howard took us straight to Goldwyn Studios and parked us in the projection room with a wide selection of movies.

I was really pleased to see my friend Carl the projectionist again. He was the first person in a long time who seemed associated with reality. I liked him because he seemed to really appreciate Howard and me as a couple.

"Now, Carl," Howard began, "don't you let these girls talk you into buying candy. You haven't anything in the booth, have you?" Howard looked up at him with a big

146

knowing grin on his face. He knew Carl kept a bottle for the all-nighters.

Carl smiled back innocently. He always warmed up to Howard. "Nothing I can't handle, boss." When he said "boss," it always had a sort of mocking tone without being disrespectful. They were always chiding each other, and it was hard to tell who worked for whom if you were standing on the outside. I have a feeling that Carl couldn't have gotten himself fired if he tried.

Howard said, "Helen, I'm going to my office right next door. You can open the door and look, or just pick up the telephone and check; I'm not going anywhere." He winked up at Carl. "Do you believe she doesn't trust me out of her sight?"

"I always thought she was a smart girl," Carl said as he shuffled off to the projection booth.

"Now, Carl, you can't leave it like that. You'll give her the wrong impression," Howard said.

"I'm sorry, boss. What is it I'm supposed to say?"

"I don't stand a chance. She's got everyone in my organization wound around her little finger."

"She's prettier than you are, boss. They all are."

I stood up to my full five feet two inches and stamped my foot. "What do you mean, they *all* are?"

"See what you've gone and done now, Carl? You've got her all upset. She doesn't know you meant all the girls in the ten years you've been running film for me."

"Upset! You bet I'm upset. Who were they, Carl? How many? When?"

"Damn it, Carl. You know how sensitive Helen is. I've got a mind to—"

"Fire me? I've been trying to get you to fire me for the last four years. I've been trying to quit for six, but you won't let me go."

Mary Jane burst out laughing, and I couldn't be angry anymore and had to join in. Even Howard laughed. I went to Carl and hugged him. "I tried to leave him too, Carl, but he wouldn't let me either."

147

"I'm glad you're back, girl," Carl said, hugging me fondly. "He needs you. Things aren't right around here when you two are quarreling."

"Start the movie," Howard said on his way out the door.

As soon as Howard was out of sight, Mary Jane and I were figuring out how we were going to get something to eat—candy bars, anything. Carl was no help; he had to stay in the booth running the movies in case Howard came back early. The drivers were no help; they were too afraid of losing their jobs.

I came up with the solution. "Why don't *you*, Mary Jane . . ."She always loved those Why don't *you*, Mary Jane's. No one was more ready for an adventure than Mary Jane. She was also loyal and closemouthed. That's why Howard always trusted her; she never broke his confidence.

So Mary Jane went to the other end of the lot where the guard sat watching the gate. She gave him some money and told him where he could buy some candy bars. Very coldly, he told her he had specific orders from Mr. Hughes that none of us were to leave the lot.

She told him, "Listen, if you don't get those candy bars, you're in deep trouble. You'd better go if you want to keep your job. These are orders from Terry Moore herself, and she's with Howard Hughes."

The poor guy was so gullible he fell for it and came back with a big sack of candy bars. Mary Jane and I happily noshed away all through the triple feature. We were sick on candy bars.

When we heard Howard returning, we quickly curled up in our huge leather reclining chairs and pretended to be sound asleep. We didn't even stir when he turned the lights on.

"Anyone hungry around here?" he asked.

We shot straight up. If we hadn't, he'd have known for sure we were up to something.

"Oh-ho-ho, I know the magic word: food!" he said, chuckling.

148

When we went outside, the car was waiting but the driver was gone. It was the wee hours of the morning when Howard drove toward the Beverly Hills Hotel. To my surprise, he drove right on by into Holmby Hills, where the mansions are even larger. We pulled off Sunset into a huge estate and drove through the gates and up a long driveway. There was an empty guardhouse on the right. Even at night, we could see that the grounds were overgrown with tangled shrubbery.

It was dark and eerie, and I thought I could see little glittering eyes peering at us from the branches. The silence was so complete that every crooked twig that cracked underfoot was deafening; and every lingering shadow held some unknown secret.

An owl screeched. I screamed and grabbed for Howard just as a lizard scampered across the porch. Howard held me close as he fumbled with the keys.

"How can you be frightened of an owl? They're good luck for us."

We followed Howard into the front hall. It was all marble, like a mausoleum, and about as warm as a Siberian winter. I felt I had walked into Juliet's tomb. It smelled as if the house had been closed up for years.

Howard's voice boomed loudly in the silence. "This is the house where Judy Garland slit her own throat."

That did it. Mary Jane and I wanted to turn heel and run away. The house had too many ghosts, but we were too exhausted and sick from candy bars to protest further. Instead, we went to bed. All night I could hear a haunting wind and branches scraping against the windows. The last thing I remember was the sound of something running out on the ledge.

The following morning Mary Jane was up early and downstairs looking for coffee. The kitchen was huge, with two refrigerators. As a matter of fact, it had two of everything, but it was completely devoid of food and coffee.

Mary Jane, who was always calm, came racing upstairs

and woke me up. She told me I had to get Howard up because she had to have her coffee. I was frightened; I'd never seen Mary Jane become unglued, ever. It was difficult for me to comprehend, because I had never even tasted coffee. She was having a caffeine fit.

I raced up the stairs to Howard's room and woke him up. Howard was so startled when he saw the state Mary Jane was in that he jumped into the car and drove like an ambulance to the Beverly Hills Hotel. He was more disturbed than Mary Jane.

In a matter of minutes, he returned with the largest caldron of coffee we'd ever seen, and Mary Jane was restored to her merry self. Howard was relieved, but after that incident he sent Frank the steward to do our shopping and cooking. "Dear Frank" was being pulled out of mothballs again, and he looked more sour than he had on Harbor Island. Who would want to work if they'd been drawing pay for thirty years while sitting at home? He had known the island would be only a short stretch, but this might go on forever . . . and who was this coffee freak?

Mary Jane and Frank took one look at each other and it was instant dislike. He knew she had his number.

Howard thought we should tell Mary Jane about our marriage, because he wasn't happy with our sleeping arrangements. He wanted me sleeping with him.

"No, Howard. I'll sneak up the back stairs after she's asleep and I'll leave you before she wakes up."

"You know you can trust Mary Jane," he said.

"With my life," I said. "But I don't ever want her to know I'm a bigamist."

Every evening after that, when I was sure Mary Jane was asleep, I crawled out of bed and hurried up the stairs into Howard's arms. I couldn't stand propriety any longer. My body was racked with sobs as all my pent-up emotions were released. Howard took me in his arms and tried to soothe me.

"Here, here, baby. Have I ever let you down? Don't you worry. We'll get that divorce. It's just going to take a little more time than we first thought. But we're together, aren't we? You know I love you, don't you? Lloyd Wright is speaking to Glenn's attorney daily."

I would usually come downstairs and slip into the twin bed next to Mary Jane about 6:00 A.M. because she was an early riser. She was usually up and in the kitchen having her coffee by 7:00 A.M. Howard wandered into the kitchen about 9:00 to eat his kadota figs and chat with Mary Jane. He'd stand over her as she was reading the newspaper. He'd never sit, just stand there. He'd question her to see if she was really reading, and he'd ask her what she was most interested in. Mary Jane told him that, besides her coffee, she must always have her morning paper, and by golly Howard was going to see to it that the paper was well read and that he got his money's worth.

I'd usually wake up around ten, and the first thing I'd do would be to run upstairs to hug Howard and tell him how much I had missed him. Howard kept his promise and did most of his business in the upstairs library, where I would check in from time to time, to see if he needed anything or just to tell him I cared. I could always tell whom he was talking to on the phone by his language and inflection.

If he swore like a trooper with every four-letter word in the book, it was Darryl Zanuck. They were good friends and respected each other immensely. That was just their way of communicating.

If he was all smiles and saying "darling" all over the place and oozing charm, it was Louella Parsons.

If he used his most intimate, confidential tone and discussed leading ladies, it was Bob Mitchum.

If he was brief and to the point, it had to be Noah Dietrich; and when his Texas accent got thicker and he teased a lot, it was Greg Bautzer, his motion-picture attorney. Greg always called Howard Sam.

I never saw anyone make transitions as rapidly as Howard; he was some actor. He would use any subterfuge or emotion to get his own way, even tears. With those sad soulful eyes, who could resist a crying billionaire?

Howard loved to cue me on my scenes. He liked to play all the parts, but his favorite was Lord Essex. While he was shaving, we'd play Queen Victoria and Albert. It was more fun playing opposite Howard than any of my leading men, because he had no ego and he thought everything I did was marvelous. He was great for my ego.

Howard became so excited over my acting that he bought me one of the largest tape recorders so we could listen to ourselves. He was pleased with the way he sounded.

"I could have been a star, you know." He said it as if he wanted my affirmation. "You're goddamned right I could. You know that son of a bitch Jimmy Stewart copied my walk."

He was becoming bigger by the minute. He even started to swagger. "You really believe I have it, huh?"

"Oh, you do, Howard, you do," I cried.

"I could have played Billie the Kid in *The Outlaw,* but I didn't think it would look right—you know, seeing as I directed and produced it. It's hard to direct yourself."

It was all I could do to hide my amusement. Because of my fondness for Howard I felt as if I would blow up and burst at these moments, he was so adorable.

"Oh, I love you, Howard Hughes. You're my real-life man. You do in life what they do in movies. I wouldn't want you if you playacted—you're the real thing."

He couldn't conceal his pleasure. "You're right, you're right," he said as he sat for five minutes just nodding his head in complete bliss.

When Howard was busy, Mary Jane and I would work on scenes from *High Heels,* the script Howard had bought for me. Mary Jane played all the parts but mine. Howard was so impressed when he heard Mary Jane that he insisted she should be an actress. She was just as insistent that she didn't want to be. Nevertheless, Howard took the tapes and played them for the casting director and told him any part that came up she'd be right for, he wanted her to have.

I still had a very high babyish voice. I worked for hours and days on end lowering it. I was determined I was going to sound like Lauren Bacall, Liz Scott, and June Allyson. It was an era of husky voices. Howard Hawks was sending all his ladies to the seashore to scream. No wonder they were hoarse—their vocal chords were being mutilated! At least my voice was lowered with good common sense.

When Howard's business became boring or he was away, Mary Jane and I spent long hours at the pool, sunning and exercising. The pool area was on our side of the house, so we could slip out our door and down the long pebbled pathway winding through the jungle blooms and dancing fountains. The pool house was Grecian in style, with statues on either side, and the pool was heated. From its warm waters we could see our majestic mansion. If it could only talk, I'm sure it would have had a lot of wild stories to tell.

Most of our evenings were spent wondering what time dinner was going to be. It was always after ten, but sometimes it was as late as four in the morning. The hours may have been strange, but Frank's shopping list was easy. One refrigerator was kept full of steaks and the other one full of salads.

Due to the nature of Howard's work, he would come and go at odd hours, but he would seldom miss a dinner with us. He considered it our mandatory family dinner, and he never thought it the least bit odd to be eating it at dawn.

The dining-room table was so long and wide that Mary Jane and I would shout our conversations. Howard liked this because he could be part of everything. He always wanted to hear every detail of our day, but he rarely talked about his to either of us.

After an early ten o'clock dinner one evening, I was doing something upstairs and happened to overhear Howard on the phone promising to meet someone at the Beverly Hills Hotel. By the tone of his voice I could tell he was talking to a woman. I went running down the stairs crying hysterically. Mary Jane finally pieced the story together between my sobs. "Okay," she said. "I'll see to it he doesn't go."

Still sobbing uncontrollably, I sputtered, "What are you going to do?"

"Well, I don't know, but I'll sneak down to that empty kitchen and see if I can find something to slice his tires with."

I loved it. A plan helped a lot, and I managed to pull myself together. "I'll come with you."

"No, it's going to be hard enough for me to sneak in and out of that kitchen without Frank the Fink hearing. Then there's the three guards at the gatehouse. Let's hope they're not sitting in the car, or they're going to feel a slump when that tire goes *whooosh*. There's one spare, so that means two tires have to be slashed."

"I'll do one and you do the other. Please, Mary Jane. If we get caught, Howard can't blame you if I'm there. I'll tell him I made you do it. Besides, I'd be scared to death waiting here in this spooky house alone."

I wouldn't give Mary Jane a chance to say no, so the two of us snuck stealthily into the dark kitchen. The floor creaked a few times and we were sure someone had heard us. We were petrified that Frank was going to see us slipping the two largest butcher knives out of the drawer. If he *had* seen us, I'm sure he'd have run for his life.

We crept out the back door, but the car was parked in the middle of the circular driveway. That meant we'd be in view of the guardhouse on the left until we reached the car. We could see that the only way we might go undetected would be to crawl on our bellies and that's exactly what we did. It looked like a scene from a prison-break movie. I have no doubt that one of those crazy guards might have mistakenly shot us. It was scary, but we were determined to keep Don Juan Hughes at home.

The next hurdle was to get the tires slashed, which was no easy matter, as the rubber was thick and the knives dull. Somehow Mary Jane poked and stabbed until her tire was useless, and then she helped me mutilate mine. Time and luck were on our side, and we managed to get back to our room, safe and sound. We sat on the bed in the dark, waiting, tense and excited, until we heard Howard coming blithely down the stairs. We both ran to the window to peek out when he crossed from the front door to the car. He was jovially swinging his keys and whistling—ready for a big night. Mary Jane and I both stopped breathing when we heard the car start and pull ahead. And then flop, flop, flop . . . it stopped.

We needn't have been afraid of Howard's reaction. To our complete astonishment, he got out of the car, looked at the tires, and started laughing his head off.

He stayed home that night and he never said a word, but after that he looked at me with a new pride.

I had successfully deterred his actions—but, reminded again of Howard's wandering ways, I was going to keep a much closer watch.

Chapter 15

ONE EVENING I WAS IN THE LIBRARY WITH HOWARD, going over a script while he was making his endless string of phone calls, conducting business and gossiping. My eyes would look down at the script and I would turn the pages, but it was more interesting listening to him. I knew he was talking with Robert Mitchum.

"Christ, Bob, every time you make a movie you've got my star in heat. What do you do to these dames? You had Jean Simmons and Ava Gardner camping on your doorstep and now Jane Russell's caught the fever. . . ." He'd laugh and laugh. "Yer wife ought to keep you tied up in the backyard . . .Yeah, I know you ignore them. That's evidently what they like. It sure never worked for me, I'll tell ya."

Howard looked over at me and winked. I stuck my tongue out at him. I didn't mind his talking about other women, as long as that's *all* he did. He thought that Bob Mitchum was the biggest ladies' man he knew. "There's not a dame around who won't drop her britches for him," Howard would say, "and to make it worse, he don't give a damn."

Howard loved gossip. He kept men on payroll to keep him advised on all the latest doings of just about everyone. His gossip network was nearly as extensive as J. Edgar Hoover's. I wouldn't be surprised if they had exchanged tidbits.

As big and solid as the house was, I heard a door slam downstairs. Mary Jane had been showering. We were accustomed to privacy in our suite of rooms and were careless about keeping the doors shut because no one was supposed to be in our wing of the house.

This night, Mary Jane, fresh out of the shower, had been drying her hair. We had mirrors on our bedroom and bathroom doors. She looked up and saw Frank in the hallway, leering at her naked body in the mirror. She angrily slammed the bathroom door as hard as she could.

When I came to bed later, she told me the story. It made me feel all crawly to think of Frank lurking about. When the lights were out, I told Mary Jane that I felt like we were being watched. We both lay there, perfectly still, afraid to even breathe. Then we heard something outside the window. Something was rustling around out on the ledge. It got louder and louder.

"I've had about enough of this," Mary Jane exclaimed, and she tossed off the bedcovers and went for the window, flinging open the drapes, expecting to see Frank.

"Rats! *Eek!*"

I ran and found Howard. I was hysterical. Of course, when he came on the scene, the rats were gone. He tried to convince us we were two little girls with big imaginations.

"There were rats out there," Mary Jane insisted. "At first I thought it was Frank, because several times I've caught him skulking around when we were dressing."

"It's true, Howard," I seconded. "I think he's weird."

Howard told us to go to sleep, assuring us he'd look into it.

A few mornings later, Howard did look into it. I was fast asleep and Mary Jane was in the bathroom about to get dressed. Through the looking glass she saw Howard. She turned around quickly. "Boo!"

Howard jumped a mile and ran off faster than a jackrabbit racing buckshot. I think that made it difficult for Howard to reprimand Frank.

We were two young girls living in an oversized burial vault with two Peeping Toms.

Feeling embarrassed over the incident, Howard had a big surprise for me the next day—my own little plane, a Cessna 140. From that day forward, all my days were devoted to flight; if Howard was too busy to take me, I flew with an instructor of his, Ray Pignet. He was one of the finest men I ever knew. Just a few years ago he was killed on a takeoff by one of his student pilots. He was the last of the stunt flyers from *Hell's Angels*.

I'm a stickler for details, and I drove poor Ray crazy with all my questions. I wasn't satisfied just to fly. I had to know why the plane flew and what kept it up there. Before I completed my training, I had read over two hundred books on aviation and had studied meteorology, airplane engines and structures, and instrument flying.

I was determined to show Howard I could make better landings than he, so I would spend weeks on perfecting them. I used to talk myself down on the landing pattern, repeating the exact words Howard had coached me down with on my first attempt.

"Pull it back—easy, easy. That's it, baby, easy. Just a little bit more. Easy does it. Baby, there you go—easy . . . *eeeeezie*—that does it!"

Soon my landings could barely be felt, they were so soft. Even Howard was impressed and proud of me, though any landing is considered good as long as you make it.

One day I flew Howard to San Diego. On the way home a fog came in. We had none of the sophisticated instruments that Howard was used to, and I ended up making a forced landing in East Long Beach, about twenty miles from Los Angeles. Howard was so proud of my navigation that I never let him know that I thought we were in Orange County.

I'll never forget my first solo flight. It was to Oxnard, California, less than sixty miles away. A fifty-mile-an-hour wind had come up that kept shifting direction. Well, my Cessna stalled at forty-miles-an-hour and my radio went out. I made three passes over the airstrip and was tossed around unmercifully. I was petrified, but I found that under stress I was extremely calm.

One of the most important attributes for a pilot is not to panic. I maintained control, but I was no hero. Sadly, I turned around and headed back to home base, where Howard, my mother, and Ray were waiting for me. It was like a wake. They were sure I'd tried to land come hell or high water. My heartbreak turned to joy when I learned my cross-country to Oxnard would still count because not landing had been the right decision.

I became Howard's first student pilot to receive her license. Later, I went on to become the third woman in the world to be checked out in a jet. Jackie Cochran was the first, and the daughter of Georges Pompidou, the former president of France, was the second.

Another time I took Howard flying and I was showing off, putting the plane in tailspins and doing everything I could think of to make Howard nervous. Nothing fazed him. He remained cool as a cucumber. I wasn't afraid to try anything, because Howard was there. It was all false bravado, because I knew he could save me. Afterward, he told me his legs were so long that he was packed in there like a sardine and he couldn't even have lifted a finger to help us. Now it was my turn to be scared. I could have killed us both.

I took Mary Jane up one day before I got my license. She was a great sport. She kept telling me how wonderful it all was, but I noticed she was hanging on for dear life. She had white knuckles all the way. That was the second time in two months that she stepped out of a plane and kissed the ground.

Flying was and is a great joy in my life. Up there, all your problems dissolve. You see everything in its true perspective. I also found pilots a friendly group of people who stick together. That, to me, was a welcome relief from the atmosphere of Hollywood, where an intrigue and a victim are born every time two people meet.

One afternoon Howard was supposed to pick me up to go flying. I waited and waited, but he didn't show. Finally I gave up and went looking for Mary Jane. She was busy writing letters and I was disappointed and bored, so I put on my swim suit and decided to go swimming. I didn't really like the idea of swimming in that pool alone. It seemed so far away, and the foliage choked the view of the house. Because of the overgrowth, it also seemed to get dark out there much earlier.

I swam for a while and then lay out in the last small patch of sunlight the day had to offer. I remember daydreaming about the first time I had gone in the pool. It was the second night we spent on the Sunset estate. It was unusually hot and dry, and the winds off the desert were blowing. I was wearing a pink baby-doll nightgown. When Howard saw me in it he picked me up in his arms without speaking, and carried me downstairs, out into the night, around to the side of the house, and down the long brick pathway to the pool.

There were torches around the pool; their flames were thrashing violently in the wind. I felt as if I were in some jungle movie a million miles from reality. Howard walked down the steps into the shallow end of the pool. We kissed. What little we were wearing seemed to dissolve in the water. We joined in passion, and the waves from our rhythm rippled across the pool and slapped against the edge. Not a word had to be said. It all seemed so natural. Then Howard gently took me underwater. We completely submerged ourselves, the two of us, the one of us. The water closed out the world. There was no longer any wind, any night. We were enveloped in liquid, enjoying worldly pleasure from the womb. I don't even remember holding

160

my breath or coming up for air, just the heightened pleasure of that night.

My enchanted memory quickly faded and I felt a sudden chill come over me. I opened my eyes, and the afternoon was gone. I was surprised Mary Jane hadn't joined me. I was frightened being out there alone, even though I could see patches of daylight sky through the trees.

Then I saw them. Rats! Not one or two, but lots of rats. They were all along the edge of the pool deck, moving about. They seemed to be swarming. I sat up in the deck chair. My presence didn't bother them at all. Screaming, I ran to the house as fast as my legs would carry me. I told Mary Jane and then picked up the phone to call Howard. She left the room, as she always did when I called him, giving me my privacy. I finally tracked Howard down, telling everyone I contacted it was an emergency. I pulled Howard from some important business to tell him I wanted to move somewhere else, home if necessary. He spent close to an hour on the phone calming me down.

Before I hung up with Howard, Mary Jane slipped back into the room. She whispered to me that Frank was listening on an extension. I told Howard what Mary Jane had said and we heard a click.

"That does it, Howard," I said. "I'm moving back in with my parents." I slammed down the receiver.

Chapter 16

We were awakened by the sound of trucks, men's voices, and general racket. Mary Jane and I went to investigate the daybreak intrusion and found that the house was surrounded by exterminators with their equipment. We looked for Frank to see what was going on, but he was nowhere to be found; his bedroom off the kitchen was cleaned out. Mary Jane asked the exterminators what they were spraying. They told her ant season was coming and it was only preventive spraying for the ants.

All those men with all that equipment? "Ants!" Mary Jane threw back. "The kind of ants you can saddle!"

From that moment on, we never saw another rat, or Frank either, for that matter. It was always funny to Mary Jane and me how a little preventive ant spraying can get rid of so many rats.

Frank was better off, too. I knew Howard would never fire him because he'd be too afraid of his talking. I'm sure he sat home for another thirty years on salary.

Since there was no more Frank, Howard told us we could take our meals at the Beverly Hills Hotel. We were elated. To be driven to the Beverly Hills Hotel twice a day and dine among the affluent, in elegant surroundings, really excited us.

What would we wear? We could wear two different outfits, a daytime and a nighttime outfit. We could wear our hair down in the day and up at night.

Howard was gone on business, so Mary Jane and I would be dining alone. We spent the entire day getting ourselves fixed up for our return to Beverly Hills society. We were a sight to behold when we stepped out of that mansion.

The Mormon boy who was to drive us was awestruck at first glance; then he rushed around the car to open the back door for us. The Chevrolet should have been a Rolls.

Past the guard shack, down and around the curving driveway, and we were on Sunset headed toward the hotel. It was great being back in town; there was no telling whom we might see.

When the driver neglected to turn into the hotel's main entrance, we protested.

"Orders from The Man," the boy said. "There's still a lot of people looking for you." He drove us to an opening in the bushes. Another Mormon boy was waiting; he led us down a service stairway, past the dry storage room, and into a hallway. It must have been a shift change, because the hallway was wall-to-wall maids. They looked at us as if we were intruders and told us the way out. The Mormon boy didn't speak but led us right on through the river of uniformed maids, up some cement steps, and into a kitchen. From there we were ushered into a large, beautiful dining room, where Bruno, the maître d', seated us. We were aghast that we were the only customers in the room and it had been closed off from the hotel by a portable Japanese room partition.

Howard had bought out the entire dining room. Mary Jane and I were all dressed up for Bruno and our escort, who diligently stood guard outside the door in the kitchen.

Our next surprise was that we received no menu. Almost immediately after we sat down, the food began coming, and we knew who had ordered. It was steak and salad.

163

These glamorous meals at the hotel continued, but from then on we demanded that we order our own food. Treating us like his children, Howard said he'd allow us to do so as long as we ordered properly balanced meals, and absolutely no sweets.

Every time we went, we were driven in a different car and never entered the hotel through the same entrance twice in a row. Howard must have sat down with the blueprints of the place and mapped it out, meal by meal. Mary Jane and I were amazed at the multitude of entryways into one building. Sometimes we'd be dropped off from the narrow drive behind the hotel and weave our way through the bungalows to some rear entrance; other times we came into the hotel through the underground parking area. There were fire exits, pipe-lined passages, and garden windows, but nothing in the least bit conventional.

Often Howard would be there waiting or would join us after we arrived, but he seldom accompanied us there. When Howard was with us, we would eat in the main dining room with the normal customers. We would always sit in the same dimly lit corner near an exit where Howard could keep an eye on the entire room. The violinist would come play three of Howard's favorite songs: "Meditation" and "E Luceran Le Stille" from *Tosca,* and "Sorrento."

We would order steak and salad. Bruno took our orders and served us himself. He would look at us with a raised brow every time we ordered broccoli, carrots, or peas. Mary Jane and I would snicker, because when Howard wasn't with us Bruno would write those vegetables down on the checks instead of the sundaes, malts, and pastries he actually brought us.

No matter how unique and luxurious our life-style was at that time, it was still a routine. The flying lessons, the swimming, the acting, and the restaurant dining were great, but it was all done on a strict schedule. Mary Jane and I welcomed any diversion with open arms.

One night, tired of our gilded cage, we devised a plan. *An American in Paris,* starring Gene Kelly and Leslie Caron, had just been released, and we were dying to see it. Though Howard had brought a projector to the house and also still took us to Goldwyn, none of the films we saw were new releases. Howard felt it was dangerous for us to be out in public alone; he told us Glenn Davis had added a private detective firm to his search force. Search force or no search force, we were determined to see the movie. Part of my old gang was in it, and I felt it was my duty to them.

We arrived in our normal manner, ordered our regular dinner (with the addition of a martini for Mary Jane and a napoleon for me), and ate our meal. As usual, a Mormon boy would check on us every minute or so by peeking through the small window in the swinging kitchen door, and we had learned that another guard always whiled away his time in the main lobby.

I'd seen to it that Howard would be out of the way for the night: I used up so much of his time (day and night) that whole week that he would never be able to get caught up with his work.

Soon the time came to put our plan into action. I excused myself and went to the powder room. There I put in a call for the Mormon boy who guarded the kitchen door. Imitating Howard's secretary's voice, I told him to go down and tell the driver to switch cars. This was a typical request, so the boy told Mary Jane not to go anywhere, that he'd be right back. Now we had to work fast. I returned to Mary Jane and we peeked around the Japanese screen and motioned our lobby watchdog in. We told him that we'd been ready to go for some time but that our escort in the kitchen had vanished. That did it. He was through the kitchen and down the stairs in a flash. Mary Jane and I went around the Japanese screen, through the lobby, down the hall, and through the Polo Lounge, careful not to draw any attention to ourselves.

We went through the back door of the Polo Lounge and into a group of tall bushes where Mary Jane's boyfriend was waiting to take us to the movie. Getting there was much more exciting than the movie itself. James Bond Hughes would have been proud of our successfully executed mission.

Late the following night, I slipped quietly up to Howard's suite of rooms to sleep with him. I was surprised to find him threading a movie projector on a table next to the bed.

"So I hear you like sneaking out to movies."

I ignored his statement.

"Oh, boy! Movies in bed," I said, jumping up and down on the bed. "You can't beat that for comfort."

"I didn't get these movies for entertainment's sake, now. I'm doing some research."

"What kind of research? Is it boring stuff?"

"I received some information this morning regarding a certain actress who got herself mixed up in something that could be quite interesting."

"Who, Howard? Do I know her? Tell me. What's she mixed up in?"

"It's Joan Crawford, but it's nothing she's involved in *now*. I heard it from a reasonably reliable source that she made some blue movies before she became known. I've got a bunch of them here to go through. I'd sure like to see what she did."

There were film cans scattered all over the room. I could see I had already missed out on some of them, so I climbed under the sheets, propped myself up with pillows, and said, "Roll 'em." I'd never seen anything like this before. I kept thinking that if my parents knew what I was doing, they would probably kidnap me and stick me away in a convent.

Howard rolled the films. At first I was embarrassed, but then I became curious. I remember a man running around in stockings and garters, wearing nothing else. Most of the films were about housewives being chased around the house by naked plumbers, icemen, and assorted deliverymen.

Those poorly made, insipid black-and-white films were funny to me, and somewhat interesting because I never knew anything like that existed. Howard ran them almost all night long. We had several of these film festivals with new

166

LIFE

A PULITZER PRIZE WINNER'S NEW NOVEL

THE BRIDGES AT TOKO-RI
BY JAMES A. MICHENER
FIRST PUBLICATION, COMPLETE IN THIS ISSUE

TERRY MOORE
YWOOD'S SEXY TOMBOY

20 CENTS

JULY 6, 1953

SHIRLEY BOOTH
IS NOMINATED FOR
ACADEMY AWARD
—"YEAR'S BEST
ACTRESS"

TERRY MOORE—
"Best Supporting Actress"

"If Doc gets fun out of running his hand
through my hair ... what's the harm!"

BURT LANCASTER
SHIRLEY BOOTH
IN
Hal Wallis'
PRODUCTION
Come Back,
Little Sheba

Co-starring TERRY MOORE with RICHARD JAECKEL
Directed by DANIEL MANN • Screenplay by KETTI FRINGS
Based on the original play by William Inge
Produced on the stage by the Theatre Guild • A PARAMOUNT PICTURE

plus

- "SPEED QUEEN"
  Sportlite
- COLOR
  CARTOON
- LATEST NEWS

MARKET near 6th   DO 2-4887

St. Francis

Terry and Richard Jaeckel in a passionate scene from Come Back, Little Sheba

Terry in one of the sweaters that were her trademark

Glenn Ford and Terry in
The Return of
October

Dining with her parents and Nicky Hilton

*Terry, John Wayne and
former husband Gene McGrath*

Terry and James Dean

Photos from Terry's Scrapbook

Photos from Terry's Scrapbook

Photos from Terry's Scrapbook

Photos from Terry's Scrapbook

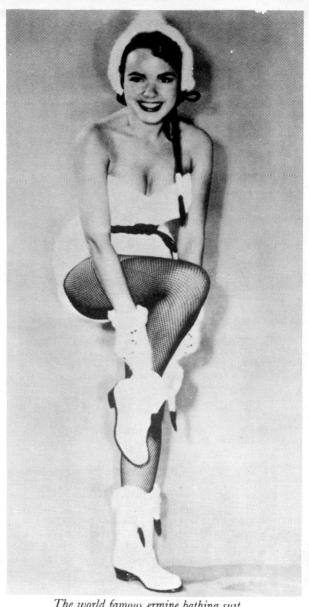

The world famous ermine bathing suit

Terry being fitted for a new dress by Mama Blue

Terry and Debbie Reynolds

Terry on tour with Bob Hope

Terry today, with the famous Spruce Goose

batches of films each time, although the finale performance was always ours.

I never did recognize Joan Crawford in any of them. If Howard ever did, he never told me. It didn't matter; the movies were, most of all, a diversion.

Howard called the Sunset House one day in the early afternoon. I answered the phone, and to my surprise Howard asked me to have Mary Jane get on an extension. He sounded unusually spirited and jovial. He told us that he enjoyed our being around, and to show his appreciation he was going to take us out for a night on the town. We would begin with candlelight and violins and champagne and the meal of our choice at the Beverly Hills Hotel.

Something had surely gone well for him that day, and he wanted to share his happiness with us. Howard told us to make ourselves look extra special, but not too fancy, for dinner at eight.

Night on the town. Extra special. Dinner at eight. That was all he had to say. Mary Jane and I spent the entire afternoon getting gussied up, as Howard sometimes called it.

To our utter amazement, Howard picked us up himself: no driver, no bodyguards (at least not in the car with us). We wondered what was happening. It didn't stop there.

Howard drove right in the main entrance of the Beverly Hills Hotel.

I was ecstatic. "Howard, did you get my divorce?"

Howard laughed. "No, baby, I'm sorry. I'm just breaking the routine. If anyone is onto us, they'd *never* expect this."

Howard was right. We hadn't expected it ourselves. He drove on past the valets to the Park Yourself section. We made a sedate journey from the car through the main entrance of the hotel and into the dining room. Our table was waiting. The candles were lit and the champagne was chilling in a silver bucket.

"Odds are in our favor to have one normal night out,

without incident.'' The perfect southern gentleman, Howard seated us and then took his corner. He discreetly eyed everyone in the room.

True to his word, Howard allowed us to order whatever we pleased. We made sure the waiter wrote down our desserts before anything else.

After the champagne was poured, Howard proposed a toast. Taking the water glass from my hand, he insisted that I clink with the bubbly.

With a touch of sadness in his voice, he held up his glass and said, ''To all the joy and humor you girls have brought into my life. May it always be as good as it is tonight.''

It was the most sentiment I ever saw Howard display in public.

Howard and I sipped at our champagne. Mary Jane swallowed hers, and soon finished off her first bottle of Dom Perignon.

The meal by violin music was delightful, and the best part was about to come. The waiter brought three large hot-fudge sundaes to the table. They were capped with fresh whipped cream and topped with a cherry.

Howard had just taken one bite when a man approached the table. He leaned over and said something into Howard's ear.

''It's time to go, ladies. A good part of the Rams football team has just walked into the hotel lobby.''

Without even touching our sundaes, we were up on our feet and walking out of the dining room into the kitchen. Howard's somber face hid his excitement as he led us along his personal escape route through a huge steamy dishwashing room and then out into the night air, where we began our descent on a series of ramps down through catacomb-like passages to the street behind the hotel. Two cars were waiting—one for us and the other for Howard.

We didn't see Howard until the following day, when he arrived with the news that he had finally arranged to get Glenn and his attorney together with Lloyd Wright and me.

From the moment Howard and I were together again, I

had felt I was no longer married to Glenn. Every time we had made love during our brief marriage, I felt I was committing adultery and I suffered the guilt and fear it breeds. I had lain in one man's arms and longed for another, and now I knew I could endure anything to live openly with Howard as his wife.

Though I was glad something was being done, I had so many misgivings about confronting Glenn that I had worried myself into a tizzy when the day finally arrived. Mary Jane and Howard did their best to bolster my spirits. They knew how hard it was going to be for me to face the monster we'd all been avoiding.

When I walked into the attorney's office, Lloyd Wright was already there. Out of the corner of my eye I could see Glenn, but I avoided looking in his direction. I could feel his gaze penetrating through my clothing, undressing me. When I had first asked him for a divorce, I was astounded at his reaction. The first thing he had cried was, "What about my sex life?"

The room was small; the air was thick and I could scarcely breathe. My head was throbbing. Fear gripped my whole body and I sat there paralyzed. I repeated over and over like prayers on a rosary, "Please, dear God, help me get a divorce. Let me be free. Please forgive me for my mistake. Please let me be free."

Voices were speaking, but the harder I tried to listen, the less I heard. I couldn't concentrate. Everything was buzzing and blurring, until I heard Mr. Wright say, "What will it take to give my client a divorce?" I looked up just in time to hear Glenn's answer. Now my eyes were glued to his; my while life rested on his answer. He looked at me now, disdainfully smug. This was his big moment and he was going to make the most of it. The wait seemed interminable. I stared boldly back at him, until a stiff grin broke at the corners of his mouth. In a slow, deliberate guttural tone that I will never forget, he said, "All I want is *money!*"

A few hours later, I was sitting in the library with Howard.

"What do you mean, we can't give him money? Then he simply won't give me a divorce. Do you understand? No divorce!" I screamed while beating the sofa with my fists. I was losing my sanity with frustration. "I can't stand it; I can't stand it another week, another day, another hour! I can't, Howard."

"Baby, you just won't listen to me. I warned you this guy was an animal. Don't think he wouldn't like to see you go to prison for bigamy."

"I'd rather go to prison than be married to him," I cried. "Oh, Howard, why can't I go to sleep and just wake up when it's over? Help me, Howard. Help me. Why can't you give him money?"

"Honey, how many times do I have to explain? If I give Davis money, it's collusion."

"So what do we do—give up?" I cried.

"Now, baby, I have a plan, but I'm not even going to tell Lloyd. Just try to be patient and let me handle it."

"You promise, Howard? You promise?"

"I promise," he said.

I crawled into his lap the way I used to do with my father when I was a little girl. I held him tight with all my might and lay there in his arms until I fell asleep. He slipped me onto the sofa and went to find Mary Jane and a blanket. She later said he covered me gently and asked her to stay with me until I awakened, explaining that the afternoon had been such a traumatic experience that someone should be there when I woke up. He promised he'd return in a few hours and we'd all have a nice steak dinner.

When I awoke, I became the silent sulker. Much to the relief of Howard and Mary Jane, my moody state lasted but a few days. A phone call brought me back to life.

Polly Bergen, who at the time was married to my Cojo, called me to tell me that there was a picture in preproduction at Paramount called *Come Back, Little Sheba*, and there was a part in it that would be perfect for me. She said they had already tested Marilyn Monroe and a score of others but I should get my agent busy on it.

I was still under contract to Columbia, so I would have to be loaned out in order to do the film. It was my beloved teacher, Lillian Barkley, who called the casting department and made the appointment for me. Usually, after starring in as many movies as I had, you go straight to the producer, but this time I started on the first rung of the ladder. I walked into casting along with dozens of other girls and was given a scene to read. They evidently liked my cold reading, because I was sent upstairs to read for the director, Danny Mann. At the completion of the reading, Mr. Mann looked pleased and called in the big producer, Mr. Hal Wallis. He ordered a test for me the very next day.

The sexy teenager opposite Burt Lancaster was one of Hollywood's most coveted roles. Well, in Hollywood, actors unfortunately always get typed. That means if you start out playing heavies you always play heavies. I was definitely typed as the little girl next door. I was never thought to be sexy. Fortunately for me, Danny Mann was a New York stage director and didn't know that Terry Moore was *never* to be sexy, so I was awarded a screen test.

I had been marvelous in the readings and everyone had high hopes for my test, but I was dreadful. I wanted the part so badly I guess I had overrehearsed.

Danny said, "We'll try one more take."

Unfortunately, the actor I was doing the tests with reminded me of Glenn Davis; and as a result in a scene fairly steaming with sexual attraction I felt nothing.

I closed my eyes for a moment of prayer, and when I opened them again the director said, "*Action.*"

I knew it had to be now or never.

The actor started changing before my eyes. He grew to be about six feet four inches tall. He became awkward and rangy; he even grew a mustache. He literally became Howard Hughes. I swear to this day I played *that* scene with Howard—at least, his spirit was with me, like Uncle Willie in *The Return of October*.

The role in *Come Back, Little Sheba* was a wonderful opportunity for me but I was supposed to do *High Heels* for

RKO. I didn't know what to say to Howard, or what, if any, conflict there would be. I wanted to do them both, but I could end up doing neither of them if I wasn't careful.

I paced and worried all evening planning and rehearsing everything I was going to say when Howard came home. As soon as he arrived, I went right into my speech without allowing him to say a word. I delivered my brilliant defense before my one-person jury. When I finished, Howard burst into laughter.

"I sold *High Heels* weeks ago," he said.

That really took me by surprise; I didn't know how to react. It hit me about a day later that *High Heels* was a project that he had never intended to follow through with. It was just another component of his elaborate plan to get me back and have his own way.

Soon after that, Mary Jane's mother became very ill with hepatitis, and Mary Jane wanted to be with her. I told Mary Jane I wouldn't stay in that big place alone; Mary Jane had me tell Howard she was leaving so he could make different arrangements. I told Howard, but he wanted a letter from Mary Jane with all the details. At the time I didn't know the reason for the letter, but later it became clear: Mary Jane had been so close to both of us, and now she was leaving; Howard wanted a memento of our time together. Her farewell letter was very touching and sincere. I'm sure Howard reread the letter periodically to bring back the caring and fun we shared for a time. Howard wrote Mary Jane a letter back and delivered it personally.

The day she left, he thanked her for the time she'd spent with us. Howard told her that she and I were the closest thing to a family he'd ever had. With tears in his eyes, Howard said how sorry he was about Mary Jane's mother. He knew just how she felt.

The moment she left was a sad moment for all of us, and the sadness didn't end there.

Chapter 17

NEWS TRAVELS FAST, ESPECIALLY IN HOLLYWOOD. THERE, gossip is a way of life. It was a daily ritual of mine to read all the gossip columns and movie society pages in all the papers and magazines. Often I would read things about people that would have been better not being written.

One morning I sat straight up in bed and felt the empty space beside me. Howard was gone!

"He's with Elizabeth Taylor," I said aloud.

I don't know to this day how I knew or why I said it, because to my knowledge they had never met; and Elizabeth was my friend and Howard was definitely not her type. It never even occurred to me that it could be my imagination. I knew! Call it a psychic phenomenon or whatever you like, but I believe there is perfect attunement in soul mates.

Damn, damn, damn, I *was* right. He *had* been with Elizabeth. It was right there before me in black and white. He had flown Liz, Stewart Granger, and Jean Simmons to Lake Tahoe for the day. Howard had had a crush on Jean Simmons for years. Evidently he didn't realize what good friends the girls were, because his flirtations with Liz canceled him out with both of them. Again, he had cooked his goose by being greedy.

Recently, on national television, Stewart Granger recounted a plot he and Jean Simmons had to kill Howard Hughes. They were going to invite him over to the house they were living in that belonged to RKO; it was on a cliff. Jean was going to entice Howard to the balcony and invite him into a loving embrace. Then Stewart would catch them and push Howard over the railing to the depths below. Naturally, it would have looked like an accident. Howard had the ability to incite people. He didn't know how close he came to being killed by *all* of us.

Howard was puritanical in many ways, but he couldn't shake his addiction to collecting women. I would not stand for it; I packed up and moved back again with my parents. My mother, who always sympathized with me, encouraged me to reactivate my social life and concentrate on my career.

At the very next meeting in Lloyd Wright's office, Howard was there waiting and offered me a million-dollar check if I would come back and stay with him. He did this in front of witnesses (Lloyd Wright, Noah Dietrich, and others); I tore it up right in front of them. I wasn't going to have him think he could buy me just like that. But I must admit that I thought many times what I would do with a million dollars.

He said, "All right, if you won't take it for yourself, you can't refuse this," and made out a check for the same amount to the Latter-day Saints Church.

I told him to mail it. The last time I heard, it still hadn't arrived.

Howard came to the realization that money doesn't mean much to an angry woman. Later he made the same offer to Elizabeth Taylor and Ava Gardner. They both turned him down too.

I was back home again in Glendale where I had started. The phone never stopped ringing. It was either Howard or

174

one of his boys, and they were always given the same answer: She's out.

This time I was determined to fight the turned-off-to-the-world feeling—the emptiness that grinds away in your midsection. The first person I turned to was Lillian. She listened for hours while I poured my heart out. She was so provoked with Howard and the devastation he had caused in my life that she said she'd run him down in her car if she saw him on the street. Cool-headed Lillian couldn't bear to see any of her children go through this kind of trauma.

She allowed me to bare my soul, and then she gave me a pep talk. She stressed my commitment to my career and said that I should throw myself into working and get out and around with the movie crowd my own age. "You have been a leader among the Hollywood set. They look up to you and they miss you. They'll welcome you back."

I decided to take Lillian's advice, though the last thing in the world I wanted was to go out with boys my own age. To me Howard was the youngest man on earth because he was ageless. I couldn't imagine his ever being old, and if he were eighty, I'd still love him.

The first few weeks I couldn't break out of the Howard Hughes shell. I told my family I couldn't date until my divorce was granted. I still couldn't bring myself to actually go out with another man, but I made some good friends. One of them was David Frame, from Dallas, whose father was vice-president of Humble Oil. He used to come over evenings and we'd just sit around with the family and talk. David was a great comfort. He thought, as did everyone, that I was suffering over my breakup with Glenn, not Howard.

I was also concerned over my career. It was now November of 1951 and I hadn't made a movie for nearly a year. I was broke, except for my weekly salary from Columbia (contract players were paid forty weeks a year); my divorce had cost me my life savings. After the meeting in the lawyer's office at which Glenn demanded more money, I had given him a check for more than seven thousand dollars, which I had to borrow from Howard; after the Elizabeth Taylor episode, my father borrowed money against my contract and I paid back every penny to Howard.

Now my option was coming up and there were no roles at Columbia that were right for me. The studio was geared for Rita Hayworth movies; she was the queen of the lot. (There was another actress at Columbia with me who had just had her option dropped: Marilyn Monroe. She had played the second lead in a B movie called *Ladies of the Chorus,* and after seeing the rushes, Harry Cohn had made up his mind that she'd never be a star. He was still claiming this several years later when he died.)

When Mother came into my room to tell me I was wanted on the telephone, she was as white as a ghost, and I knew something was dreadfully wrong.

"Harry Cohn wants to speak to you. He sounded awfully nice. He even asked how I was."

I gasped. "That probably means my . . ." I stopped; neither of us dared voice what we were thinking. I was probably being let go. Mother's hands were trembling, and so were mine, when I picked up the phone.

"Hello, Mr. Cohn." Mother held my hand for support. She didn't see how I could take another disappointment, and I still owed the studio money.

His voice boomed. "Have you been seeing any more football players?"

"No, Mr. Cohn, my football days are over."

"Good—now maybe you have time for your career."

"Oh, I do, Mr. Cohn, I do. That is, all I ever want to do is keep working. I don't even want a day off."

Cohn gave his ironic laugh. "That should make Paramount happy."

"Paramount?" My hopeful voice was barely audible. Mother's ear was at the receiver trying to listen too. She was squeezing my hand so hard I let out a scream when he told me Paramount was borrowing me for *Come Back, Little Sheba*.

Harry Cohn sounded truly pleased to be giving me the great news. However, his last words stunned me: "Stay away from that son of a bitch Hughes and you might even become a star."

That's all he said; I would think that one over later.

We called up Daddy at the office. He said he had felt I was going to get the part all along.

The next thing I did was run to Carolyn and Harriet to share the good news. They came over to the house, and our neighborhood committee decided it was time to change my little-girl image. They started making plans, then and there, for all the exciting, more sophisticated clothes they were going to make me. The next few days, we went on a shopping spree, buying the latest fashion magazines, patterns, materials, and yarns.

Harriet's magic needles started whipping up sexy, tight-fitting sweaters in every style and color. They were very formfitting; she practically knit them on me. Mother and Carolyn used every shred of their imagination concocting original skirts. I became the skirt-and-sweater girl. Lana Turner, the former sweater queen, was now into slinky nightgowns and men. Ann Sheridan, the oomph girl, was giving it all up to become an actress.

Eat your heart out, Howard Hughes; I'm becoming a sex symbol. If that's what you want, then that's what I'm going to be.

"I don't ever want to see you again, Howard Hughes," I yelled. It felt good just saying it. Then the doorbell and the phone started ringing at the same time. Mother ran for the door and I went for the phone.

"Hello, Howard," I was saying as mother walked in carrying a vase with four dozen long-stemmed American Beauty roses.

He sounded genuinely surprised when I told him I had the costarring role in *Come Back, Little Sheba*. I told him he'd better keep his hands off my career. I didn't need his help. He was all broken promises. The only time my career flourished was when he wasn't there to mess it up. And as far as *High Heels* was concerned . . .

"Yonk." Howard gave his alligator love call.

"Stop that. That won't work this time," I said.

"Yonk, yonk." I could tell he'd been practicing; it was near perfect.

"How is it?" he asked. "Am I doing it right? Yonk, yonk."

"You sound like you've had a lot of practice," I said sarcastically.

"Helen, no matter what you think, I could never make the alligator love call with anyone but my baby."

"You're too late, Howard. I'm not interested."

"Then let's be friends and just let me take care of you."

"I can take care of myself, thank you," I retorted.

All the while I was talking, Harriet, Carolyn, and Mother kept marching by with more vases of flowers. The man in the florist's truck kept going back for more and more and more.

"Who died?" I asked.

"I did," he murmured meekly. "I haven't been anywhere since you left."

"I'm sure you've had lots of company," I spit out.

"You know what day it is?" he asked.

"Yes, it's Monday."

"It's our anniversary," he said softly. "We were married two years ago today. Helen, no matter how you feel about me, you're the only family I have. Thanksgiving's coming up and you can't deny allowing me to spend it with Mama Blue and Lamar and Wally. Now, if you don't want to come, I'll understand."

"If *I* don't want to come! Howard Hughes, you have your nerve."

He went on. "Just listen. I've made plans to take your family to Palm Springs. If you stay home, you know Mama Blue will wear herself out cooking. She's tired; she deserves to get away and have some fun. You know how she loves Palm Springs and the Chi Chi. Irwin Schumann has planned a whole dinner in her honor. Now, if you want to deny your mother a relaxing holiday with her own family . . ."

"All right, Howard, I give in—but just Thanksgiving."

This was one time I was happy I'd allowed Howard to manipulate me, because Mother and Daddy were truly excited about spending Thanksgiving in Palm Springs. (Wally was in school in Utah and decided against coming home because of finals.) Howard wanted to fly us down and have us stay at picturesque, and expensive, La Quinta. We declined the offer. Instead, we drove down and registered at the Sunny Sands Motel, with swimming pool and continental breakfast included. Mother and I had stayed there several times before, when Howard and I were dating. Eddie, the proprietor, knew us well by this time and took special care of us. He was quite proud that the elusive Mr. Hughes had visited his establishment when he called for me or brought me home.

The weather was beautiful, and we spent a relaxing day at the pool until Howard called to say business had held him up; he would be late, but we should go to the Chi Chi and enjoy ourselves until he arrived.

I wanted to show both my family and Howard how little I cared what he did, so I acted as though it didn't matter that he was going to be late. But I spent the whole day resting and getting exactly the right amount of suntan.

I had brought all the new clothes in my wardrobe and tried them on over and over trying to decide what to wear. Howard hadn't seen any of them yet. I finally decided on a royal blue accordion-pleated skirt with a matching tight turtleneck sweater. Harriet had knit a poodle right in the sweater to represent Little Sheba, the dog in the movie I was about to make. My stockings had a bluish hue, and my shoes were made from the fabric of the skirt. Mother combed my hair into a beautiful upsweep.

My father remarked, "You didn't go to this much trouble

when you went to your senior prom or Harry Cohn's formal New Year's party. Why are you getting all gussied up for Thanksgiving?''

"Because I want him to eat his heart out. I certainly don't care otherwise," I threw back.

I saw Mom give Dad a knowing look and a gesture that meant Leave it alone or you'll be sorry.

After a full day of getting ready, we drove to the Chi Chi. Mother had helped me and then spent ten minutes getting herself ready; she looked gorgeous. She was forty-two years old and didn't have a line or wrinkle in her face. Her blue-black hair had started turning white at eighteen, which only made her look more interesting. She could do anything with her hands. She even tailored suits and made lampshades. She always managed to look chic, though she never spent any time on herself. Her life was dedicated to her family and my career.

When we arrived, Irwin and his beautiful about-to-be-wife Virginia looked as though they were waiting just for us. Irwin always had a beautiful smile and dressed elegantly; I would have to describe him as a stunning Cary Grant type. No one was ever more gracious or made us feel so at home.

Howard didn't arrive until ten; naturally, my father hadn't waited to eat and wouldn't allow my mother to because of her ulcer. Mother and Father joined their friends at the Chi Chi for a game of canasta, so when "the Man" finally arrived, Irwin put Howard and me at our own table. I acted as if I hadn't even noticed he was late. I was furious but absolutely charming.

The dinner was so delicious that I overate. Howard only picked at his food, but I marked that off to his being nervous at seeing me again. He stared and admired me openly, even more than he had at our first meeting. He had no embarrassment about showing his true feelings in front of all those people, and he hadn't cleared the dining room. I doubt he could on Thanksgiving; it was the Chi Chi's biggest holiday.

I loved his many compliments, and the way he looked at me and desired me. I knew the whole room was discreetly watching us. I kept the conversation light and gay; even when Howard slipped a bunny rabbit pin with diamond eyes on my shoulder I nonchalantly said, "Oh, thank you." I played the whole dinner like a scene between Vivian Leigh and Clark Gable; and Howard played Rhett Butler to perfection. He was too good, too perfect.

After dinner, the family joined us in the next room for the show. It was one of the few evenings that Howard didn't have a phone in his hand. He was all attention. We laughed ourselves sick at Bob Blake's impersonation of Louella Parsons. It was perfect, and every time he said "scoop" or "my first exclusive," a Parsons byword, it brought the house down. Several people, including Jimmy Durante and Jimmy Ritz, one of the Ritz brothers, stopped by our table. Howard laughed and joked with everyone. His happiness was short-lived, however.

While Mother was playing canasta, she overheard a lady at the next table say, "Oh, look, there's Howard Hughes. How could he ever eat another Thanksgiving dinner? I saw him earlier this evening at the Doll House with a girl, wolfing down a huge dinner."

Another lady spoke up. "My dear, I saw him just an hour ago at the Palm House with a young lady eating Thanksgiving dinner."

The fact that they later said he'd spent the entire time eating or on the telephone, and paid no attention to the girl, was little consolation when my mother repeated to me what they had said.

Head high, I walked out with dignity. "You, Mr. Hughes, have just lost your family *and* your best friend."

He didn't even allow me my dignity; he followed me out. "What's wrong, honey?" He was obviously panicked.

"Did you have an enjoyable Thanksgiving dinner with me?" I asked sarcastically.

"Of course I did," he said.

"Tell me, was it as enjoyable as your other two Thanks-

181

giving dinners tonight—the one at the Doll House and the one at the Palm House?''

He said innocently, ''Those girls aren't fortunate the way you are. They don't have families.''

''Oh, 'The Orphan Story.' ''

''Well, if you gotta know; I didn't think you were going to show up today and I thought I was going to have to spend Thanksgiving alone.''

''Well, you got that part right. 'Bye, Howard,'' I said just as Mother and Daddy's car pulled up. Perfect timing.

I went home crushed. I still loved Howard inwardly, but I was strong and as tough as nails on the outside.

This time when Nicky Hilton called, I said yes. Nicky was the eldest son of Conrad Hilton, the hotel magnate and recently divorced from Elizabeth Taylor. He was also tall and gorgeous, which made it even better. He was a scratch golfer, and I loved to walk around the golf course and go to the tournaments.

Nicky was also one of the kindest, sweetest human beings I've ever known. I never heard him say anything against another human being or talk about other women. He had scores of women but wouldn't even admit going to bed with Elizabeth before they were married.

He had one big drawback: no matter what woman he was with, he was always looking around for the next one. I think I captivated Nicky's heart because I didn't care. I loved Howard—but I was going to do my darnedest to forget and let him eat his heart out.

I knew Nicky fit the bill in every way. Howard was ragingly jealous. Nick not only had many of Howard's virtues, but he also had the one thing Howard couldn't compete with: youth.

I started dating Robert Evans, Johnnie Ray, and many of the glamorous stars at that time. It was only to forget and make Howard jealous. It worked too. Howard tried to dig up dirt on whomever I went out with so he could call me up and attempt to discredit them in my eyes. I never knew what

182

was true and what he was making up, but most of his defaming gossip eventually proved true. Unknown to Howard, he really didn't have to go to all that trouble on my account. Though my mind wandered, my heart never did.

Mary Jane called me. I could hear Mother on the phone. "Oh, no . . . I'm so sorry, Mary Jane. What can we do?"

"What's happened, Mother?"

She had tears in her eyes as she told me, "Mary Jane's mother died. The funeral is Friday."

Died. I couldn't believe it. Just a few months ago she had been in radiant health, excitedly entertaining those football players on her front porch. I knew her mother had hepatitis but I never knew that anyone could die from it. I felt guilt-ridden that Mary Jane had spent all these months with Howard and me when she could have been with her mother. I was determined to always spend as much time with my mother as possible. I thought of Howard and the great void the early death of his mother had left in his life. My relationship with him had often become very maternal. I was the mother figure, and he was my bad little boy; he loved me dishing out orders and making demands.

I remember little about the funeral, I was so blinded by my tears and remorse. I remember the funeral parlor was overflowing with friends and family; I remember Mother saying she'd never seen so many flowers. The most beautiful of all was a blanket of white roses. I thought white roses were the most beautiful flowers on earth that day.

Mary Jane held me tight the moment she saw Mom and me. We were all too emotional to speak. Even my huge dark glasses couldn't hide my sorrow.

After the funeral, I dropped Mother off at a friend's house and drove home alone. There was an old green Chevrolet parked in front. My heart skipped a beat. I wondered whether it was one of the Mormon boys, and was astonished to see Howard step out of the car and walk over and climb in next to me. His eyes were red; he quickly said he'd been up for days. I'd never seen him look so

183

woebegone; I was devastated by his appearance. He was more irresistible and vulnerable than the most innocent child.

The next moment he was in my arms and I was holding him like the big baby he was. My baby.

All the beautiful white roses that formed a shield around the casket had been from Howard. He had sent Mary Jane a letter that expressed his deepest feelings of sympathy for her mother and his undying gratitude to her.

Howard got behind the wheel of my car and drove me away. We drove far into the night. I snuggled up close to him as he drove and drove and drove. I didn't even pay attention to where we were going. I'm sure an hour went by without our uttering a word, but we were together again. When we talked, we were two young lovers without a care in the world and with rich, full lives ahead of us.

We drove uphill for what seemed the longest time. First we hit fog and then drove into rain. As we climbed, the rain grew more and more intense. Howard pulled off the road so we could just hold each other and listen to the rain pound down on the car. It was a wonderful feeling being there with Howard, completely isolated from the world by nature's sovereignty.

As the rain died down and the sky grew light, reality became visible to me once again. Thoughts of Liz and the girls in Palm Springs began invading my dream world.

"Why, Howard?" I asked. "Why, when we have something as beautiful as this, do you have to tear us apart and hurt me with all these other women?" And the argument began. It was loud and heated, venomous and tearful. Then both of us took notice of a tiny green worm, measuring itself across the windshield. We were both silent as we watched the worm move until, almost magically, we both burst into laughter and found our way back into each other's arms.

Upon heading home, Howard turned to me, grinning, and in a lighthearted, singsong tone he said, "If ever we anticipate another altercation . . . let's always remember our measuring worm."

I would have thought that something like that would sound corny coming from Howard, but it didn't. I can hear him saying those exact words even now.

On the drive back to Glendale he asked, "Did you ever see the play *Private Lives* by Noël Coward?"

"No," I answered offhandedly. Years later, because of this conversation, I starred in *Private Lives* as Amanda.

"Well, in this play the man and woman are madly in love but they're always fighting, so they find a word. I don't remember what the word was—something silly. But they decide that whenever they start to argue, one of them will utter this word and neither of them will speak for a whole minute. When the minute's up, they usually have forgotten what they were arguing about. They stayed together. I think our word should be 'measuring worm.' Do you like that?" he asked.

"Oh, Howard, I do, and we'll always think about that little worm and never fight again." I snuggled up closer to him.

"Now baby, it won't be that easy, but you'll see, it will help."

Howard reminded me that it was the middle of December and his birthday was Christmas Eve and we'd never been apart for the holidays. And then there was my twenty-first birthday coming up a week after New Year's. All my reserve was broken down; I couldn't bear to spend the holidays without Howard.

Howard then presented me with a belated anniversary present; he had intended to give it to me in Palm Springs on that disastrous Thanksgiving. It was a boat pin, a replica of the ship we'd been married on. It was yellow gold; along the bottom was a row of moonstones, sapphires, and rubies.

I asked Howard what he wanted for his birthday, and he said, "Only you—I want you."

The following day I went to Edith Head, who designed a

Terry Moore doll, wearing an exact replica of the navy blue sweater and tree-of-life skirt that Howard loved.

Howard and I were family again. The sorrow we shared proved that. We gave ourselves to each other in mutual need.

When the holidays were over, it was time for me to go back home and proceed with my reentry into the public life of a young movie star. Howard wanted me for himself, but I was determined to hold out and establish myself. I did a great deal of talking to convince him that *Sheba* was the vehicle I needed and that the preparation for it would require most of my time. Still hurt from his past skirmishes with infidelity, I told Howard that living together in complete secrecy was impractical.

He drove me back to Glendale, and I left him with the notion that the sooner the Glenn Davis annulment came, the sooner we could live together again. When he finally realized he wasn't going to win, he reached in his pocket, pulled out a folded sheet of paper, and handed it to me.

"Here," he said. "It's a list of the finest drama coaches in town. Now, you choose one and work hard. You've been away from it awhile, and I want you to be the best."

I threw the list of drama coaches away, but I slept with my boat pinned to my pillow.

Chapter 18

PRIOR TO THE FILMING OF *Come Back, Little Sheba*, THE
studio sent Johnnie Ray and me out on a flurry of publicity
dates together. Photos of us eating together, going to
parties, and holding hands were in all the papers and were
accompanied by the standard innuendoes and engagement
predictions.

Even though Howard often used the press in his own
manipulations and knew that most of Hollywood's gossip
was hype, my exposure with Johnnie Ray had still made
him jealous. He would go to any length to discredit a man
whom he felt I had an interest in, especially a younger
celebrity, and could never believe I had no interest in any
man but him.

Johnnie Ray and I always remained good friends, and the
press had a field day writing romantic stories about us.
When Johnnie married, I became good friends with his
wife, whose father owned the famous Mocambo nightclub
on the Hollywood strip. Whenever I walked in, even if the
place was overflowing, they put an extra table on the dance
floor for me. Sometimes I'd be sitting under Eartha Kitt's
or Edith Piaf's nose.

Hollywood was an inner circle and without Howard I was in the center, at least for now. . . . But I never knew what Howard had up his rolled-up white sleeves.

Production of *Come Back, Little Sheba* was not set to begin until the last day of February. I thought that if it would only come sooner, it might take my mind off the thing that was haunting me every day: my mistake in marrying Glenn Davis.

Glenn was blocking our every effort to dissolve the marriage. Our best hope now was an annulment, which only took three days. It would erase the specter of bigamy which was constantly preying on my conscience. The crime of bigamy carried with it a jail sentence and the ruination of my career—a career that had been carefully planned and nurtured since the tender age of eight.

Through our attorneys, I tried to impress upon Glenn how clean and easy an annulment would be. But for some reason Glenn felt an annulment was a blight against his manhood and divorce wasn't.

Howard, on the other hand, wanted the world to know that I had chosen him over the All-American Boy. He used to remark over and over, "I can just see the headlines: Terry Moore leaves Glenn Davis, America's sweetheart, for Howard Hughes."

When the idea of annulment had been flatly refused, we turned to Mexico. Divorces were granted in one day there, but unless both parties agreed, such divorces weren't worth the paper they were written on.

The legal system and the American press had just had a field day with Laraine Day, who had divorced a husband in Mexico to marry the Giants' manager, Leo Durocher. It became a front-page scandal—and she had had an *un*contested divorce. Ours would have been *very* contested. Glenn was going to get his pound of flesh and his money—or rather, *my* money—come what may.

I was disconsolate; the only avenue left was a California divorce. After a settlement was made between the two parties, it usually took six months to get on the court calendar, then a full year before the final decree became effective. Only then could Howard and I be married again.

Howard knew that if I didn't soon get my divorce from Glenn, I'd be lost to him forever. The pressure was too much for me, and it was tearing us apart. Howard wanted to marry me again just for the sake of propriety; this way no one would ever be the wiser that I'd committed bigamy. We could then live together openly and that would end my dating other men, even just for publicity. He was becoming increasingly annoyed over Nicky Hilton's attention toward me.

Howard diligently continued trying to get me divorced. Each time a scheme fell through, he came up with another one. We thought the latest one was his best. He was like an excited child when he told me.

"I don't know why I didn't think of it before. Use Davis's weaknesses against him," he said.

"What are his weaknesses, Howard?"

He smiled. "He's vain, he's money-hungry, and he's stupid."

Howard had pulled an old, unproduced RKO script off the shelf and sent out his smartest assistant, Cubby Broccoli, to Utah where Glenn was in spring training with the Rams. Howard said that he had promised to make Cubby a real producer if he could pull this caper off. Howard coached Cubby carefully and warned him never to mention his name or RKO. He was to say it was an independent production.

Cubby dusted off the script and offered Glenn the starring role, the romantic lead. There was only one condition: If Glenn were to be accepted as a sex symbol, he would have to be single. "Would Mr. Blackstone, manager-agent, dream of letting his up-and-coming boy, Eddie Fisher, get married? Never! Every girl in the world must go to bed nights dreaming that she might be the girl who would grow up and marry Eddie Fisher or Glenn Davis.

"Don't make your mind up now, kid. Think it over for

forty-eight hours and I'll call you back. Marlon Brando and this new kid, Tony Curtis, are dying to do it. Their agents are hounding me night and day, but this part is right up your alley.''

Cubby was one of several men who introduced Howard to other women. You cannot imagine how difficult it is to be in love with and married to a billionaire who loves women and who owns a studio and his own production company. Every agent, lawyer, and acquaintance is trying to make points by introducing him to a beautiful woman. I doubt that any girl, the world over, who had come of age, was gorgeous, and wanted to be in pictures didn't come to Howard's attention. Howard would either see them in person or see their photographs. I felt as though I were in constant competition with the whole female sex. And I was. In spite of this, Howard saw more of me than anyone.

Howard wanted me terribly now that he only had me part of the time. His business had to have suffered with all the time and attention he was giving me.

He even began bringing Noah Dietrich, his number-one man, with him when he drove to Glendale. They held their meetings in the car driving to and from my parents' home. In an interview that appeared in the *Hollywood Citizen News* in 1972, Noah said that with the exception of Jean Peters (and that was only on one occasion), I was the only woman he ever met with Howard. I began seeing almost as much of Noah as I did of Howard. I liked him because he was all business and never interfered with our lives or introduced Howard to other ladies. I always looked up to Noah as being a brilliant man who was responsible for Howard's having the freedom he did. This meant that Howard had more time for me.

I thank God for movies. All of the problems that Helen Koford and Terry Moore were going through came to a halt when *Come Back, Little Sheba* went into production. I was able to leave almost everything behind and submerge myself in the character of Marie Buckholder, the student

190

boarder who comes to live with Shirley Booth and Burt Lancaster.

Sheba was one of the hardest pictures I ever made. Danny Mann, the director, had to have a scapegoat. He started with Richard Jaeckel who was low boy on the totem pole; but he became so unglued that Danny decided to leave him alone. I became the next target, but I wasn't going to let him see my hurt or tears if it killed me, which it almost did.

One day, Burt stumbled over a line for eight takes. On the ninth take *I* flubbed a speech and the torrent of Danny's temper was unleashed on me. I had been really brave until now, but this time I didn't trust tears not to fall if I opened my mouth to speak. That beautiful cameraman, James Wong Howe, and his crew came to my rescue. They pretended something had gone wrong with the lights and started moving them all around. Every time a crew member passed me he'd give me a pat on the back, but the director couldn't see. God bless those men; they were stalling to give me time to recover because they knew how close my emotions were to erupting.

I'll never forget the understanding and kindness shown me by Burt Lancaster. He took me aside one day. "Hang in there, kid. Danny's mad at me but he's taking it out on you."

The situation became so tense that I was happy only when Hal Wallis was visiting our set; then Danny had to behave himself. Luckily, Wallis always came by for my big scenes; he was the best producer I ever worked for and a master of his profession.

I was still having problems with my love scenes with Richard Jaeckel. Every time I looked at him, I could see Glenn standing in front of me. I used all my ingenuity and imagination to turn him into Howard in every scene we had together.

In the evenings, Howard and I would giggle about it over dinner or on the telephone when I was too exhausted to eat. He loved to hear how I had actually made love to him on the set all day. I'd even have to describe what he'd worn and give him mine and Jaeckel's dialogue.

We rehearsed *Sheba* for a week with the actors, director and cameraman. When we'd finished shooting at the end of four weeks, it was already cut and ready to go to the music department.

I had cried myself to sleep every night; but now it was over and I knew we had a good product. I learned a great deal from Danny and felt my performance definitely justified the means, though I'm sure he would be shocked if he knew I had taken his mode of directing so hard.

At the end of every movie there's a wrap party, so called because all the cables and everything are wrapped up and put away. Howard didn't want me to go, because he was afraid there'd be ice cream and cake; I had to get a note from the assistant director that no sweets were being served. Then he didn't want me going because there would be alcohol.

"But, Howard, I don't drink," I said.

"I know; it's the other drunks I'm worried about. I've made enough movies; I'm well aware what goes on at these set parties."

In the end I put my size-four foot down and went. Just as the party was just beginning to roll and I was having a wonderful time, Howard called on cue and said he was waiting for me at the drive-in gate of Paramount. I left reluctantly, feeling very put upon. The moment I saw Howard's face, I forgot how disgruntled I was; he could never hide good news. His face was all smiles when he said, "Well, Cubby's back from Utah."

My heart skipped a beat. "What happened, Howard? Tell me what happened."

"Everybody wants to be a star. Davis fell for the movie crap, hook, line, and sinker."

Impatiently I said, "That's great about the movie, but do I get my divorce?"

"I'm coming around to that. When Davis finally agreed

to the terms, he was mouthing off to Cubby that he was going to show Terry Moore what stardom was all about."

"Did he sign the divorce papers?" I cried.

Howard proudly stated, "Yep, he was holding up production; he either had to sign or lose the part."

I threw my arms around him. "Oh, Howard, I love you, I love you."

He pushed me away. "Wait a minute, that's not all. Lloyd already has your divorce on the schedule. It's set for April 14. That in itself is a miracle. You've got to call Lloyd and thank him, because I've really been pushing him on this matter."

"Oh, Howard, you went to all that trouble, even putting Glenn in a movie."

"He's not going to be in the movie," Howard stated flatly.

I couldn't hide my surprise. "He's not going to be in the movie? You mean Cubby's not really going to star Glenn?"

"Hell, no. Davis isn't going to be in that picture or any other picture. Ever."

The day that the divorce was granted was one of the happiest days of my life. In 1952 it was very difficult to get a divorce; the two most common grounds were adultery and mental cruelty. I chose to sue on the grounds of mental cruelty. Because of an agreement I'd made to go easy on Glenn, I used as reasons for divorce such things as the fact that Glenn had lied to me and publicly criticized my acting. I was frightened that the divorce would not be granted, but I should have known that if Howard was involved, I could have gotten the divorce by saying Glenn sometimes snored.

Not only did I feel freed from the mistake I'd made, but I also felt loved. Howard had kept his promise to me; his method was creative, elaborate, and expensive, but he had won, and that's what mattered.

Howard had Lee Murrin, a trusted assistant, out looking for a house for us. I was so excited. I felt as if I had just been married and I was feverishly anticipating the honeymoon to follow.

Chapter 19

IT WAS ONLY A FEW DAYS AFTER THE DIVORCE WAS granted when Howard phoned me and said those magical words, "Come on home, baby. I need you."

Lee Murrin had found us a nice home in Coldwater Canyon, set back and not visible from the street on acres of beautiful grounds. It was a large Spanish-style stucco hacienda surrounded by a porte cochere with long hanging plants. The furnishings were Mexican and the paintings were done by the lady who owned the house. Everything was overly bright but cheerful. It was a jazzy, happy house. I loved it.

The first day en route to our new home, Howard and I were winding through Coldwater Canyon. I was startled when Howard suddenly came to a screeching halt. He noticed a little dog that had managed to crawl to the side of the road after having been hit by a car. Howard got out, and to keep the poor delirious little creature from wandering back into traffic, he held it in his arms. I went off in the car to find a veterinarian; Howard stayed behind, cuddling the bleeding, shaking puppy.

When I returned with the vet some time later, there was Howard, still kneeling at the roadside, his clothing covered with blood. He remained right there as the doctor ministered to the puppy. Howard was so concerned; he didn't think about another thing until he was told the dog was going to be fine and was on its way back to its owners. As usual, Howard had a box of clean white shirts in the car but no money. I paid for the vet's road call and we went on home.

At first, we had no servants and I never remember seeing a single bodyguard. We were alone and isolated from the whole world; Howard said we could make love all we pleased and I could scream my head off if I wanted to and nobody would hear.

When we made love, Howard was the one who always took precautions, but he forgot that night. He suggested that I take care of it immediately. I hadn't the vaguest notion what he meant.

"What do I do, Howard?" I cried.

"Go douche. Hurry! You can't wait or it will be too late."

I started to cry. "You never told me, Howard, and I don't have one."

"Where is it?" he asked.

"I've never had one. I'm sorry, Howard."

"Good God, do I have to teach you everything? I forget you're still a baby." He jumped out of bed, and in a total of ten minutes he was dressed and out of there and back from the drugstore with the proper equipment. He also had to teach me how to use it.

"What if I did get pregnant?" I asked teasingly. "Just think, we might have a little Howard running around the house."

"We always have to be careful," he reprimanded. "That must never happen. Before we were ever married, I discussed all this with you. There's no room in our lives for children. No one should have a child or a pet unless they have the time to devote to them. We certainly don't. You want to pursue your career, and I've got a tiger by the tail that I can't let go of.

"Besides," he said, "we wouldn't have all this time for each other."

"But, Howard, when I saw you with that little puppy today, I never saw anything so dear. You're a natural father. If you're so sweet and tender with animals, imagine what you'd be like with a real live baby."

He then went on to tell me that God put each of us in this world for a different purpose. Howard believed that his abilities to make money and control things were God-given gifts and would be taken away unless used to help mankind. He feared that a child who didn't have the full benefit of both parents' complete devotion would go astray and might use the wealth he had accumulated for different purposes than he intended.

Howard had ordered a Swedish couple to cook for us, but they hadn't arrived yet, so for the first week Howard had a wonderful time doing the cooking for us. One of his greatest discoveries was Mary Kitchen's corned beef hash, which he liked to serve with a poached egg on top. Another favorite was the thinnest pork chops dipped in apple sauce. He even had hot dogs cut up and mixed with a can of pork and beans; he called it his Welsh goulash. I couldn't believe it; Howard had never ordered or eaten any of these foods with me before. He said he'd been the cook's helper when he was a child in summer camp and these were the dishes he remembered. He loved donning his apron and prancing around the large kitchen. His biggest kick was shopping unrecognized at the market; he became absolutely mesmerized at the assortment of colors and displays.

Howard became enthralled with the cookie department. He'd spend ten minutes making a decision and then buy one box. He probably ate the cookies before he got to the checkout counter, because I'm a Dick Tracy when it comes to sleuthing and though I hunted high and low I never found any.

Every morning when the milkman made his delivery, he saw Howard in his apron, scrambling eggs, and assumed he was the new cook. The milkman told Howard lots of stories about the previous tenants, Marlon Brando and his wife, Movita. After Howard listened to all his tales, he made sure the milkman never showed up again. Howard loved to hear gossip about others, but he abhorred being gossiped about.

That April, May, and June, we went everywhere together and we didn't care who saw us. I wore all my beautiful clothes, and Howard bought me a gorgeous piece of jewelry for each outfit. Carolyn, Harriet, and Mama Blue worked hard to keep ahead of him. They waited eagerly for my weekly visits to Glendale to see what new bauble Howard had given me.

Every evening Howard took me somewhere we'd never been before. We went dancing at the Coconut Grove. Freddie Martin, the famous bandleader, played special dances for us. Howard loved the tango; he danced elegantly, yet very close and seductively. Freddie played our song, "Again," again and again for us. We dined at the famous Perino's and Chasen's and La Rue's. We began flying to Las Vegas to see all the shows.

It was during our idyllic interlude at the Coldwater house that Howard started talking about making a permanent move to Las Vegas.

"Why Las Vegas?" I asked him once.

"The air's clean, for one thing," he replied.

"Yes, but you're always winding the car windows up so tight because you can't stand the dust," I reminded him.

"Beats smog," he replied. He continued talking, more for himself than for me.

"Yep, I want to get us a ranch. I know you'll like that because you're always talking about your childhood on your grandparents' farm in Idaho. I can run my business as well from Las Vegas as here and it will afford us the privacy we both crave." He laughed. "You'll probably be off making movies."

"Only if you direct them, produce them, or are with me. I don't ever want us to be apart." I snuggled in under his arm.

"Wait a minute. Have you washed your hands?" He pushed me away and started examining them closely.

"Yes, Howard, about five minutes ago, and I brushed my teeth too. See." I made a silly toothpaste grin. He laughed and I repositioned myself on his shoulder.

"All right, but you were chewing bubble gum earlier and you know that gets your hands all sticky."

I knew his thoughts were elsewhere.

"I'm going to buy Nevada," he said.

"That's nice," I quipped. "How much is it selling for?"

He looked down at me as if I had appeared out of nowhere.

"How many senators does New York have?" he asked.

"Two," I answered in a bored tone. "Do I win the sixty-four dollars now?"

"California?" he questioned.

"Two, Howard. I didn't have to make the honor roll to know that."

"How many senators does Nevada have?"

"Let me guess; could the answer be two?" I retorted sarcastically. "Come on, Howard, enough is enough. Now, do I get forty-five more tries?"

"Exactly," he went right on. "Little Nevada has just as many as big New York and California. Nevada is controlled by gambling. If I buy up the casinos and move my operations there, I'll have two senators in my pocket, a governor, and the next president of the United States. That son of a bitch Brewster or no one is ever going to disgrace me like that again."

Howard was thinking about Senator Owen Brewster and the 1947 Senate investigation of the National Defense Program. He never forgave Brewster, the chairman of the special committee, or Juan Trippe, who was then head of Pan American Airlines and who Howard felt had instigated the investigation.

198

Howard was like Mr. Smith in Frank Capra's famous film *Mr. Smith Goes to Washington*. He fought for what he believed in, regardless of cost or consequences. He had fire, but it had to be ignited, and woe to those who stood in his way. Howard fought to win or die.

The Special Committee to Investigate the National Defense Program wanted to know what Howard had done with the millions of dollars that had been invested in building a flying boat. The entire nation was looking forward to Howard's appearance and testimony, but no one knew where to find him. (Howard said he was with gorgeous Cyd Charisse in Santa Barbara—before her marriage to Tony Martin—and was whipping up public sympathy by leaking his side of the story to the *Los Angeles Herald Express*.)

With the news media proclaiming his innocence, Howard flew to Washington, D.C., and walked into the Senate hearing unannounced. Since he had flown all night, they allowed him to appear the next day.

Howard turned his appearance before the committee into a personal triumph and cleared his good name. But he never really recovered from the accusations and the public insult.

We didn't meet until a year after this political confrontation, but the scars were still deep and time never erased them. Howard was very thin-skinned and was hurt far more than I thought he should be by the press. He took great care to make them his friends; Louella Parsons and Hedda Hopper always said that Howard could charm the birds right out of the trees.

Late one evening Howard called me at the Coldwater house. I'd been there alone all day and I was a bit distressed about it. I was ready to tear into him, but his exuberance made me forget all that.

"It's all happening, baby. Nevada is in the works. Be ready in fifteen minutes. We're flying to Vegas. I've got a day of meetings tomorrow, but we'll be able to see a show together."

I was ready and waiting when one of the Mormon boys arrived at the house fourteen minutes later. He drove me to

Culver City where Howard was waiting in a P-29 he'd bought from Convair. This was the military model, which he'd purchased off the line, minus proper instrumentation. That didn't matter to Howard; he'd fly anything that had wings.

We were off to Vegas by sense of smell. All the way there Howard performed his aeroacrobatics, testing the limitations of his new toy. I was thrilled by it; I was never scared with Howard. He had nine lives and three to go.

When we arrived in Vegas, we went straight to the Desert Inn, where Howard put me into a room he already had the keys for. He told me to get my rest, order anything I wanted (except sweets), and he'd meet me at the show that evening. I was so exhausted I slept until the phone woke me in the afternoon. It was Howard.

"Someone just told me that Bob Neal's in town. He checked into some cottages at the El Rancho Vegas with his mother and a girlfriend of yours."

"Who's with him, Howard? Tell me."

"Debbie Reynolds. I'll be a little late for the show so it might be a nice thing for you to call and invite them. That way you'll have company until I get there."

When I called Debbie and the Neals and invited them to the show at the Desert Inn, I learned that Johnnie Ray was performing at their hotel, so we all had dinner at the Desert Inn and then went back to the El Rancho for the show. After the lights were down and the show was in progress, Howard slipped in, unnoticed by the crowd, and sat at our table.

Of course, Howard knew Bob Neal; they were both from Houston. The Neal family made their enormous fortune from Maxwell House coffee. Howard told me that after the Lindbergh kidnaping little Bob Neal was transported to school in a limousine followed by an armored car.

Bob and Howard respected each other, but they were always competitors, usually competing for the same girl. That night, Howard met Debbie, who was Bob's date for the first time.

Bob was Nicky Hilton's best friend, and through Nicky

he had gotten me to introduce him to Debbie some time before. They had dated, and Bob wanted to marry her. Looking back, Debbie says she was much too young.

During the show, while I made a trip to the powder room, Howard took Debbie out into the casino to teach her how to gamble. When I returned to the table, Howard and Debbie were gone.

"What is Debbie doing with Howard?" I demanded angrily.

"He invited her to go to the casino. What's wrong?"

"What's wrong is he's with me," I replied.

"He's just showing her how to gamble."

"Well, that won't be all," I retorted.

"It better be, because she's with me."

"Well, you can tell him when he comes back that I've gone to see Johnnie Ray and he can take a hike."

Bob went out to Debbie and whispered in her ear, "You know, Terry's very angry with you for being out here with Howard."

"I'm sure she's not," Debbie said. "She knows I'm not a flirt. I wouldn't do anything like that. Besides, he likes girls with big boobs."

"She's not worried about you. She's worried about Howard, and she's leaving."

"Well, that's not nice. She shouldn't get upset. We'll stop." Debbie turned to Howard. "Mr. Hughes, let's go join Terry because she seems upset about something and she's going to leave."

"But I'm just teaching you how to gamble," he said, surprised.

"Let's go back to the table. Terry's my friend and I don't want her mad at me."

When they came back, I'd already gone up to my room. When Debbie came up to check on me, I was packed and ready to leave for Los Angeles. She talked me into staying with her at the El Rancho. Only a few minutes after Debbie came into my suite, the phone rang; I let Debbie answer. It was Nicky Hilton, obviously tipped off by Bob that I was angry with Howard. Nicky was sweet and understanding and offered to fly up and join me right away.

The phone in the adjoining room began ringing. Debbie answered it.

"Mr. Hughes is on the phone, Terry."

"Let him wait until I finish talking with Nicky," I said.

Five minutes went by before I picked up the phone. The first thing I did was yawn several times.

"Don't pull that on me," Howard said.

"I don't know what you mean," I said innocently.

"I don't know why you're so upset. I was only nice to Debbie because she's your friend and has never gambled before. Now come back down here, baby. This alligator misses you." He gave two "yonk yonks."

"That's not going to work, Howard. You seem to know how to occupy your time without me well enough. Besides, I just promised to go teach Johnnie Ray how to gamble." And I hung up.

Bob was in his car waiting for us in front of the Desert Inn. Debbie and I climbed in and Bob sped away. After a minute or so of driving, Bob noticed we were being followed, so he took the highway all the way out to McCarran Field, which was later purchased by Howard. Most of the casinos like the Tropicana, Caesars Palace, the Riviera, and the MGM hadn't been built yet, so the highway was dark and deserted.

At the edge of McCarran Field, Bob wheeled and cut off the car following us. He stopped the car, got out, and aproached the blue Chevrolet.

"You tell Howard that I don't want to be followed anymore. Understand?"

The two Mormon boys in the car nodded.

"Now get out of here."

They backed up, turned around, and were off.

On our way to see Johnnie Ray's late show, we stopped at the Flamingo and the Old Frontier to take in whatever entertainment they had. At both places, Bob said he saw

Howard in the wings, peeking around curtains, plants, and pillars.

When we finally arrived at the Johnnie Ray show, he was on his break, so he came and sat with us.

This time, *I* saw Howard spying on us from the shadows. I was accustomed to sitting close to Johnnie because, even with his hearing aid, he sometimes had difficulty hearing. I think part of the reason I was fond of Johnnie was that he was tall, thin, and lanky and hard of hearing like Howard. I also loved talking with him on the phone. He had the most darling speaking voice I've ever heard; it was just a little husky, yet boyish. Like all girls, I loved singers, and Johnnie was certainly my favorite at the moment. He had a very dramatic style; he actually cried when he sang. I liked his emotionalism because I always had a tendency to overdramatize every element of my own life.

I snuggled in even closer to Johnnie. I even put my head on his shoulder a few times and cooed as he talked to us, knowing Howard was taking it all in. Debbie later told me she thought I was being very bold for a Mormon. She was a strict Nazarene and also had rigid rules of behavior. She had no idea, at the time, that I was acting to make Howard jealous. It worked, too, and we didn't see Howard for the remainder of the night.

It was quite late when we got in and finally went to sleep. That night I stayed with Debbie in one of the cottages at the El Rancho. Bob Neal slept in the cabin next to us. He wasn't very happy being awakened by a phone call from Howard before dawn.

"Bob, why don't you get the girls and I'll take you all flying? This is the most beautiful time of all watching the sun rise. The girls will love it."

"Howard, the girls are sound asleep, and so was I until you woke me up," Bob told him, annoyed.

"Wake them up," he begged. "Believe me, they'll love it."

"Believe me, they won't. They probably have their hair

up in curlers and their makeup off. Go to sleep, Howard, because I'm not waking the girls and I'd advise you not to."

Bob said he hung up and then really felt sorry for Howard. He had sounded like a disappointed kid who had a big airplane and no one to play with. All that money and power, and he was all alone.

The following day, Howard was at the El Rancho to pick me up. I flew back to Los Angeles with him, but I gave him the silent treatment and cold shoulder all the way. A couple days of this, I thought, would teach him not to flirt. As I look back, though, I think that was the type of thing that caused many of the problems between Howard and me. He was insecure and felt unloved most of his life. It never occurred to me at the time, but I'm sure each time I became angry at Howard, he thought I had stopped loving him. Poor Howard, the genius, was being crushed by not understanding the convoluted logic of a little girl. And this poor little girl was unknowingly driving her husband into the arms of others.

Chapter 20

Wrong or right, I felt humiliated over Howard's attention to Debbie. It was hard enough that no one knew we were married, but to be pegged as another "Hughes's girl" nearly killed me and my family. The least I expected from him was his complete love and devotion, especially in front of my friends. I returned to my parents' home in Glendale and I accepted dates with Nicky Hilton, who never stopped calling.

Howard realized he was wrong because he even used Debbie Reynolds to call me to plead his innocence, but I wasn't ready to listen to Debbie's or Howard's pleas. My ego was too bruised to accept them.

Howard and I played a game of one-upmanship in every aspect of our relationship. I couldn't even accept a present from him without giving him something better. After he gave me a gold pin of our "dream ship," I had gold cuff links in the shape of measuring worms designed and made. Now I could not stop my retaliation this time by remembering the measuring worms, or the owls or hearing his wailing alligator love calls.

It was time to return to my home lot, Columbia Studios,

and the schoolroom. They had another Mickey Rooney picture ready for me where all I had to do was stand around in a bathing suit and look pretty. I turned it down and ended up on permanent suspension—in other words, fired.

The timing was absolutely perfect. Everyone had seen the rushes of *Sheba* at Paramount and decided I was going to break into the big time. Here I was in an Academy Award–quality movie and free to sign with any studio. Paramount, Hal Wallis, and Twentieth Century-Fox were all waving contracts at me. So was RKO, but I wouldn't allow my career to fall into Howard's hands.

Paramount started an unequaled publicity campaign that turned me from the girl next door into a teenaged sex queen. I did layout after layout in every pose and every style of bathing suit. I loved it but could hardly believe it. Wow, me, *sexy!* Instead of having my arms around a gorilla named Mighty Joe or a dog called Lassie, they were around real live men.

The big cardboard heart for Valentine's Day, the firecracker for the Fourth of July, and the Christmas tree were brought out in the merry month of May and I posed with them all so the photographs could be released for all the holidays. I pressed my arms tightly to my sides and showed cleavage; I did so many leg shots I was heralded along with Dietrich and Grable.

Photographers started following wherever I went and I was mobbed by autograph seekers. That was exciting for about one week. Once I realized I'd lost my privacy, it was terrifying.

I must have over a thousand pictures taken with Conrad Nicholas Hilton, Jr., better known as Nicky. My father adored him because they shared the same hobbies and vices: fishing and gambling. Daddy would have bet on anything that moved if he had had the money. He attended the horse races at Santa Anita and Hollywood Park with his good friend Eddie Winckle, who would come over in the evening with his slide rule; together they would handicap the next day's races. You've never seen a more serious undertaking;

yet after all their homework they only managed to break even.

My father was even more serious about fishing. He and Nicky would spin fish stories by the hours. I don't know how Daddy finagled it, but Nicky lent him all of his most sophisticated fishing gear. My father became the permanent custodian and Nicky borrowed it back when he needed it.

Nicky had two different personalities. Sober, he was shy and retiring—one of the most modest men I've ever known. But when he drank, he liked to throw his weight around and remind everybody about his family and money.

He said I was the only woman who understood him. I do now, but I doubt if I did then. I was never jealous when he flirted with other women, perhaps because I wasn't in love with him, though I did adore him. I would have killed Howard if he had done the things I allowed Nicky to do when he was with me.

There was rivalry between Nicky and his brother, Baron, even though Nicky seemed to allow Baron (who now runs the Hilton Hotel chain) to rise above him. I've always thought that was because Nicky felt responsible for the childhood accident which left Baron blind in one eye. Nicky never got over it. Baron did.

After visiting Baron's beautiful home and his family of many children, Nicky would always say to me on the way home, "I'm going to marry you and we're going to have ———— children." It was always one more in number than Baron and his beautiful wife Marilyn had at the time.

Nicky was a playboy. He was a great golfer, hunter, and fisherman. I never knew him to work a day in his life, but he took his sporting excursions more seriously than most people take their jobs. He was out to marry me, and this time he thought he had a good chance, until he left on a prearranged fishing trip.

While Nicky was out of the way, I received my first phone call from Greg Bautzer. Greg was probably the only man around who had more women swooning over him than Howard. He was not only tall, dark, and handsome, but he was also one of the most successful attorneys in town. He represented Howard and a lot of other show-business bigwigs.

Greg was of Spanish-German descent, with dark, wavy hair and a year-round tan. He and Ginger Rogers were so good on the tennis courts that they were now taking on professionals like Gussie Moran of lace-panty fame.

Today I would have to compare Greg to Tom Selleck or the men in the Marlboro ads. He had a rich, booming voice that scared me to death, unless he was talking about love. And he was.

Greg had a penchant for Academy Award winners and seemed to date all those who weren't otherwise spoken for; he was the lawyer that Joan Crawford loved and lost in *Mommie Dearest*. At the time of her Academy Award, Jane Wyman, former wife of President Reagan, was dating the great Bautzer, and so was Academy Award–winner Ginger Rogers. Howard always said Greg wouldn't bother with a star until she had the statue. I knew I had arrived when Greg finally got around to me. I was thrilled; dating Greg, I thought, would drive Howard wild, and that's just what I intended to do. The timing was perfect.

A big bouquet of roses arrived from Greg, with a record placed in the middle and tied up with a ribbon of movie film. The record was called "I Want to Be a Friend of Yours, Umm and a Little Bit, Umm and a Little Bit More." Corny? You bet, and I loved it.

The following night Mr. Bautzer arrived in his chauffeur-driven limousine. He was the most dashing man, in a buccaneer sense, I had ever seen. His vibrations were so strong they rattled a whole room. My knees rattled, too, I was so frightened of him.

Let Howard read about *this* tomorrow, I thought. Things were definitely looking up; Howard was much too worried about me to even think about other women. I really didn't want to hurt him, but this time he was going to get a little of his own medicine.

As was to be expected, the most glamorous man in

Hollywood took me to Hollywood's most glamorous restaurant, Romanoff's. Romanoff's was on Rodeo Drive, the Via Veneto of Beverly Hills. Its owner and proprietor, Mike Romanoff, was a self-proclaimed Russian crown prince. He had fooled Hollywood for many years and when his ruse was discovered, people loved and respected him more than ever. After all, Hollywood was supposed to be reel, not real. The prices were astronomic, and the reservation book read like *Who's Who* every night of the week; you shared your meals with Bogart, Boyer, Gable, and Flynn. Prince Mike played weekly poker with the Zanucks, Goldwyns, and Warners. If your option was about to be dropped, you heard it at Romanoff's before it made Louella's column.

We had no sooner been seated than the headwaiter came rushing over. "Mr. Bautzer, Mr. Howard Hughes urgently wishes to speak with you." Greg turned to me and immediately started pleading his innocence.

"I didn't tell Sam [Greg always called Howard Sam] we were here, honest. I want you to listen to the conversation so you *know* I didn't tell him where we were going."

I was completely puzzled because it hadn't even occurred to me that Greg would tell Howard; he was one man that I thought even Howard couldn't use. I declined vehemently, but he insisted and practically carried me along to the phone booth. He put the phone between both our ears and said, "Yes, Sam?"

I heard Howard's distinct Texas twang. "Christ, Greg, what are you doing with Helen? I told you she wouldn't be with Hilton. He's out of town."

I couldn't believe my ears. I have rarely seen a more embarrassed man than Bautzer. He realized he'd been had: Howard was using Greg to try to keep me away from Nicky.

All this renewed my faith in how much Howard really cared for me. I was finally seeing the Debbie Reynolds incident for what it really was. I decided I couldn't punish Howard any more.

The next phone call I received from Howard, I became the sweet little girl he loved again.

"There are four more articles about you today. Why do you continue this charade with Hilton? And this thing with Greg will be in the papers tomorrow. I'm at my wit's end."

"Oh, I'm sorry, Howard. You're the one who told me how important publicity is in my profession. Whatever Nicky and I do is news, and, anyway, he's my best friend," I answered innocently.

"I thought *I* was," he said.

"Oh, darling, you're different. You are. You're everything. You know that," I told him.

"Well, you've spent enough time with your folks. I need you back here," he stated.

"I'll come home tomorrow, Howard, I promise. Oh, and darling, I've got some good news. I've been offered the lead in a wonderful play in La Jolla that your friend Mel Ferrer's directing."

"Well, we'll talk about that."

The next day Howard sent Bill Gay to pick me up and bring me to our usual in-between meeting ground at La Cienega and Holloway Drive.

After an hour I became impatient waiting. Bill told me that Howard was in a business meeting at Walter Kane's apartment and he would join us at any moment. Nearly two hours went by and I was fuming. Howard's thoughtlessness made me so angry that I ordered Bill Gay to drive me to Walter Kane's apartment. He complied.

When we arrived, I jumped out of the car and tried the door. It was locked, so I impatiently started ringing the bell. To my surprise, Howard answered the door, and I could see a beautiful young starlet standing behind him. Howard looked as though he'd been caught with his hand in the cookie jar.

I was livid, and without thinking I hit him with all the strength I had, forgetting I carried a heavy plastic handbag in my hand. Instinctively Howard swung and hit me with his open hand across my face. I was too shocked by what I had done to have any reaction. Howard was bleeding profusely from my blow; the catch on my bag was similar to the metal latch on a lunch pail and it had cut him seriously enough to require several stitches. I was scared to death that I had marked him for life. He was more shocked that he'd struck me.

Since his last airplane crash, Howard had had an aversion to hospitals, so we immediately drove back to our Beverly Hills Hotel bungalow and called a plastic surgeon. I put cold compresses on him until the doctor arrived and made the necessary repairs, leaving when the doctor assured me his injury was minor.

I don't recall how many stitches it required, but my scar lay right next to one Ava Gardner had left with a bookend.

The first phone call I received when I returned home was from Gregson Bautzer. I had erased the Romanoff incident from my mind, but he insisted on apologizing again. He told me that he hadn't been able to get me out of his mind and if I would allow him, he'd like to take me out for himself this time, not for Sam. I was delighted.

Greg and I saw each other a few more times. He began calling me as often as Nicky and Howard. Greg and I would mostly talk about movies and movie stars. I talked a great deal about Howard, and yet Greg's affections toward me seemed to be increasing. One night he called to ask me out, saying he had something important to discuss.

We made a date for the following Saturday night, but I had to cancel because I accepted the part of De De in *Season in the Sun*, the play in La Jolla, and rehearsals were to start immediately. I was sitting tight, without a studio contract, and I thought a stint on the stage would be good for me and would keep my mind off Howard.

When I went to my agent's office to sign the contract, he introduced me to Kirk Douglas. He was so ruggedly handsome. I actually felt my knees weaken. He promised to come to La Jolla to see my play, which he did.

One evening, after the play, Kirk showed up. I was thrilled, but I felt completely out of my league for the first time. I don't know why; he couldn't have been kinder to me. It was probably because I had seen him in too many movies and associated him with tough, domineering roles. I was impressed being out with my first movie star who wasn't of my generation.

I felt that Kirk was too powerful for me and I couldn't handle him. He was just too sophisticated and I felt I wouldn't know what to say. Or worse, I'd be too scared to say no. I never accepted another date with Kirk. It wasn't because I didn't want to; I was crazy about him. The crux of the matter was that I was too naive for a man like Kirk, but I wasn't for Howard. He had a lot of boy in him.

A good part of the time I had felt like mothering Howard. He is the only man who ever brought out the maternal instinct in me, more so than my own children. Perhaps that has been the secret of his lifetime hold over me, because I feel that there is no stronger instinct in a woman. I always called him "my baby," and Grandma used to shake her head and say, "How can Helen call that big galoot 'baby'?"

One day, in the middle of the play's run, my agent, Norman Brokaw of William Morris, called, "Terry, I want you to get the first plane out of there because I have an interview for you with Elia Kazan. It's at Twentieth Century-Fox and the film is called *Man on a Tightrope*. Fredric March, Adolphe Menjou, Richard Boone, Cameron Mitchell, and Gloria Grahame have already been cast. The lead girl's role hasn't been cast yet and I think you're perfect for it."

"Kazan!" I gasped. "He's the most brilliant director in the whole world. I'd give anything to work with him. I'll call you back just as soon as I make my reservations."

This was a dream I could hardly fathom: to work for Elia Kazan, or Gadge as he was known to his close associates. To me, he was the greatest director in the whole world, though he was considered extremely controversial. He had directed everything that Tennessee Williams had ever written for Broadway, and most of the screen adaptations too. He'd discovered Marlon Brando, Rod Steiger, and Karl Malden. I thought I was the least likely actress to ever work for him, as he hated products of Hollywood, but I had to take the chance. To meet Kazan was the fulfillment of a lifelong dream. I had seen everything he'd ever made at least twice; my favorites were *A Streetcar Named Desire* and *Viva Zapata*.

I immediately called the airlines, but there wasn't a single carrier that could get me there on time, and, worse still, there wasn't one that could get me back in time for my evening performance. I didn't dare ask my producer for permission to leave because I knew the answer would be no.

I finally came up with a solution. I was a pilot; why not charter a plane? There was only one problem: I called San Diego and there were none available, not at the last minute, anyway. I knelt down and I prayed; then I called my flying instructor, Ray Pignet, explaining my dilemma and how much this meant to me. He had a Cessna 140 available and he said he could leave immediately. He had some friends he could visit in La Jolla while Mama Blue and I flew to Los Angeles and back.

Mama and I were ready and waiting when he touched down one hour later. He took the car and I took the airplane, promising to be back in three hours. I made my flight plan and we were off. I wore my oldest Levi's, my "good-luck" gray leather flight jacket, and cowboy boots but brought along a white silk shantung dress to change into. Mother held it in her lap, but by the time we arrived it was ruined: she was so nervous flying in a single-engine plane that she chomped on chocolate-covered peanuts all the way and used my beautiful dress as a catchall.

When we arrived, Norman, my agent, was waiting impatiently for me at the airport. "You don't have time to change your clothes," he said. "You'll have to come as you are or you'll miss Kazan."

I looked like a female Brando—real tough. This isn't unusual today, but it was unheard of then; we were still in the hat and white-glove age.

As we drove off, my agent said, "The only thing I can

tell you about the role is the girl can break horses and she's real mean.''

We breathlessly entered Mr. Kazan's outer office, where there were dozens of young actresses waiting, all in beautifully starched cotton summer dresses, and all looking like a breath of spring. There was standing room only, so I stood, amidst the snickers and the critical mutterings of my peers. We had no more than arrived when Kazan himself popped out of his office and took one quick look around and said, "Hey, you. Come here.''

I took a deep breath and followed him outside and down the studio lot. He put his arm on my shoulder, man-to-man style, and asked, "Okay, what can you do?''

"I can fly, break horses, and I'm *real* mean.''

"You're okay, kid,'' Kazan said. "You've got the part.''

I gulped; I didn't know what to say.

"By the way, I hear you're good in Danny's picture,'' he added.

"I'm sure Paramount would let you see it,'' I stammered.

"I don't have to see it. You're what I want. I can't stand girls with all that fuckin' makeup and every fuckin' hair in place.'' (It was crude language to me, but it seemed all right coming from Kazan.) "You stand out cuz you're different and you're real mean.'' He laughed hard at that. "You're really a pilot?'' he asked.

"Yeah.'' I was acting street tough with my head hanging down and my thumbs tucked in my belt. "Glad you reminded me. I've got to get my little flying machine back to La Jolla. I'll buzz you on my way back.''

He seemed pleased as a child. "You really will?'' he asked.

"Sure will. I'll even tip my wings.'' And I gave him a wink. I don't know when in my life I've been so deliriously happy.

"I'll tell Zanuck you've got the role. He'll probably want to sign you to a fuckin' contract. Do you know who Darryl wants to play this part?''

"No,'' I answered, in a way I hoped sounded mean.

"Debra Paget. She's good, but I do my own casting." He laughed again. "He also wanted Hildegarde Neff for Gloria Grahame's role and Rory Calhoun for the Cameron Mitchell role. Next time, I'll bet he doesn't make any suggestions. We'll do all the shooting in Germany because I don't like studio executives butting in."

This was 1952, and not only was I going to work for the great Kazan, but we'd be on location in Germany. I was in movie heaven.

Twentieth insisted that I sign an option for a seven-year contract. Howard was pleased because he was close to Darryl Zanuck, the studio chief; I *wasn't* pleased with the fact that many of the contract stars were Howard's former sweethearts: Jean Peters, Ann Francis, Mitzi Gaynor, and Debra Paget, to name a few.

The first week I was home after the play closed, I accepted that date with Greg Bautzer. The morning of our date, flowers arrived with a record snuggled into the arrangement. This time it was a song called "You'd Better Go Now, Because I Like You Much Too Much." I was thrilled with all the attention, but the mere thought of Howard still brought an immediate sinking feeling to my stomach.

I told myself, "Keep busy, girl. Don't think about him. Think about Bautzer, Bautzer, Bautzer. That's your answer. Howard, damn it, where are you?"

Everyone was participating in my stardom; it was a neighborhood affair. Before every date, some of our closest neighbors came over and consulted about what I should wear. Then, when I was all dressed and ready, they came over to see the finished product and to give their approval. Everyone had to be in complete agreement or I would have to change my outfit.

The morning after a date, we met again in our living room and I reported all the exciting events of the night before in the most minute detail.

"Did Humphrey Bogart like your sweater?"

"Was Marlon there?"

"Was your dress the prettiest at the party?"

"Did he ask you out again?"

I enjoyed revealing everything that happened as much as they enjoyed hearing about it.

As Greg and I walked toward the big, black limousine that was so conspicuous in our neighborhood, I noticed that most of the neighbors' curtains were parted and they were peeking out their windows at us. I straightened up a little taller as Greg helped me into the limo. As we rolled sedately down the street, I waved at the car with Howard's detective in it.

We drove for a few blocks, then Greg asked his chauffeur to pull over to the curb and stop. He took me in his arms and gave me a long, lingering kiss.

When he released me he said, "What I'm about to tell you is one of the most difficult things I've ever had to say."

I was breathless with anticipation.

Greg went on. "I saw Howard earlier today and I was shocked. I have never seen any man so grief-stricken. Let me finish, because I already know what you're going to say. You wouldn't know Howard if you saw him. He's lost nearly thirty pounds. He told me that for the first time in his life he's in love, and for the first time I believe him. I admit I never thought he was capable of it. It puts me in a difficult position, because I love you too. You're going to have to make a choice, right here and now. Is it Howard or me? If it's Howard, I'll drive you to the Coldwater house where he's waiting for you. If you choose me, then we'll continue. . . ."

Before he could even finish his last sentence, I blurted out, "Howard. I choose Howard. Oh, Greg, take me to him. I love him. He needs me!"

Chapter 21

I WAS SHOCKED AT HOWARD'S APPEARANCE. HE HADN'T lost thirty pounds, but he was much thinner and terribly gaunt-looking. There was an air of inner sadness about him that hadn't been as evident before. He had grown a beard and I was amazed how Christlike he appeared.

When Greg left, Howard took me in his arms and just held me. Our thoughts and inner feelings flowed one to the other and we didn't spoil them with words. All I knew was I was home again.

The next day, I poured out my feelings to Howard.

"Howard, Grandpa told me that I've spent my whole life building a reputation and now I must spend the rest of my life polishing it. Please try to understand me, Howard. I want to be with you forever, but people out there are going to find out we're living together. We can't tell anyone the truth."

"Would it make you feel better if your mother and father moved in here with us?" he asked.

"Yes, Howard, it would." I thanked him.

"Now you won't go to Germany, will you?" he asked.

"I want to go—just as much as you wanted to fly around

the world. You did what you had to do and now, I have to do what I have to do. Remember how you told me that Katie Hepburn tried to stow away on your plane? Well, you can stow away with me,'' I told him.

"But I have my stockholders to worry about,'' he replied.

"Then fly over whenever you can. I'll just work doubly hard when you're not there, and I'll take Mom with me so you'll have nothing to worry about,'' I promised.

"Kazan's the one I worry about. All his leading ladies fall in love with him, and he's never used any of them in more than one film.''

"I'm not interested in other men, Howard. Something's changed inside me; I realized it when Greg brought me to you last night. You looked so sad I wanted to take care of you. I made up my mind that I'd never leave you again.''

"You'd better be careful. That's a pretty big order for you,'' he laughed.

I dragged Howard into the bathroom and between fits of laughter we shaved off all those horrible long whiskers. He hated to shave because his skin broke out in a rash, and he told me that when he got old, he was going to grow a long beard and never shave again.

"Okay, Santa Claus,'' I piped up. "I can see the manicure course I took at Glendale High is going to come in handy.''

Next, I headed for the kitchen.

"Oh, no,'' Howard yelled. "Not the kitchen. That's a danger zone for you. You're not going to try to cook again, are you?''

"Ohhh, aren't I? I'm making a steak and salad, and you're going to eat it and like it.''

Howard followed me to the kitchen and pulled up a chair straddling it backward. He watched my undertaking greatly amused . . . until I pulled out the lettuce drawer of the refrigerator and dumped everything on the floor. I nearly blew up the kitchen when I left the gas on too long lighting the stove. When I picked up the sharp butcher knife to cut the lettuce, Howard let out a yell. "Oh, no, not my tires."

Now it was my turn to laugh.

Luckily for Howard, the Swedish couple arrived the next day and my parents moved in with us.

I loved the script for *Man On a Tightrope*, written by the famed author Robert Sherwood. It was a true story about a little flea-bitten circus and its people who make a great escape from Czechoslovakia to free Germany. I played the circus owner's daughter who falls in love with a young Czech, played by Cameron Mitchell, who is thought to be a spy.

At my next meeting with Kazan, I happened to mention my pet snake, Midnight, the large boa constrictor that Bob Cummings and I had brought back from our picture in Florida. He thought it was a great idea for me to use Midnight in the movie. The studio took great care to ship her over early.

Howard promised to visit and take me touring after the movie was completed. I dreamed of visiting all of Howard's favorite places; he said it would be even more fun for him seeing Europe for the first time through *my* eyes.

The morning of the day we were to leave, the studio called to break the sad news to me. Midnight, my snake, who had been shipped over with the crew, had died from exposure. Germany was too cold for a snake used to a Florida climate. Midnight's brief career ended in tragedy.

Howard marched into the bedroom while Mama Blue and I were packing.

"This is the biggest production I've ever seen," Howard told us. "This is worse than the assembly line at my factory. You're only going for ten weeks. If you've forgotten anything, I'll send it over on TWA."

I started to pack the sexy black jersey dress Howard had designed for *High Heels*.

"Wait a minute, you're not taking that. You're going there to work, not to excite men. All you need are some warm sweaters. Better take your long johns."

"Yes, Howard." I was too happy to argue, but when he wasn't looking I slipped my dress into the bottom of the suitcase.

Howard was in and out, annoying us all day long until it was time to leave; then he disappeared along with the car and all the suitcases. Mother and I were panic-stricken, thinking that Howard was trying to make us miss the plane. At exactly takeoff time, Howard came in, whistling "Sorrento."

Mom and I were having hysterics by this time, but Howard said, "Don't worry, they're holding the plane. I had a personal crisis at the factory and had to straighten it out myself. Gloria Grahame isn't there yet either. She had some kind of car trouble," he said.

"Don't just stand there, let's go," I cried. "You have to be the most frustrating man in the whole world. What would you do if you couldn't hold up an airline?"

Howard just chuckled.

"What you've put her through isn't fair to either of us," Mother scolded. "You know she's an actress and highly emotional."

When we arrived at the airport, Mother and I learned that Gloria Grahame had just checked in and had a heated argument with the airport official about her overweight luggage. We were only allowed forty pounds; she had two heavy trunks and was told she'd have to leave one behind. One trunk was full of clothes and the other full of Wella Balsam, a hair conditioner. To my amazement, Gloria took the Wella and left her clothes behind. She figured she could buy clothes in Germany but she couldn't afford to have her hair break off from the harsh bleaches. Later, Gloria discovered Wella was made in Germany and she could buy all she wanted at a much lower price.

Howard helped Mother and me all the way through the airport and onto the plane. When we walked down the aisle, I could hear everyone buzzing, "What's holding the plane up?"

When Howard followed us in, everyone's mouth dropped open. There was a unanimous "Ohhh." Now they knew why the plane was late for takeoff.

Howard kissed me good-bye for our longest separation. He was unhappy I was leaving, but he was glad my mother was accompanying me. He did not trust Kazan, Zanuck, or anyone else for that matter. When a man is in love with a girl, he thinks every other man is in love with her too.

The headquarters for our shoot was Munich. Most of us stayed at the Vierjahreszeiten Hotel, which was still partly bombed out. Mrs. Herman Goering was also a guest at the hotel, and everybody there still treated her as though she were a queen and Germany had not been defeated.

The country still showed the ravages of war. There were few automobiles; almost everyone rode bicycles. Lederhosen, the short leather pants with embroidered suspenders, were common attire. Mother thought they were the cutest costumes she'd ever seen, so we went into the first store we could find and each bought a pair. We came out of the store wearing them and nearly caused a riot on the streets. People were pointing at us and laughing because they had never ever seen women wearing the national dress of the *men* of Bavaria.

All the stores were selling the most precious antiques I'd ever seen for practically nothing. The Germans thought they were worthless and made fun of us for buying these old things. They'd point at them and yell, "Junk, junk." Howard couldn't believe I bought him a Dresden monkey band and a five-hundred-year-old Meissen clock for five dollars. I was constantly shopping and shipping him beautiful antiques for our new home.

The first week in Munich was spent looking for and fitting my movie wardrobe. I'll never forget my introduction to Fredric March. I had gone to Kazan's office to get my various outfits approved. After the last one I struck a pose and asked Gadge, "Do you like them?"

"I don't like them. I love 'em," a voice from behind

said, and two hands out of nowhere grabbed my breasts. I let out a scream and whipped around to face Freddie. He had a big happy grin on his face.

I was mortified and angry, but later I came to love and respect Freddie. When I met him he was the original dirty old man, who became as meek as a pussycat when his lovely wife was around. I don't believe he ever did anything; he just liked to scare the ladies.

I'll never forget how thrilled Mother was when she told me Mr. March had asked her to help him with his lines; it was a dream come true. He had been her favorite actor since she had seen him in *A Star Is Born*. Mother was a frustrated actress; she felt this might be her big chance.

A few minutes after she left to meet him, there was a long scream that could be heard all the way down the hall. Mother raced into our room and barricaded the door, shaking all over; Freddie had scared her half to death by making a pass at her. I think he truly loved making women squeal.

Freddie was the most professional actor I'd ever worked with. He would travel thirty miles to the location on his day off just to give us his offstage lines. He realized that delivering a line the way it was intended made for a better reaction from whomever the scene was being played with. He gave so much of himself that my scenes with him were always genuine and spontaneous. The greatest compliment I ever had was when he told me I was the best young actress *he'd* ever worked with.

I loved the rehearsals that stage directors like Danny Mann from *Sheba* and Kazan require before filming. They gave the cast a chance to get acquainted and get a feel for the part before the filming began.

I thought Freddie was marvelous in the rehearsals with Richard Boone, but Kazan kept accusing him of overacting. "You're eating the scenery up, Freddie," he chided. March became so frustrated and angry that he practically whispered his part. Freddie was having fun, but Kazan yelled,

222

"That's it; that's what I want." He played it Kazan's way, and the critics loved and praised him.

Gadge told Cameron Mitchell and me to go off and rehearse by ourselves. "Remember the scene from *Streetcar*?" he said, "where Stella throws her arms around Brando's legs?"

"Oh, yes," I recalled. "That was great."

"That was Brando's idea, but I got credit for it," he said.

This typified the direct honesty of Kazan. He would never ask his actors to do anything he wouldn't do himself; if he felt anything was too dangerous, he woud try it first. He personally rode every horse and tested the elephants before we were allowed to go in the ring with them. He instilled so much confidence in us that if he had told us to fly we'd have probably tried to do it.

Gadge brought out a performance from me that was better than I could ever imagine, and he accomplished this without my even being aware he was directing. To this very day, he is one of my best friends. Once you work for Elia Kazan, he spoils you for other directors because he knows how to draw the best out of you. He can turn even a dull scene into something wild and exciting.

The cameras started rolling on September 1. I was as happy as I'd ever been on a production. Howard had called me early to wish me luck and strength with an alligator love call. I threw up before going to the set that day and felt a bit lightheaded, but I attributed it to the excitement of working with all these wonderful people.

In *Man On a Tightrope*, I performed an act with horses and an elephant; I don't know how many times I was thrown from my little horse, but if Gadge was watching and the cameras were rolling, I always climbed back on. Like Howard he admired women with guts.

I insisted on doing all my own stunts because I so desperately wanted Gadge's admiration. I didn't tell Mother or Howard about the dizzy spells I was having because I was afraid there was something seriously wrong and they would try to keep me from finishing the picture.

It rained all through the movie. Most directors would have waited for it to stop, but not Kazan: he kept the cameras rolling. Since a regular falling rain doesn't register on film at 24fps (movie speed), I'm sure there were those who wondered why my hair was wet at the end of a scene when it had started out dry. Rainy weather became known as Kazan weather. I wore absolutely no makeup, and before every scene Gadge would say, "Hang your head over." Then he would mess my hair up, I'd throw my head back, and that's the way I'd play the scene.

We moved from Munich and its elegant hotel to a brothel somewhere in the Bavarian Alps between Munich and Salzburg, Austria. It was a difficult location, but our fondness for one another helped carry us through.

The American GIs stationed there would come at night, and if they caught a glimpse of Gloria or me, they'd shout at us to come down. When Gloria discovered the place had been a whorehouse until the day our movie crew moved in, she'd stand on the balcony and wave down to them. They would throw stockings and candy bars up to her, trying in their best German to persuade her to sell her services. Gloria played the role to perfection. Sometimes Freddie would play the irate innkeeper or her procurer, and some- times Cameron Mitchell and I were brought into the act. We loved those boys and were too patriotic to keep their gifts, though we did eat some of the candy bars; I think they were disappointed that the gifts were returned. It was all good- natured entertainment, until Howard heard about it.

There were forty of us with access to one bathtub and one telephone. The story went that Hitler couldn't get through on that phone during the war; Zanuck could never get through after we arrived, nor could the forty of us; but Howard never had a problem. His alligator love calls came through loud and clear; the only time the phone was working was when Howard was "yonk-yonk-yonking." I made the mistake of telling him how cute the American soldiers were and, of course, put all the blame on Gloria, but Howard was irate.

"How can you be so foolish?" he asked. "You have to be taken care of every minute. The next thing you know, there'll be a riot and those men will break the door down to get at you." He lectured me for over forty-five minutes.

From that day forward, we never saw another GI. No one understood why we had suddenly been placed off limits.

I did.

During these postwar years, things were still in short supply. We lived on Wiener schnitzel, cabbage, and potatoes for over two months. Even with this three-item menu, everyone said I was eating more than usual. I didn't think so, but every week the wardrobe girl had to let out my clothes a little bit more. Once, while talking to Howard on the phone, I told him he would love the consistency of the menu and I accidentally slipped about my gaining weight. He scolded me and made me promise to cut out the potatoes. "I don't want to have a plump fräulein meeting me when I get over there," he said.

I had put on ten pounds and it had all gone to my bust; I had gone from a full 32C to a 36D cup. This was quite impressive on my five-foot-two-inch, one-hundred-pound frame; I had to lean forward to see my toes.

I had a craving for sweet California Valencia oranges, so as an encouragement to keep me thin and trim, Howard had a large crate flown from California via TWA. I think they were the first postwar oranges in all of Germany. My popularity with the crew reached new heights.

I was living my part onstage and off. I came to love those circus people, who worked harder than anyone on earth for a paltry four marks a week, which was the equivalent of the American dollar at that time.

One day, we were working in the beautiful Valley of the Alps. We were crossing a suspension bridge near King Ludwig's castle between scenes when a sirocco, the fierce, hot, dry wind that blows up off the deserts of northern Africa, suddenly came up out of nowhere. Everyone ran for cover, but I was delighted. I always reveled in the greater elements of nature; rainstorms, heavy snows, the crashing surf, and wild winds always seemed to energize me. They have always been reassuring hints of the true magnitude of God's infinite power.

I was shocked out of my euphoric state when I was abruptly, roughly tackled and thrown to the ground by the very handsome lion tamer, Heinrich. The wind had excited the elephants and they were stampeding across the bridge; Heinrich rolled me out of the way of the charging beasts and held me until they were past.

Heinrich spoke no English and my German was still scant, but I thanked him the best I could. I gave him a big hug and told everyone how wonderful he was. To show my gratitude I bought him a beautiful golden lighter at the PX and had it inscribed "Thank you for saving my life."

A few days later, Gadge called me into his office to reprimand me.

"Don't you know how serious it is to play with the feelings of these people? I'm surprised at you, Terry. Don't you know our lion tamer is a married man?"

I could feel myself turning red; I couldn't believe my actions were being so misunderstood. I poured out my heart to Gadge; when I had convinced him that there was nothing between us and explained why I had given Heinrich the lighter, he finally told me what all the fuss was about. It seemed the lion tamer had gone home and asked his wife for a divorce because he decided he was going to the United States of America to take care of Terry Moore's tigers. We had a good laugh over that.

I was elated when Howard called and said he was coming to see me as soon as we finished our locations and returned to Munich. I started counting the hours and minutes until we would be reunited.

The day arrived for my big love scene with Cameron Mitchell in the Isar River. Mother had bought herself a Leica and a Rollaflex camera at the PX and had somehow become a photographer. Her pictures were so good that they were eventually used in advertising the movie.

Bavaria was cold in October, and the Isar River, from the

melted snow waters, was freezing. It was so cold that our doubles refused to do the long shots, so Cameron and I did them ourselves. I wore a nude-colored two-piece suit, and we coated our bodies with heavy oil like channel swimmers to insulate ourselves from the cold.

Kazan had us making passionate love in a whirlpool. There were five cameras filming at the same time from different angles so the scene would only have to be shot once. It's a good thing, too, because my breasts were frozen solid after that scene and they took eight hours to thaw out. We were never as cold in our lives but *Newsweek* said it was the hottest love scene ever filmed.

The day after I took a particularly bad spill from my little pony, we returned to Munich. I had been fasting for two days in anticipation of Howard's coming.

The first thing I did when we returned to our grand old hotel was to draw my bathwater. I dumped in all the bath oil and bubble bath I had left.

The last thing I remember was lowering myself into the steaming tub.

Mother came in shortly after and let out a scream. I was unconscious in a bathtub of bloody water.

Chapter 22

THAT NIGHT AT THE HOTEL RESEMBLED A SCENE FROM A Fellini film; being unconscious, I've had to piece together what happened from people who were there.

Mother, ever quick in crisis situations, pulled the plug and let the water out of the tub and quickly threw some blankets around me. Her next instinct was to run for help. We had made friends with William and Della Hahn, an American couple who lived a few doors down the hall and spoke fluent German. Mother knew William could handle the situation.

The hallway was complete madness. Gloria was out there screaming, using a trick that Howard Hawks had taught Lauren Bacall and the others to make their voices husky. The only problem was that the word she was screaming at the top of her lungs was "Fire!" Someone had translated the word into German and called the fire department. Now firemen were in the hall with all their equipment, searching for the fire. The guests on that floor were out in the hall, too, making mad dashes through the crowd with their belongings in an attempt to escape whatever holocaust was coming.

Fortunately, Mother found William Hahn, and he instructed the misdirected fire department to take me to the nearest hospital. She then ran to the phone to call Howard, who assured her that both he and his personal physician, Dr. Verne Mason, would be there within twenty-four hours.

The previous weeks had been wonderful, but our schedule had been hectic. Most of the time I felt as healthy as I ever had in my life, but even when I was sick and feverish, I had insisted on working and giving offstage lines. I had done all my own stunts, including the long shots floating down the icy Isar River. I put everything out of my mind that interfered with my character in the script. Normally, there was nothing unusual about this, but I'd been having intermittent bleeding and dizziness the last three weeks on location.

What I had consciously refused to even consider had become a startling, shocking reality. Howard and I were having a baby. On the way to the hospital my water broke. I was screaming out Howard's name as I went into what seemed an endless labor.

Mother arrived at the hospital and assured me Howard and Dr. Mason were on their way. I held on. She checked with Kazan, and he told her he wouldn't be needing me for at least five days. I only had a few scenes left to do.

Mother remained with me until Dr. Mason arrived. He came into that foreign hospital and immediately took charge.

"I'm so glad you're here, Dr. Mason," I said. "I'm so scared. I've never been so frightened in my life. Where's my mother?"

"I sent her back to the hotel," he told me.

"Why? I want my mother!" I cried. "I want Howard. I can't have a baby without Howard," I screamed. "Where are you, Howard? Where are they, Dr. Mason? Why aren't they here?"

Dr. Mason's reply was completely unexpected.

"Don't you care about anyone but yourself? Your mother

229

is ill over this; she's in no condition to be here. And Howard . . . if he set foot on this continent he would be blamed for this mess. How would that look?''

I realized he was thinking only of Howard. I mustered up every last bit of strength I had and I lashed back at him. ''Blamed? Tell him not to worry,'' I cried. ''I'll tell the whole world he had nothing to do with it. Believe me, it'll be all mine.''

Verne lowered his voice, but each word he spoke cut into me like a whip. ''Howard doesn't want this baby. Are you trying to use it to hold on to him?''

Those words have haunted me all my life. Until now I've refused to even remember them and the irrevocable damage they did to me.

I heard my own bloodcurdling scream and my whole world disintegrated. For the first time in my life I was alone. Completely alone. I dreamed I was soaring off into space and I saw my mother and my father and Gadge and Lillian and Mary Jane and Cojo all reaching for me. I tried to grab hold of them, but they were just out of my reach.

I heard the cry of a baby. Our baby. I passed out.

Once, I half awoke and was told I'd given birth to a boy. No one spoke English except Dr. Mason, so I could have been mistaken or dreaming. Verne told me it had been a girl, who had been too premature to survive. He later told his wife and children that my baby had lived for twelve hours and died of septicemia.

When I awakened, Dr. Mason was waiting at my bedside. He seemed quieter, more relaxed.

I looked around expectantly. ''Where's Howard?''

''He should be calling again any minute now,'' he said.

''Calling? Calling from where?'' I anxiously inquired. ''What's happening? Why isn't he here now? Doesn't he know our baby is dead?''

Before he could answer, the phone rang and it was Howard.

''Where are you? I needed you. I feel just awful—'' My voice broke.

Howard's voice was strong and self-assured. "Before I even sent Verne over there, I said I was afraid this was what was happening. I started thinking it when you told me you weren't getting your period. I know you've been irregular before, especially when you travel. Then this gaining weight. It's a terrible thing. It shows you can't be too careful. Like I told Verne and your mother, we should just be thankful you're well."

"I didn't want to lose the baby," I cried. "When are you coming, Howard?"

"I'm in New York; I'll wait for you here. Under the circumstances, it's better for you if no one knows I'm involved. Verne has gone to a lot of trouble to keep your identity secret at the hospital; this type of publicity could put a quick end to your career. You get some sleep now and I'll call you later tonight."

I had my first real misgivings about Howard. Why isn't he here? I kept asking myself. Why isn't he by my side? He should be holding me in his arms. It was his child too, and he doesn't even care enough to be here. I almost wanted to die of shame. I had lived for this man who tried to con me out of my virginity on Mulholland Drive, this man who demanded our legal marriage be kept a secret, this man who continued to see other women after I married him. This was the man who, I saw now, had allowed me to go through with an illegal marriage to Glenn Davis; this was the man who let me pay over seven thousand dollars of my own money so he could have me back. He knew I'd be crushed by my loss, and yet he wasn't here. He was hiding, thinking of his own reputation, not mine. All these things were going through my mind, and I couldn't even cry. A change had taken place in me. I couldn't even cry.

For five days I slipped in and out of a comalike sleep. I was unable to distinguish what was actually happening and what I had imagined. After I gave birth I had a horrible dream of a hypodermic needle coming nearer and nearer to the head of an infant. I woke up in hysterics and had to be sedated.

231

I was so exhausted I couldn't make sense of my experience. During the moments I was awake, I would attempt to grasp bits and pieces of information. The hospital personnel weren't very helpful, and though Dr. Mason checked on me every few hours, day and night, whenever I'd ask about my baby he would change the subject. He kept telling me that if I wanted to recover soon, I'd have to keep my mind clear. He limited our conversations to the movie I was making, but I kept asking him about Howard, wondering why he couldn't come in secret if Dr. Mason could.

Mama Blue was overwhelmed and immobilized herself. I hadn't seen her since Dr. Mason had arrived to take over. Her love for me ran so deep that she was unable to face my immeasurable loss. It was her loss too.

Out on location, the cast and crew were maintaining the hectic pace to bring the picture in on time, so they were unable to come around. Howard seemed a million miles away, and the uncertainty of my child's fate haunted me.

As the time for my release from the hospital neared, I began to receive some cheering company. Adolphe Menjou, Richard Boone, and Freddie March came to see me. They had been told I had a bladder infection, so they showed up with a douche bag full of flowers. It was so typical of Freddie, who Gadge always said was going through the change of life. Little did Freddie realize what a reminder his gift was of the night in the Coldwater house over six months ago when I had become pregnant.

Howard had my room constantly full of flowers. I was surprised when a bouquet of blue roses arrived; Howard's flowers, like his meals, seldom varied. The roses weren't from Howard; they were from Kirk Douglas. To this day I have no idea how he knew I was in the hospital, but I was happy he remembered me.

I checked out of the hospital, and Dr. Mason disappeared as mysteriously as he had arrived. I looked at my body and could see no visible signs that I'd had a child. I was even slimmer than I'd been before, but no one even noticed because we were all so bundled up against the cold.

The only ones who knew about my loss were Gadge and a German actress, Edelweiss Malchin, whom I had become friendly with. Gadge had no love for Howard, who had tried to interfere when he directed Jean Peters in *Viva Zapata*. He was amused that Howard worried so much about him, because he never gave Howard a thought. It was during this time that Gadge and I swore we'd be friends forever and would always come to each other's aid. Thirty years later that bond still stands stronger than ever, and Gadge has promised that I will be the first woman to work for him twice. He is now a famous author, but I'm sure he'll direct again and I will have a role.

I couldn't believe Howard when he called and said, "I don't want you to finish the movie. Tell Kazan he can get a double or shoot around you." He was adamant.

I was just as adamant. "Howard, I only have a few scenes left and they're in the studio. Nothing is going to stop me, do you hear?"

He had suddenly become the solicitous husband and father. "Helen, I'm not letting you finish this picture. It's up to me now to take care of you. I've already spoken to Zanuck. He'll be there tomorrow."

I was devastated. Could Darryl Zanuck really be coming all the way to Munich to stop me? I was sure Howard was making it up; he'd do anything to get his own way. I was stunned when Zanuck did arrive. I walked right up to him and told him I had every intention of finishing the movie.

I found an unexpected ally. "You're goddamned right you will," Darryl roared. "You think that son of a bitch tells me what to do with my picture? I'll charge all the airline tickets to him and you'll tell him you spent the last three days lying down with your feet raised and a hot-water bottle on your belly. Believe me, he'll never know the difference. He's happy and I'm happy. Simple, huh?'' He laughed and gave me a wink. I liked him from that day on.

Zanuck was right; I did my remaining scenes and Howard believed he had won. Mother and I left Germany after a round of parties and sad farewells. But along with the good memories, I also took home much pain and uncertainty. I often wonder if there is a young woman somewhere that bears a strong resemblance to Howard and me.

Upon my return, Howard was shocked at my appearance; he couldn't believe how emaciated and wan I had become. I was run-down and susceptible to any infection that might come along. Howard was extremely patient and kind, and he pampered me despite my on-edge, snappish disposition. He didn't mention the baby and would shy away from anything that might lead into that subject. I felt his love but was unable to show any in return; he had not been there when I needed him.

Once back in Beverly Hills, I was glad to be home. Howard had planned a Thanksgiving dinner for the two of us, one of his famous late-night meals. The dining room at the Beverly Hills Hotel was closed to the general publc and waiting for us.

I felt twenty years older than the young Helen who had spent Thanksgiving a year before in Palm Springs with this same man. We sat down to a beautiful turkey dinner at our usual corner table. The violinists softly played the selections Howard had requested for the one hundredth time: ''Sorrento,'' ''Meditation from Thais,'' and the tenor arias from *La Bohème* and *Tosea*. As usual, Howard pointed out the similarty between ''Sorrento'' and *Tosca* as if he were the only one whoever discovered it.

As we finished our meal and were alone in the dining room, I felt I could ask Howard to quell the uncertainties that were eating away at me.

''Tell me something, Howard.''

''What, baby?''

''What happened to our child?''

"I don't want to discuss that."

"Why don't you?"

"You've got to put all that behind. Your health is still fragile. You know what Verne said about that."

"Or what you *had* him say," I said accusingly.

"What do you mean?"

"Verne wouldn't talk to me about it. I want to know why. I have a right to know what happened."

"The baby died. It had blood poisoning and died, and that's all there is to it. There's no mystery. It happened. Now let's drop it. It's over. Nothing we say can bring it back."

"How do you know it died?"

"How do you think I know? Verne was right there."

"Were you there, Howard? Did you see our baby die? Did you see a blood test? I didn't, and I was right there. I don't *know* if our baby is dead."

"The infant died of septicemia. You're going to have to face that and put it out of your mind or you're gonna make yourself sick."

"*Sick?* I'm already sick. I'm sick of all the secrecy. What are you *not* telling me? I've got to know the truth. Tell me, Howard. Is the reason you know it's dead because you had it killed?"

His face blanched a little, and his voice rose unsteadily. "Stop it, baby. Why are you doing this to yourself? You know how much I love you."

Nothing he said could deter me or relieve my doubts. "You didn't love our baby, though, did you, Howard? You hated it. You were so afraid of our child growing up and soiling your precious name, spending your precious money. Did you have it killed?"

"Honey, don't," Howard pleaded.

I looked into his eyes; mine were beginning to flood with tears. Howard was feeling my pain; it showed in his face. I was hurting him and knew I would hurt him more. I didn't want to believe that he had anything to do with the baby's death, but every time I looked at him it came to my mind. Howard loved me too much. I had to stop my mind from thinking. I got up and ran.

This time I wasn't running from Howard; I was running from myself.

On the way out of the dining room, I grabbed a magnum of Dom Perignon champagne from the display at the door as a last defiant gesture and told a waiter to charge it to Howard.

Chapter 23

WITH THE MAGNUM OF CHAMPAGNE TUCKED UNDER MY arm, I waited at the entrance of the Beverly Hills while they summoned a taxi.

On the way out I called Edelweiss Malchin, my actress friend from Germany, who was visiting the States, and told her I was on my way over. Edelweiss had fallen in love with our production manager on *Tightrope* and had followed him back to Los Angeles. He was going through a divorce and had to spend Thanksgiving with his family, so that had left her alone. She had decided to go ahead and cook a turkey with all the trimmings and invite me and a few people from the apartment complex where she was living. I told her I had wanted to be with Howard but we had quarreled and I had changed my mind.

When I came on the scene, dinner was over and only the young apartment manager and his girlfriend were left. I told everyone to get ready because we were going to have ourselves a party.

They were delighted, especially with the champagne. The rest of the story had to be told to me because after a certain point I drew a blank. After my second glass, I lost all awareness and memory. I do not and cannot drink, and I have an extreme allergic reaction to champagne.

They told me that when the first magnum was gone, I called up the Beverly Hills Hotel and demanded they send over another. To everybody's surprise, the hotel limousine arrived with the champagne. Before that was gone I called again. The hotel limousine promptly returned with another bottle. Afterward, I became so violently ill that Edelweiss called the hotel and found Howard. Both Howard and the ambulance arrived about the same time and rushed me off to the Good Samaritan Hospital.

The first thing I remember was awakening to the sound of muffled voices. I heard the words "exploratory operation." As my eyes began to take in the room, I realized that the men were doctors and that I was in a hospital about to be operated on. The doctors were beginning to leave, but I motioned for the last doctor to come back.

"*Pssst!* In the name of heaven, I don't need any exploratory operation. I had too much too drink. In fact, I drank everything in sight."

The doctor was young and adorable. He threw back his head and laughed. "That's the only thing we didn't check your blood for, because your mother told us you never touch alcohol."

"Doctor, I'll tell you one thing. I've touched it for the first and last time. If you're going to amputate, please take my head."

That incident resulted in five days of intravenous feedings, yet my hospital stay turned into a very pleasant experience. I was suffering from complete exhaustion, but I wasn't what you call *sick* sick. I needed rest, vitamin shots, and a lot of tender loving care, and the doctors gave me plenty of that. They were always in my room, checking and kidding with me. Everyone liked to congregate there, including John Barrymore, Jr., who was a patient down the hall.

The nicest surprise of all came when Jane Withers, one of my favorite childhood actresses, called and said the shah of

Iran's brother would like to meet me. The moment we hung up, Prince Mahmoud Pahlavi called and asked if he could visit me at the hospital and wanted to know if there was anything I would like him to bring.

I said, "Oh, thank you so much. I'm so tired of vitamins and intravenous feedings; could you please bring me some candy bars?"

Howard had given strict orders that I was to have no sweets and had my menu closely monitored after the tube was taken from my arm. He would never suspect a prince of delivering candy bars.

A few hours later Mahmoud arrived with a shopping bag with every variety of candy bar. He sat on the side of my bed and together we happily gorged ourselves. I don't know what I expected him to look like, but I certainly didn't expect him to be tall and movie-star handsome.

Mahmoud loved America and just being one of us. However, he couldn't stand publicity and had stopped seeing Rita Hayworth when the papers mentioned their dates. I later introduced him to my friends as Juan Lopez from Cuba, because I knew how his family felt about his becoming involved with another actress. He was later forced to come home and marry one of King Farouk's daughters for political reasons.

Mahmoud had been sent to the States to attend college at UCLA, not to date beautiful Hollywood actresses. I was very content to keep our friendship quiet just as long as Howard knew about it. The larger my cloak of secrecy, the more detectives Howard hired to snoop. For every detective he hired, Mahmoud (not to be outdone) hired one of his own. It soon looked as if I had the Secret Service following wherever I went. It grew ridiculous.

The prince continued to be my constant visitor long after I left the hospital. He even offered to move my whole family, including my French poodle, Little Sheba, to his palace on the Caspian Sea, but even a prince with a palace couldn't dim my ardor for Howard.

Years later, my friends asked, "Whatever happened to

that handsome Cuban, Juan Lopez?'' I never told them. Today he is hiding somewhere in the world with a contract out on his life by the Ayatollah Khomeini.

While my prince kept me in candy bars, Howard kept my hospital room filled with long-stemmed red American Beauty roses and white gardenias. He received a daily report on my condition, but since he felt like the offended party, he didn't phone. He waited daily for my call and apology. However, when he learned of my visits from the prince, he came to the hospital himself and immediately checked me out. It didn't help matters when the hospital personnel mistook him for my father and called him Mr. Moore.

He commented in the car, "Christ, you're not even safe in the hospital with tubes attached to you. Doctors are notorious wolves and you had them all in your room, all the good-looking ones at any rate. How does a poor old working boy like me stand a chance? I saw what was going on back there, and that doesn't even count this prince guy.''

Howard was always trying to build a case against me as he thought it gave *him* leeway. He had the memory of an elephant and kept track of every time I looked at another man.

Howard had rented a new home that had belonged to Howard Hawks, in which we were presumably to start a new life together. He had a stack of papers with the reviews from *Come Back, Little Sheba*, underlined in red. I danced up and down when I read them and Howard grinned from ear to ear at my pleasure. He hugged me, happily sharing my triumph.

The ads read, "Terry Moore, who put the *She* in Sheba." The ad in the *New York Times* didn't show a photo of the stars, Burt Lancaster and Shirley Booth, even though Miss Booth had been mentioned for every possible award. Instead, they featured a picture of Richard Jaeckel and me in a passionate embrace.

The *San Francisco Chronicle* said, "What we're coming to see are the love scenes played by Terry Moore and

Richard Jaeckel, as torrid as any yet passed by the Breen office.''

I glanced up, and Howard was grinning like a Cheshire cat. He took full credit for my talent in all matters.

"Looks like this could be Academy Award—quality material here. They really loved you,'' Howard said.

"Don't make fun, Howard.''

"I'm not. That's me on the screen you're making love to. That's worth an award in itself. Anyway, Greg was after you after he screened the picture. He has a nose for these things.''

"Stop it, Howard. You're teasing me.''

Howard liked to praise my acting to bolster up my confidence. He loved my being a movie star, but he was unhappy having to make the sacrifices it entailed. He didn't want anyone to suspect we were married, but he loathed the magazine layouts and the necessary publicity dates I had to go on.

Howard kept reminding me that we were going to be married in public as soon as my divorce was final. He liked it when I announced to a reporter that I planned to marry him the following May: the pictures in the papers showed me courted by every handsome young anybody around, but the copy said I would be marrying Howard.

Minna Wallis, the sister of Hal Willis, introduced me to a young actor named Laurence Harvey. Minna was a Hollywood agent who was well known and liked by everyone, and she thought Larry Harvey was the perfect escort for the opening of *Come Back, Little Sheba*, and the subsequent parties the studio insisted I be seen at. Looking back, I'm sure this was done with Howard's approval; he and Minna were friends. I didn't know that Larry preferred men but Howard did. Larry also kept me away from Nicky Hilton and producer Bobby Evans.

Laurence Harvey was brought to Hollywood by producer Jimmy Wolfe; the Wolfe Brothers were one of the hottest producing teams in London. Jimmy and Minna saw to it that Larry and I were included on the guest list of every important party that Christmas season, and soon a party wasn't considered a success without Larry and me present. I had made my first movie more than ten years earlier, but this was the first time I felt part of the Hollywood scene. I had entered the world of the people who were the stars when I was a child. The all-time greats, the last of the Hollywood superstar system.

Humphrey Bogart and Clark Gable both came up to me at the same party at different times and told me how much they had enjoyed my performance in *Sheba*. Bogart actually said that he would love to work with me.

Gary Cooper told me that he was giving me his vote for best supporting actress. I just laughed. It never occurred to me he might be serious. I couldn't believe that these people seemed to be as happy to meet me as I was meeting them. I was much too shy to ever introduce myself, so they introduced themselves to me.

One morning Mother came into my room all excited. She caught her breath and exclaimed, "Jack Benny's on the phone. He must want you for his show." I was caught up in her excitement; I was a lifelong fan of Mr. Benny's. I picked up the phone and said, "Hello."

"Hi, this is Jack Benny."

I nearly fainted when I heard his famous voice. "Yes, Mr. Benny," I answered breathlessly.

"Call me Jack," he said lasciviously. "Do you think you can get away from your mother long enough for me to meet you somewhere alone?"

I could scarcely speak I was so disappointed. It was just that he'd been bigger than life to me and I believed in him and Mary Livingston, his wife, like apple pie à la mode.

Mother was waiting anxiously to hear what he wanted. I couldn't let her down. "He thinks I'm so talented that he's going to try to find a show for me. He just called to see if I'd be interested."

That story satisfied Mother and she ran to call Harriet and Carolyn with the good news.

The old gang no longer existed. Jane Powell was happily

242

married to Geary Steffan. Liz Taylor was off with the English crowd with her husband, Michael Wilding. Cojo was married to Polly Bergen, Richard Long to Susan Ball. Marshall Thompson was married to Richard's sister Barbara, and I was having dinners with the Ray Millands, the Robert Taylors and the Ronald Reagans.

The party circuit always included Larry and me. Judy Garland often brought her little girl, Liza, who loved to stand up and sing. Her talent wasn't developed yet, but she was adorable. She honed her skill in front of the hardest audience in the world.

I knew I'd made it when Julie Styne, the songwriter, called me and asked if I'd like to go out with Frank Sinatra. Frank was living with him while he divorced Ava Gardner.

"Thank you very much, but I don't go out with married men."

Even if he had been divorced, I was too unsophisticated to go out with him yet, and Sinatra was the one man that Howard would not have forgiven me for.

I was the youngest addition to the board of directors of the Screen Actors Guild; Ronald Reagan was at the helm of the organization. I went to a few meetings but my mind wasn't there yet. I was working too hard and having too much fun. I didn't take it very seriously.

Behind the scenes of these glamorous Hollywood social functions, another life went on that I'm almost embarrassed about not having realized. I was still an outsider in that I still rarely saw past the facades that the Hollywood dream machine had created for the superstars. The undercurrent of drug abuse, bizarre sexual practices, and the myriad of affairs in the inner circle seemed to pass over me. I'm amused at my naiveté as I look back, remembering how flattered I was that some of my celluloid heroes took the time to pick me out at the parties, complimenting me on my skills as an actress. I thought they were just the nicest people in the world and was never aware that their kindness and attentions were, in actuality, sexual advances. At least Howard said they were. It seemed to me that the bigger the

243

star the nicer he was, and most of them were as they appeared to be on screen.

In retrospect I see that staying abreast of all Hollywood's dirt would have been a full-time job. That's why Howard had his spy network to gather the dirt for him. But if I say so myself, I was Little Miss Clean.

As Jan Ford, Judy Ford, Helen Koford, and Terry More I have been in more than seventy movies. I have worked from a $5.50-a-day extra, plus carfare, to the top studio salary. I have never been to bed or had an affair with anyone *I* have ever worked with on those movies. I was never intimate with anyone at any studio with the exception of Howard, whom I married. There are many reasons for this. First there was my religion. I was brought up to believe sex without love was a sin. I sinned with Glenn Davis, and found out I didn't enjoy sin.

I was always with the number-one something in the world. Name the sport, football, baseball, or soccer star, and he went to great pains to get a date with me. My list of singers was growing too: Eddie Fisher, Johnnie Ray, Al Martino, Julias La Rosa, Bobby Darrin, James Darren, Dick Contino, and Vic Damone. Someone else had called for Sinatra and Bing Crosby, a sort of surrogate suitor.

Bing had seen me at his agent's office, Berg-Allenberg, when I was fifteen years old (but looked twelve). Mr. Allenberg called my mother and said, "Mr. Crosby saw your daughter Helen in our offices today and may call and invite you to see his rushes at Paramount. Mind you, I could lose him as a client for telling you this, so please protect me by not revealing what I'm going to say. I would not take your daughter to meet him."

Bing Crosby called. We were busy. We kept our word and honored Mr. Allenberg's confidence until his death. Mother and I were crushed by the destruction of another image. Bing with the pretty voice, Bing with the funny lines, and the Bing in priest's clothing was really Bing the ladies' man.

Jack Warner usually had large sit-down parties with stars

like Charlie Chaplin, Mae West, William Holden, Glenn Ford, James Mason, and Joan Crawford. Joan was always nice to me. When I met her at one of these parties, she offered to take me under her wing and teach me the style she had taken years to perfect. She felt my hair and makeup could be improved. She was right, because I never wore any makeup and my hairstyle was usually too long to be chic. Joan lived and breathed chic and was every inch the star, but it was Greer Garson who stopped the room when she made an entrance. She was regal and elegant and entered a room with her head held high. Jack Warner was a charming host, but he must have been a tyrant at his studio because I never met any of the Warner players, the stars he helped create, at his parties, like Bette Davis, Errol Flynn, Olivia de Havilland, or Ida Lupino.

I was once accused of being a name-dropper, but I could barely mention anyone I knew without being one.

In the midst of all the partying on the West Coast, I had to fly to New York for an opening of *Come Back, Little Sheba*. As always, Howard insisted I take Mama Blue along. Poor Howard took me to the airport so he could be with me; I hadn't spent much time with him lately and he was feeling rejected. I knew he was still trying to look after me, though, because thirty minutes after I arrived in my hotel room, one of the Mormon boys arrived with my mink coat. I had left it in Howard's car in mild-weathered California. Afraid I'd take sick in bitter-cold New York, Howard sent a special plane out right after ours with the mink.

The following day I was in for a real surprise: Howard himself flew to New York. I believe the German incident was beginning to bother him. He had promised to show me all of Europe after the movie. When my health wouldn't permit it, he said he would take the money and have a wardrobe designed especially for me by the great Valentina, the Russian designer who had created all the clothes for Katharine Hepburn in *The Philadelphia Story*; she also made most of Garbo's clothes. Six dresses cost ten thousand dollars; that was astronomical for 1952. I still have and wear these clothes; they look far better on me today than they did then. I wanted so much to look like Garbo and Hepburn, but I didn't stand a chance. I'm afraid I was too petite and pixieish to ever capture that lean, elegant look.

Howard watched as I modeled my new wardrobe. "I think you look almost eighteen," he laughed.

Christmas came and went amidst more parties and gifts from Larry Harvey, Jacques Sernas (the French film star), and Nicky Hilton. Nicky told his friend Bob Neal, "Whenever I give Terry a gift, she always says, 'Oh, thank you.' It never occurs to her that a guy might expect more."

Howard and I spent Christmas together with my family. It would be the last one spent in the Glendale house; the little girl from Glendale and her family were getting ready to make their big move to Westwood.

We spent Howard's birthday, Christmas Eve, at the Beverly Hills Hotel with the usual menu, with cherries jubilee added for the occasion. Howard hated each birthday with a vengeance and would have forgotten them altogether were it not for me. He was now forty-seven years old and beginning to feel it.

All my running around the big-league movie world didn't seem to touch me adversely. The phone rang, the press was at the door and telegrams began arriving from all over the world. They all seemed to know what I never even suspected. In January of 1953, I was nominated by the Academy of Motion Picture Arts and Sciences for best supporting actress in *Come Back, Little Sheba*.

Chapter 24

WINNING A NOMINATION ATTRACTED SO MUCH ATTENTION and so many new friends that it could have made the rest of my days seem lonely by comparison. Unfortunately, they were nearly all false friends, the ones who only last the duration of your fame and money. The ones who "always knew you were going to make it" are with you when you do and are long gone when it's over.

Not too surprisingly, it was Greg Bautzer who first called and told me I'd been nominated. If it had been anyone else on earth, including Howard, I'd have thought they were pulling my leg. I don't know why, except I can, in all honesty, say a nomination had never entered my mind.

My tragedy of 1952 was pushed into the background by life's miraculous system of balance. I became too busy to dwell upon the past. We were in a new year, and I was with my family in a beautiful new home. Howard had meticulously designed and furnished a gorgeous bedroom in my parents' home befitting my new image and "single" star status. I had arrived at a new plateau in my career, a candidate for the Oscar.

The Academy Award is the most important recognition in

the world of motion pictures because those who vote are fellow professionals. I was awestruck by the Academy. It was like the hand of God touching me, and I didn't feel worthy, especially for best supporting actress. This award was harder to get than best actress. There is only one leading lady, one star, in each motion picture, but there are many supporting roles, which makes the competition on that level much greater. I did not believe that I deserved to be in the same league as great actresses like Thelma Ritter, Helen Hayes, Mercedes McCambridge, and Ruth Gordon.

I was thrilled with all the attention, so I pushed my insecurities aside to bask in all the glory.

Howard, bless his heart, called the moment I hung up with Greg. I didn't burst his bubble by letting him know that Greg had already told me.

"Helen, we've got to make careful plans. The eyes of the whole world are on you now. There is nothing like an Academy Award to make people take you seriously. We've got to handpick your roles from here on out." He laughed. "I'll bet Harry Cohn is shitting about now. Ho-ho-ho, here he's let you and Monroe both go, and you're the two hottest properties in this whole goddamn town."

I was hanging on to his every word with pure delight. He went on talking about Marilyn Monroe. I'd never heard him mention her before, though I'd known her for years. Publicitywise, Marilyn and I were the two hottest females that Fox had. There were rumors out that I was jealous of her and that we were in a competition feud. Of course, the rumors were ridiculous; we were the best of friends, and had been since 1948. We were complete opposites; in fact, *Life* magazine once contrasted us by calling Marilyn "indoor sex" and me "outdoor sex."

I was the first girl that Marilyn shared her good news with when she found out that John Huston had picked her for *The Asphalt Jungle,* the movie that put her a giant step toward stardom. I was walking down Hollywood Boulevard with my mother when Marilyn spotted us. She threw her arms around us and kissed Mother on the cheek.

"Oh, Mama Blue," she cooed in her breathless voice. "I'm going to be a star just like Terry. John Huston wants me. Imagine, he wants me!"

When I remember Marilyn and that day and so many others we shared together, my eyes fill with tears. All she needed was to be needed. She was so radiantly happy during those days. The whole world was reaching for her, but soon it started tearing her apart. She wanted to be taken seriously, and ironically, she turned out to be one of Hollywood's finest comediennes. Marilyn was serious about her acting and worked hard at it. I was always defending her against people's remarks to the contrary. Later Marilyn apologized for her little fling with Howard. She told me she had no idea I was in love with him and they had not made love. I believed her. I never knew Marilyn to lie.

"I always thought Marilyn was a joke," Howard said. "But she's turned it around and now the public's eating her up. I'm not going to permit that to happen to you. Somebody must have told Marilyn her upper lip is alive or something. Damnedest thing I've ever seen. She moves it around like a snake."

"Howard, that's very sexy," I interjected.

"You're always defending her, but that's nice. That's what I like about you."

It was most likely Howard himself who told her that her upper lip was alive. Later, Natasha Lytess, Marilyn's drama coach, told me that Howard had given Marilyn a sapphire and ruby brooch. They immediately had it appraised at their jeweler's. When they discovered that it was only worth five hundred dollars, they decided that Howard Hughes wasn't worth bothering with, so the romance died a quick death.

Howard must have taken my silence for concern and, always being guilty, he blew me a kiss and said, "Come on, you don't have to worry your head about anyone else. At least not where I'm concerned. My little admiral gives an order and I jump."

"I wish that were true, Howard."

"My boys follow your instructions before mine. Why, just yesterday I told them to take a package to the airport and they told me they had to deliver a script to you. Damnedest thing I ever heard of. Now, with this nomination, you'll really have them dancing."

By this time some of my resentment had eased.

"Stop teasing, Howard. I'm not like that."

"You're not, huh? Well, we'll see. They all change. Pretty soon you'll be too big for me."

"Boy, I sure hope so. Nothing would make me happier than if you lost all your money and I had to help you start all over again. Then, maybe, you'd finally know I love you. And as far as the nomination goes, I'm grateful, but I don't feel I deserve it yet."

"Take it and run. I think you're going to win and I think you do deserve it."

If Howard's reaction was happy, then my family's reaction was ecstatic. The funniest one in the whole family was my father. I knew my mother was a frustrated actress, but who would have suspected Daddy? Naturally, I had gotten my talent from him.

"Didn't you know I did the lead in the school play at Box Elder High School in Brigham City, Utah?" he bragged.

"No, Dad, you never told me."

"Well, I did. Do you know the play *Hamlet?*"

"Sure do. As a matter of fact, I'm studying *Hamlet* right now with Marie." (Marie Stoddard was eighty-seven years young. She was the actress I studied voice, Shakespeare, and drama with for two and a half hours a day, five days a week, and had been John Barrymore's last coach.)

"I'd like you to teach me one of those soliloquies so I can recite it when people come to the house. They're going to expect something from me now."

I started to laugh, but Mother put her finger to her lips and I realized Daddy was serious.

Mother was behaving like the mother of the bride again.

250

She had gathered the neighborhood together to help decide what she should wear.

"Wear where?" I asked innocently.

"Why, to the awards. Edith Head is going to design your dress, but I don't have anything long."

"Wait a minute," I said. "How do you know Edith will design me a dress?"

"Because we called and asked her. She already has Hal Wallis's permission . . . and, Terry, she was so pleased you asked her. I think she's almost as excited as we are. Edith is a big booster of yours. She really loves you."

I was lucky. I had a lot of mothers. There was Edith, Marie Stoddard, Lillian, and, of course, Mom.

Mother was much happier than I was. This was the moment she had spent her whole life preparing me for. She had done everything from painting ceramics to making lampshades to pay for my lessons, and she and the neighbor ladies worked late into the night making my clothes. This was the first time she had ever worried about what she would wear. Mother's big moment had arrived. If I didn't deserve it; she did!

Unemotional Lillian cried for joy. Her "child" was up for the highest tribute our industry could pay. She locked up the schoolroom and took me to lunch, along with Cojo and Jocko Mahoney.

We went to Britingham's, a restaurant that was tucked in between CBS Radio and Columbia Pictures. We celebrated with milk shakes and Monte Cristo sandwiches.

Everyone treated me with an air of reverence that I wasn't too sure I liked. I always had a great fear of falling off pedestals.

Lillian couldn't wait to get me alone. "Guess who first told me about it?" she asked.

"I thought I did."

"No, that's what you were supposed to think. Howard called me first and then spent ten minutes explaining how I should act surprised when you called. That man is crazy about you. You could get anything you wanted out of him if you were like the other girls.''

I started to object.

''I know you don't want anything now, Terry, but I hope you won't regret it one day. Never let him keep you from acting. I know he's thrilled you're finally being recognized for your abilities, but even you don't realize how talented you are. I don't ever want him to destroy that or keep you off the screen. He loves you, but he's also deeply jealous, and that jealousy could be destructive.''

It wasn't Lillian's words that frightened me but the seriousness with which she said them.

The person I was the most anxious to see was Marie.

I hadn't expected her reaction. ''Hmph,'' she said. ''You're still a baby. You're not old enough yet to appreciate the meaning of this award, and you don't deserve it. This will just slow up your progress because you'll think you can stop working now.''

''No, Marie, I promise I'll work twice as hard.'' I burst into tears. ''And I know I'm not good enough.''

''Wipe your tears and quit dribbling. You're as good as most of those you're up against, but don't measure yourself against motion-picture actors. I'm going to give you the tools to be a great actress in any medium. What you do with them is up to you. Then you can thumb your nose at me and everyone else and claim you did it all yourself like all the others do.''

''Marie,'' I said soberly, ''I promise before God, when I win that Oscar, it will be for us. I'll never forget you.''

When I went to Paramount, I felt I had gone back to Glendale High. It was like a welcome-home party. A. C. Lyles, whom I had met at a mailbox years before, was the first to greet me with his bright smile. Ace had worked his way from the mailroom to producer. And without relatives in the business, that's not easy.

''You've got my vote,'' he said. ''In fact, I've taken a poll and you have this studio locked up. We're all pulling for you. Now you're going to be too big a star to play in my movies."

"I only hope you're right," I kidded. "I'll never be too big for a friend."

Ace leaned over and whispered in my ear, "Tell me, is it true what they say about H.H.?" he kidded seriously.

"You bet it is, Ace, and if anyone wants to know—I've got it all," I threw back with a laugh.

I headed on down the studio lot where Wally Westmore, the famous makeup artist, called down from his window. "You can't miss, kid; you've got the Westmore turned-up nose."

I laughed gaily and continued on to Edith Head's office to see the sketches for my Award night dress. It was a showstopper, an ankle-length pearl pink satin. It was fashioned with a full wraparound skirt featuring a one-sided fullness that looked like a pocket overflowing with pink satin poppies. It had a long matching full coat.

I threw my arms around Edith's neck. "Oh, Edith, it's a dress for a princess. I know I'll be the best-dressed girl there."

"Who's your escort?" she asked.

I felt my heart sinking. Oh, dear God, who *is* my escort? Howard will never go. It certainly wasn't enjoyable attending all the premieres and functions I was at last being invited to, without the man I loved.

Edith could feel something was wrong and quickly covered up for me. "Don't tell me. Let it be a big surprise. He's a lucky man, whoever he is."

I panicked. It had to be someone special for this special night. Laurence Harvey had returned to England and was to marry Margaret Leighton. It should be an actor, because then the press coverage was far greater. My mind began scanning the available males, who are always scarce in Hollywood. There was a gorgeous new Greek god named Nico Minardos at Twentieth, but Marilyn Monroe was head over heels for him. There was also a new young actor at Fox

253

who had just started in a new movie called *Titanic*. The word was out that the studio had ordered a big buildup for this kid, Robert Wagner, but I couldn't just walk up to someone I didn't know and say, "Excuse me, my name is Terry Moore. I don't have a date for the Academy Awards."

I decided to ask Howard, even though I thought it was futile; he hadn't made a public appearance in many years. Complete pandemonium would have broken loose had he shown up with me or anyone else. The newspapers would have bannerlined the story, and *Time* and *Life* magazines would have blown it up out of all proportion. It would have been a devastating violation of Howard's privacy. And he was steadily becoming more complicated and private at this stage of his life.

Howard was really flattered and boyish when I asked him. After his firm refusal, I thought that, in view of my dilemma, he would offer Robert Mitchum or somebody else exciting to take his place.

"Why don't you take Bill Gay?" he suggested.

I could have killed him. "You'd really like that, wouldn't you? Why don't I just take one of those detectives you have following me? It would make it a lot easier for you. I'm not going with one of your lackeys." I stamped my foot for emphasis. "Everybody would think I was a Howard Hughes girl."

"What's wrong with that?" he asked, surprised.

"Everything. I'm not one of your girls. I'm your wife!" And that was the end of that. Except I was still without a suitable date.

Careerwise, I could do no wrong. To the disappointment of Hal Wallis and Paramount, Zanuck picked up my option. My first assignment under my new contract with Twentieth Century-Fox was to be *Beneath the Twelve Mile Reef*. It became a milestone in motion-picture history because it was the first CinemaScope movie. I was to costar with Robert Wagner, Gilbert Roland, and J. Carroll Naish. I was happy that the studio immediately began to pair Bob and me for publicity. My problem was solved. We were the press agent's dream: two single, attractive youngsters brimming with vitality.

When the big night finally arrived I was in the clouds. I took great care in dressing. I was so proud of my Edith Head original and wanted everything to be perfect. Wally Westmore had made up my eyes and Nellie Manlay, who did Marlene Dietrich's hair at Paramount, had done my coiffure.

The whole neighborhood and the private eye parked outside were watching when Bob Wagner arrived in a chauffeured limousine to pick me up. I was running a little late and he had to wait. The moment I was ready and on my way out the door, Howard phoned to wish me luck . . . and to tell me how to walk and what to say and how to sit and how to act and how to pose for the cameras. I was beginning to get flustered by all his instructions and was about ready to hang up when he stopped, gave an alligator love call, and told me he loved me. That was all I needed to hear to get me calmly through this night. But Howard couldn't leave it on a high and happy note.

"There's just one more thing," he said. "There's something funny about this Wagner kid, and I want you to be on your guard. Unless your parents are with you, I want you to go directly home after the awards."

I hung up on Howard, took Bob by the arm, and was off.

Bob had brought me a corsage. I had nowhere to pin it and wanted to leave it behind, but Mom was afraid his feelings would be hurt, so she tied a ribbon around my neck and pinned the flowers on it. It instantly became the chic thing to do in this period of the strapless gown.

The whole night was like something out of a fairy tale. We stepped out of the limousine onto a red carpet in front of the biggest gathering of fans, autograph hounds, and photographers I'd ever seen. Arc lights crisscrossed in the evening sky. There was an army of policemen just to keep the crowd back. Every television channel and radio station was fighting for an interview.

255

Inside, the beautiful gowns and jewelry the women wore astonished me. I saw everyone; everyone saw me. I was Cinderella with the most handsome of princes, and this was the royal ball.

As soon as the ceremony began, I began to get so nervous that Bob took my hand and gave me an understanding look; he knew what I was going through. I finally felt I maybe deserved the nomination, but not the actual award. With every presentation I became more and more nervous. I knew that if my name were called I'd pass out. When they finally came to best supporting actress, I was the happiest and most relieved girl in the world. The award went to someone I felt did deserve it, my good friend Gloria Grahame.

After the awards, there were more fans than ever waiting outside. People had to wait thirty minutes for their limousines. Bob decided it would be better to brave the crowd, go to the lot, and find our driver. If we stood there, we'd soon be crushed by the fans.

Even though I hadn't won, Bob and I stole the show. Bob may have been the prettiest boy to come out of Hollywood since Tyrone Power. His eyes were beautiful, his nose exquisite, and his lips full and sensuous. His body was perfect by my standards: he was tall and wiry, strong and boyish, without an ounce of fat anywhere. Bob had everything: he had looks and wealthy parents who couldn't have been nicer or more gracious. They made their money in the steel business so they could afford to raise R. J. in Bel Air where he caddied at the famed Bel Air golf course for Clark Gable, Randolph Scott, and other notables. Bob had a well-bred, happy-go-lucky personality and the self-assurance that comes with wealth. His favorite expression and his answer to whatever question you asked him was "How do you mean that?"

Defying Howard, I went with Bob for late-night scrambled eggs at Romanoff's. The waiter overcharged him fifty dollars, but Bob was too embarrassed to make a scene in front of me and didn't say anything. I caught the mistake and spoke right up; believe me, they made amends, apologizing all over the place. Later I read in a fan magazine how much Bob appreciated it.

The next day Howard picked me up and we went driving. He thought I'd be depressed over losing and began pampering me, so I played along to get my way. He put aside all of his work for the day, and we made love to cure me of depression. Even then it wasn't completely cured. We were in the Beverly Hills Hotel, so I made him order me a hot-fudge sundae as my final treatment. As soon as I was back in great spirits, Howard was complaining about Bob Wagner and me. He didn't want me to go to Florida, but he knew that I would.

His big attempt to shake me up was when he said, "You're going to be in Florida when your divorce becomes final. That just might throw a monkey wrench into the works."

"What works?" I asked.

"My plans for our second wedding."

"Third wedding," I interjected.

"You're right. Third wedding," he repeated, a little amazed. "I've got time set aside, and now you'll be gone. You know how busy I am. This movie could foul things up and delay us for who knows how long."

"If you love me enough, you'll find time," I said wondering what he was doing now.

Chapter 25

IT ALWAYS SEEMED THAT HOWARD NEEDED MORE ATTENtion when I was on my way somewhere; he stuck to me like glue as I tried to get packed and ready. He kept saying that there was something funny about "pretty boy" Bob Wagner and he didn't like the idea of my being down there with him. He made sure Mama Blue was going and told us both that Gilbert Roland was a stud who shouldn't be trusted.

Howard always had his store of gossip. He told me the story of old Joe Schenck, who was the granddaddy of the movie industry. Old Joe was married to the great love of his life, silent screen star, Norma Talmadge. According to Howard, she had a love affair with Gilbert Roland. For this one mistake, Howard said, Gilbert was blackballed by the major studios for nearly twenty years.

From the moment we boarded the plane for Florida, things went badly. I fastened my seat belt and went to sleep. There is no way I can stay awake on anything that sails, flies, or moves unless I am the pilot myself. I awakened eight hours later wondering why everyone was laughing.

"Are we in Florida?" I asked.

To my embarrassment, we were still in Los Angeles; the

plane had developed engine troubles. My coworkers had let me sleep while they had gone to the airport bar and partied.

Our first location in Florida was Tarpon Springs, a Greek sponge-fishing village. We stayed at a rooming house that didn't serve meals, so we ate nightly at Pappas' Restaurant. Bob and I had become so popular with the fans that we were unable to enjoy a single meal without having autograph books pushed in our faces. One evening after fans had followed us, peeked through our blinds while we were dressing, and handed us pencils between every mouthful, I ran to the ladies' room and I locked myself in the cubicle. When fans started poking their autograph books under the door, I snapped and started screaming.

From the moment the first photographer snapped Robert Wagner's picture with me, we became America's sweethearts. Nothing could have been further from the truth. Bob was madly in love with Barbara Stanwyck, whom he had met when they made the movie *Titanic*. The two lovers of the decade were each in love with people who could be their parents. Howard called me every night, and R. J. called Barbara. Bob was such a cutup; when he first heard Howard's wailing love call, he let out a big wail of his own. Howard answered back thinking it was mine. Mother, R. J., and I spent the whole night laughing over that.

Looking back, it seems such a waste to have been in all these romantic places with Bob and be pining away over Howard. Besides being lovesick, most of the time we were all seasick. We'd get up at five in the morning and they'd take us out to sea and put us in an old sponge boat. We were left there all day long while the cameras photographed us and the boat bobbed around in the ocean waters like a cork.

Bob, Amigo (as Gilbert Roland was called), and J. Carroll played a Greek family who made a living fishing for sponges. I played the daughter of Richard Boone, a conch fisherman from Key West who competed with the Greeks from Tarpon Springs for sponges. Peter Graves played my boyfriend, whom I run away from to marry Bob Wagner. I was surrounded by all those beautiful men, but I never gave them a second look, because every night Howard's call came right after supper. We would talk for two or three hours, and by then I only had time to learn my lines and go to sleep.

When we finished our locations in Tarpon Springs, we moved to Key West. Summer was closing in, and Key West was so hot and humid I felt as if I were breathing under water.

President Truman gave us his boat, *The Good Will,* to fish from on weekends. It was a welcome change from the smelly sponge boats, but we all still suffered from seasickness. Bob or Amigo or I was always throwing up between scenes. The director would wait for us to finish, and then he'd roll the cameras again. Even today I can't watch *Twelve Mile Reef* without getting nauseous.

Two things happened almost simultaneously. First, the day I had been waiting for over two years arrived: my divorce from Glenn Davis became final and he remarried. The second thing that happened was that the world press carried the story that Robert Wagner and I were engaged to be married.

We were all too engrossed in our moviemaking to see the newspapers, but the phone calls and the telegrams began pouring in. The first ones I received were from my girlfriends Susan Zanuck and Debbie Reynolds. I knew they'd much rather wring my neck, because both of them had a huge crush on R. J. Bob's parents couldn't understand why they were the last to know. Barbara Stanwyck and Howard seemed to be the only two people in the whole world who didn't believe the story.

I had been extremely depressed leaving Howard for such a long location. When he put me on the plane to Florida, he had promised me the sun and moon if I'd marry him as soon as the movie was completed. Now he called me up spewing his anger.

"I should have learned my lesson the first time. Now you've done it to me again. First it was Davis, and now this

260

kid Wagner. You've made me the laughingstock of Holly-wood."

"Please, Howard, stop it," I screamed. "Damn it, just stop it. You know there's nothing between Bob and me. You also know that the press can write whatever they please about someone and there's nothing that can be done about it. Even if they are forced to print a retraction, it wouldn't matter. People have already read it and accepted it as fact. We're all victims of the press. Nobody knows that better than you, Howard."

"You must be carrying on or the press wouldn't have picked up the story. If we were publicly married now, think how embarrassed I'd be with my TWA stockholders. We're just going to have to postpone the wedding until this dies down."

"Howard," I screamed till my throat throbbed. "We're already married."

"I know, I know. Keep your voice down. We just have to put off the public ceremony . . . temporarily. You don't seem to realize what a great source of embarrassment this is for me."

The moment we hung up I called Harry Brand, the head of the publicity department at Fox. He assured me that they had not planted the story but he would check the source and let me know. A few hours later he called back to relay that the story had broken in Chicago—just like the Johnnie Ray story.

My reaction was to immediately tell the press that I planned to marry Howard very soon, while I continued to wonder if Howard would ever let the public know. I became so depressed for the remainder of the movie that I even found it difficult going up and down stairs. The humidity was smothering me and I was drowning in my own tears.

The whole company moved to Nassau to film the underwater sequences. Bob and I did all our own underwater love scenes, some of which required us to hold our breath for nearly two minutes. Our lungs were bursting and our feelings smarting, but somehow we managed to make our kisses look real. In one scene, just as we were about to kiss, a fish swam between our lips. Bob pushed it away and went right on with the kiss. We also filmed scenes in which we had to dive and bring up sponges. When you are at least twelve feet underwater without a face mask, you can barely see your nose, let alone a sponge; but after about twenty misses I made a grab for something and, thank God, it was a sponge.

Being so far away from Howard, I was able to think without being swayed by his influence. Why did he have to hurt me so? Postponing the wedding was like a knife in the back. I often thought that he would take what he knew were innocent situations, such as R. J. and me, and fantasize them so far out of proportion that he would strike out at me. Howard wasn't one to leave himself open for hurt or failure. No one would get the best of *him*. No one ever had. Why couldn't he see that I wasn't trying to?

At that time, more than ever before, I needed some reassurance, proof that he really loved and cared for me. I needed something more than a talk on the phone and an alligator love call. I needed Howard with me so he could hold me and show me, instead of telling me, how real and special our love was.

I called him. "I need you, Howard. Fly down here right now. I need you tonight."

"Well, honey, that's just impossible right now. I can't get away."

"Don't say that, Howard. I need you. You can do anything you want, any time you want. Please fly down here. I can't take it anymore. The shooting is finished tomorrow and we can be together. We can have our wedding. Did you see where I told the paper I choose you over R. J.?"

"I saw it, but, baby, I just can't drop everything and fly off to the Bahamas. I'm in the middle of an important government project that's already behind schedule. We've got a serious situation there in Korea and I can't let our boys down. Please understand. It's not that I don't want to be with you. I'll be at the airport when you come in."

When I hung up from that conversation, I found myself facing all the past scars of our relationship. My uncertainties were snowballing. The lies, the mistrust, the cheating, the mystery of our baby, and now this; it was all there in front of me. The magic of our love was fading, and it was going to take nothing short of a publicized wedding to bring it back to full bloom again.

As he had promised, Howard was waiting for me when we touched down at LAX. I was exhausted from the whole experience; the only feeling I had left was desire. He still looked better than any man on earth to me.

At the airport, he seemed more alive than I had ever seen him. He acted like a young man who had just fallen in love (with someone else, I thought). I was worn out, sea-shaken, sun-beaten, salt-dried, and felt like a dead fish.

"Am I taking you home with me, or are you going with your mother?" he asked.

"I'm going home," I responded.

"Which is . . . ?"

"I'll never live with you a day, a night, an hour, until—"

"Don't start that again," he interrupted. "Tell her, Luella," he said, turning to Mother, "that this time it's not my fault."

Mother looked uneasy. "You two kids work it out. Don't put me in the middle. I can tell you there was no romance between R. J. and Terry, and I was right there all the time, Howard."

"That's what you say, Luella, but the press got a smell of something. Maybe the love scenes were too real."

"Mother, don't even talk to him. Howard, you could have saved yourself a trip, because we're going home in the studio limousine. Let's go, Mom, Please, Mom." I ran off, with my mother following right behind. She knew my mind better than anyone else in the world, and her heart was breaking for me.

The following day, Mother awakened me with her bright

smile, singing "Good morning, merry sunshine" and carrying a glass of fresh-squeezed orange juice. The first thing I did was go straight to the Fox lot to find out what pictures were scheduled. Out of all of them, the only one that had a strong female lead was *King of the Khyber Rifles*. I had to get that picture. Just because Howard wasn't fighting to keep our love alive didn't mean I was giving up. I loved him and wanted him and knew that to keep him I had to stay on top; this picture would keep me up there, and I was determined to land it. Mother thought I should take a breather and not jump right into another production, but I had to. I wanted to be the most desirable woman in the world for Howard. I had to outshine whomever he had found while I was gone.

The film was to star Tyrone Power and Michael Rennie; they wanted an English actress. If I could be mean for Kazan, then, by golly, I could be English for director Henry King. If I could convince the producers, Zanuck and Mr. King, I had it made. I spoke to my agents, and they told me to forget it. Why didn't I try out for the role of a polar bear at Disney? I had a better shot at it. Between that remark and Howard's attitude the night before, I was ready to tackle the universe.

The first thing I did was to introduce myself to Michael Rennie in the commissary. I told him I was testing for *Khyber Rifles,* and I needed an English accent, so would he mind if I hung out with him and his English friends?

Would he mind? I had just introduced myself to the most lecherous man at Twentieth Century-Fox. No, he wouldn't mind. I never even suspected; he looked so properly English.

True to his word, Michael introduced me to the English colony in Hollywood. It was too bad that Laurence Harvey had returned to London, but Robert Newton offered to help, and so did Commander Whitehead of Schweppes. I got free Schweppes for years.

I was now ready to tackle the great Henry King, who had directed such spectacular films as *Nightmare Alley* and

Blood and Sand. Mr. King didn't know it yet but he had given me my first role; I was the little girl he had chosen in 1940 to play Walter Brennan's granddaughter in his movie *Maryland*.

My courage came from my desperation. I went bravely into Henry King's office and used all the pizzazz I had, combined with my most persuasive charm, to try and talk him into giving me a screen test. Stars seldom tested, but I was willing to do somersaults if necessary. He loved my nerve, and then, when we discovered we were both pilots flying out of Clover Field, there was an instant camaraderie. This turned the trick. He agreed to give me the test, but no one was to know. He would use some leftover film so there could only be one take.

I came out of that meeting and went directly to my dressing room. I cried and cried until my whole body relaxed.

True to his word, Henry King snuck me in between some other screen tests, and when the film was run for Zanuck, he jumped out of his chair.

"Send for that English girl. I don't care what she costs. Hire her."

"I already have," Henry King gloated.

All the papers carried the story of how Henry King and I had fooled Darryl Zanuck into giving me the coveted role in the second CinemaScope movie. I was suddenly the most talked about girl in Hollywood. Everything I did made news.

Howard was all over me again now that I was on the rise. Whatever I was doing, it was the correct thing to do. I had my playboy husband panting after me again, and I loved it.

Howard visited me several weekends in Lone Pine, California, where we filmed *Khyber Rifles*. Lone Pine was a town that had two of everything—two cafés, two service stations, two movie houses. I couldn't imagine how Tyrone Power would fit into this locale after his glamorous life. I needn't have worried. Ty was the most adaptable person I'd ever met. He found and gave happiness everywhere.

I'll never forget the first time I met him. It was on location and I was all dressed up in my 1890s costume, waiting to rehearse our first love scene. He arrived, we were introduced, and we began. Well, I was so nervous that first my eye started twitching, then the entire side of my face. I was so embarrassed I wanted to die. But Ty understood and tried to put me at ease. He said he needed to run lines with me, which gave me more time to get used to him. He had always been my favorite star, and I was overwhelmed; actors can also be fans.

Tyrone Power was responsible for *Khyber Rifles* being one of my most treasured experiences. I loved him deeply, but I never fell "in love" with him. We exchanged philosophies, novels, and books of poetry. He became one of my closest friends.

One day Ty said to me, "Terry, you're very special. Wherever I am, I'm always going to be watching you."

I can't tell you how many times I feel he is.

Once, in a conversation with Howard and me, he said, "I've lived such a full and happy life, I wouldn't mind if I died tomorrow. No, that isn't quite true. Before I go, I'd like two things. I'd like to die onstage like my father, and I would love to have a son."

A few years later, at the age of forty-four, Ty died of a heart attack on the set, in a fencing scene. Three months later his wife had a son. His two last wishes came true.

After *Khyber Rifles* Howard dated me like a lovesick teenager whenever he wasn't working. My publicity was increasing daily, and Howard kept saying he'd be free soon for our wedding and a honeymoon.

I received an offer from Johnny Grant to do the USO Christmas tour in Korea. The soldiers had voted me the actress they would most like to meet. This was the highest honor ever paid me. I was so excited at the idea of entertaining our troops that I couldn't wait to call Howard and tell him. He was so red-white-and blue that I thought he would be proud of me for accepting. I remember his reaction.

"Absolutely not. All I need to put me in the grave is knowing you're running around Korea with a million horny soldiers. Christ, why do you have to be such a constant problem to me?"

"I've already told them I'm going," I said.

"Well, if you won't tell them you're not, I'll call them myself and cancel for you."

"You'll do nothing of the kind. In your own words, Howard: 'We've got a serious situation in Korea and I can't let our boys down,'" I laughed. I knew I had him.

Chapter 26

ANOTHER YEAR WAS COMING TO A CLOSE. I WAS ABOUT TO embark upon 1954, the year that I was to receive more publicity than anyone in the world with the exception of Nikita Khrushchev.

Before I was to leave for the USO tour, Twentieth Century-Fox decided to give me a gigantic sendoff for the simultaneous Broadway openings of *Beneath the Twelve Mile Reef* and *King of the Khyber Rifles*. I was to be photographed entering the Roxy Theatre, rushed out the back and into the Criterion, exit, catch a plane to Los Angeles, and hop on another plane to Korea to entertain the troops.

That afternoon I squeezed in a visit to Eddie Fisher on his Coca-Cola television show. Eddie gifted me with a gold-disc bracelet with a sapphire in the center of each record. He promised to call me every day in Korea and sing "Oh, Mein Papa" over the wire.

Later I met Kirk Douglas for cocktails at the Sherry-Netherland Hotel. I hadn't seen him since La Jolla, and I wanted to thank him for the blue roses he had sent me in Germany. He was living in Europe now and had just come in for a few days to see his children. He buoyed me up and wished me luck. Such a nice man!

I was off to the races. Theatre one, flashbulbs and cameras. Theatre two, repeat!

I stopped off in Los Angeles long enough to leave one set of luggage and pick up another and have my tearful farewells with Howard. The big baby . . . ohhh, he was adorable when he wanted to be. There was just nobody like him when he turned on that little-boy charm and that pout that said, "How can you go away and leave me?" Howard drove Mother and me to the airport. Every time there was a delay in leaving I ran back and kissed him good-bye again.

Just as we were leaving there was an SOS from the publicity department: they had received word from the Hollywood Coordinating Committee that I was to leave my ermine bathing suit home. But there was nothing anyone could do because all the luggage was on the plane.

I had lain in bed one night thinking about what I could wear in Korea that would be glamorous and warm at the same time. The Fox wardrobe department had designed a special wardrobe for Susan Zanuck, who was entertaining on the show. I couldn't afford the time for anything like that, so I had to think of something glamorous and clever.

I thought nothing was lovelier than a girl in a bathing suit, but that wouldn't keep me warm in Korea. Then I came up with the idea of an ermine bathing suit because that's what Santa Claus's suit is trimmed with. I added white mittens and a white bonnet all trimmed in ermine tails for warmth and white majorette boots worn over my tights and black fishnet stockings. I looked like a snuggly little bunny in my one-piece suit, which my friend, Edith Head, had designed for me and furrier Merrill Lowell had made.

Before I left, Ailene Mosby, a columnist, interviewed me and asked me what I was going to do on stage.

I told her, "Ailene, the guys in Korea have stated that they're really disgusted that the Hollywood stars and starlets have come to Korea and have appeared onstage in combat clothes. It's a lot of fun for the actresses to dress like soldiers, but the soldiers hate it. I thought it would be great to come out onstage in a GI trench coat and let them all think, 'Ohh, another one.' Then at the appropriate moment, I'll whip off my coat and say, 'This is the new GI underwear.' I'll be wearing my adorable ermine bathing suit, and they'll love it.''

Our DC-7 stopped at Higgam Field in Honolulu. While our plane was still rolling down the runway, I was being paged to the telephone. Naturally, it was Howard. It soon became the favorite joke among our gang; no matter how often or fast we moved, Terry was always paged to the phone. Howard kept better tabs on me in the Far East than he had at home.

At each base, we'd visit the armed forces radio station and give a call to Eddie Fisher, who would sing "Oh, Mein Papa" for me and the troops. The bracelet that Eddie had given me was engraved, "To Mommy from Eddie," after the song.

Johnny Grant was our leader and MC in the Bob Hope style. The cast consisted of Suzie Zanuck, Sheila Connolly, Penny Singleton, and me. Mama Blue was our beloved den mother. She became the first woman to visit the Punch Bowl, and Heartbreak Ridge, where some of our bloodiest battles of the Korean War were fought, escorted by none other than General Harvey Fischer.

Johnny opened the show and I closed it. I'd come onstage, and Johnny would greet me with a line like: "I like the sweater you're almost wearing."

Then Johnny would choose the shyest guy in the audience and bring him onstage. Before thousands of his buddies, I would sing and flirt, "Gimme a Little Kiss." At the finish, I would plant a big kiss on him, sometimes lasting two minutes, while every guy out front screamed and snapped pictures. In fact, they started hollering from the first "Gimme," which was extremely lucky since I'm tone-deaf.

Even today, when I'm traveling anywhere in the world, someone will come up to me and say, "Remember me? I'm the boy you kissed in Korea.'' Their picture with me kissing them always ended up in their hometown paper. I loved each and every one of them.

I spent all my free time dancing with the soldiers in the Noncommissioned Officers Club until I dropped with exhaustion. Howard's call usually came while I was at the club, and I'm sure he wondered why I was always out of breath. Those boys sure could dance, and I was trying to keep up with every one of them.

The first few shows came off as planned with me wearing my white felt skirt appliquéd with Christmas trees and my fur-trimmed cashmere sweater. But the boys had read that I was coming to Korea with a fur bathing suit, and everywhere I went they had huge canvas pipes pumping in hot air backstage. They were so disappointed that I wasn't wearing the suit that finally I couldn't take it anymore. I went ahead and wore it, disobeying the Hollywood Coordinating Committee, whoever they were.

I walked out on that stage in my trench coat to a lot of boos. When I whipped it off, ten thousand men stood up and cheered and went crazy. I think that was the moment we began to win the war. *Stars and Stripes* said I was the biggest boost the army ever had.

The word was out and our show was a smash sensation wherever we went. Boys waited in the snow for eight hours to see our show and hot air blew out from every stage. In fact, it was so warm onstage, in that 40-degree-below weather, that the other performers were perspiring.

Suddenly, word came that I was to be shipped stateside. The Hollywood Coordinating Committee was demanding the armed forces send me home immediately: Ailene Mosby had printed a story that I was wearing a mink bikini and doing a striptease.

I was crushed. My bathing suit wasn't even that revealing.

When Howard called me, I was distressed at a tinge of humor in his voice.

"You've really got yourself in a mess this time," he said.

271

"Every paper in the world is running your striptease front page. You've got the studio going crazy. I just talked to Darryl, and he's mad as hell. You'll be lucky if you ever get a good role from him again. He called it a major public disgrace for Twentieth Century-Fox. I told you that you shouldn't go over there. I think you ask for trouble."

I exploded—slightly. "Howard, it was nothing. It's all a lie. I'm just sick over it. How did it get so big? I don't want to be sent home. I haven't done anything wrong. I haven't. It's not fair."

"Well, whether or not there is any substance to it, it's made actress Terry Moore a household word. We should be able to capitalize on it somehow."

During the next few days, riots broke out in Korea. Men risked their stripes by broadcasting and printing demands that I be allowed to stay. GIs marched, carrying me on their shoulders, crying, "If we're old enough to fight, we're old enough to see a girl in a fur bathing suit."

The press had a field day. Headlines blared, "Terry Moore Kicked Out of Korea." I became known as the second front and pushed every war headline off the front pages.

My fellow performers were ordered to proceed to Seoul without me. There were a lot of tearful farewells when they flew on at my insistence and left Mother and me behind.

While the whole American army rallied behind me, friends were deserting me back home. Eddie Fisher's calls, which had been coming daily, stopped. His manager, Milton Blackstone, felt I was now the wrong image for his boy, the king of Coca-Cola and the goodie-goodie boy of the teen set.

Debbie Reynolds went on record by telling the press that she felt it was terrible that I was using the boys in Korea for publicity. I didn't believe it until Tab Hunter said he was there when she said it. Something like that coming from a friend hurt me deeply.

I was in very low spirits, and so was Mother. We were both wondering if Howard didn't have his hands somewhere in this international episode; he was enjoying it much too much. He said, "Baby, you're right where Marilyn Monroe was a year ago. All you have to do is march down the aisle."

Just when we thought we couldn't endure any more, some boys stormed into our barracks with the great news that our demands had been granted. They had fought tooth and nail for me and we were allowed to continue with the show and stay in Korea for the remainder of the tour.

Mom and I forgot all of our troubles. We hugged each other and jumped up and down jubilantly. The boys hoisted us on their shoulders and carried us around; everybody was kissing one another. We had won our war.

Mom and I were flown to catch up with our troops. She was a great sport because the pilot was doing aerobatics all the way in celebration of our victory.

When I walked backstage at the next show I could hear Suzie Zanuck, who had become my best friend, saying during her introduction, "This is for you, Terry, wherever you are. I know it's your favorite: 'Won't You Come Home Bill Bailey'?"

At that moment I walked onstage. Out front it sounded like VJ Day. The applause crescendoed while we hugged and cried. It was one of the most wonderfully emotional events in my life.

I must give special thanks to Private Butterworth, who wrote for *Stars and Stripes* and lost his stripes to keep me in Korea. He went to the chaplains, the priests and rabbis, and got signed statements that my fur bathing suit was decent enough to wear in church. Alan English worked overtime sending messages worldwide over the airwaves. They were all there fighting to keep our spirits up as we tried to raise theirs.

Part of our tour was spent visiting army hospitals. The sight of young men without arms and legs made me realize the importance of our mission. Many men placed my picture beside them during their amputations. When I came home I wrote a poem, "The Medal of Honor," and

273

dedicated it to them. It was my way of exclaiming, "War is hell."

The Medal of Honor

Dear Uncle Sam,
Give me back my daddy. Mommy says he's gone to war.
Where is war? Why don't his letters come no more?
Why does Mommy cry and hold me tight
When I say my prayers at night?
Please, God, help Mommy get rid of her fears.
The little spots on this paper are tears.
I asked God to take care of Daddy
And bring him home to me,
Cuz I wanna hug and love and kiss him,
And ride horsey on his knee.
Everyone says he's a hero, my dad,
So why is Mommy always actin' so sad?
And Grammy says when everything's settled,
The president's gonna give my dad a medal.
We're having a big party,
With lotsa flowers and grown-ups and girls and boys.
My daddy wouldn't miss it,
Cuz he loves to take pictures and play with my toys.
And there's a big long box in our livin' room
That's come from overseas,
So hurry on home and open it, please, Daddy, please.
I love you,
Lisa.

While I was in Korea I fell in love with a wonderful orphaned child. The Tenth Corps had taken a little seven-year-old Korean boy under their wing and let him live and work at the noncom club. They called him Chisai, which means "little" in Japanese. I became so attached to this adorable little boy that I didn't want to see him have to stay in that war-torn country and decided I would not be happy until I was certain he was afforded the best life possible. I thought it would be great if Howard and I adopted him and gave him a beautiful new life in America. When I excitedly called Howard with my idea, he surprised me. He didn't say we would do it, but he didn't say we wouldn't either. He just said that we would check into it as soon as I got home.

It was back to Honolulu from Korea for rest and recreation. Not long after we were there, the front pages were carrying pictures of me surfing on the shoulders of a handsome bronzed beach boy. That did it. Howard didn't appreciate my competence as a surfer or the fun I was having. He wanted me home badly; it aggravated him terribly to read about me every day and not be with me. I was having loads of fun playing in the islands, and I enjoyed making him wait a few extra days, until Howard phoned me with some wonderful news. He said that he'd checked things out and it was possible to have Chisai sent to us in the U.S. as soon as we were married again. We would be responsible for giving the child a stable environment and a good education. He closed by saying he'd arranged for me to be brought home right away. He wasn't kidding. The air force was at my side in a matter of minutes. They tucked me under their protective wing, thanks to Howard, and flew me home, pronto.

I was happy to be home once I got there. I wrote to Chisai in his language, GI prose, and told him of Howard's and my intentions. He wrote back, and our correspondence continued on a regular basis.

There was a Sergeant Albert Truman White with Tenth Corps who was especially fond of Chisai. He and his wife were unable to have children of their own and they wanted to adopt Chisai very much. Howard and I conceded to these lovely people. Chisai grew up happy and healthy in the U.S.A.; his name is now Link White. After the death of his American parents, we renewed our communications, and I've become a sort of mother to him.

I get a chill when I think about how much good can come out of people during something as horrible as a war. It even affected Howard.

Chapter 27

HOWARD WAS THERE TO MEET US WHEN WE TOUCHED down in Los Angeles.

"Hello, Miss Famous," he said. "Every newspaper and magazine in the United States is blazing your name or picture. You're receiving more publicity than any other woman in the world. Bob Hope and every other comedian are cracking jokes about it or wearing an ermine bathing suit in their act. How can one little girl cause so much commotion?"

"Oh, Howard, we had no idea. We haven't even seen a newspaper since we left three weeks ago. Is it good or bad?"

"Bad? I just wish to hell I'd thought it up. I spent millions getting Russell out front, and you don't even have a PR man," he said.

"Are you sure it's good?" Mom asked uneasily.

"Come on back to the bungalow and I'll show you. I had Carl Byoir send over some of your clippings today. You've had headlines across the nation for nearly two weeks. *Time* magazine called Zanuck and wants to do a cover story on you. You're already slated for stories in *Life, Cosmopolitan* and *Redbook*."

"All I'm interested in knowing is what my next picture is going to be. All my films are in release now," I reminded him.

"Let's get the hell out of here before someone takes my picture." He laughed good naturedly. "I guess you're going to your mother's house until we're married, huh?"

I nodded my head affirmatively.

"I thought so. Well, we might just be doing that sooner than you think."

I couldn't resist giving him a big hug and kiss right on the spot. After he embarrassedly pushed me away, we followed him to his car; he had special permission to drive right up to the plane. He told Mother and me to duck down as we sped past the gate and the waiting photographers.

My phone never stopped ringing from the newspapers and periodicals wanting interviews and pictures. I couldn't go anywhere I wasn't recognized. Every public relations firm and agent wanted me to go out with its clients. Hugh O'Brian and Tony Curtis called for dates. Tony was so gorgeous and sexy I just couldn't turn him down. We were halfway to a local movie theater when I spotted one of Howard's detectives following us. I made some excuse to Tony and had him turn around and take me right back home. He never asked me out again, and I don't blame him. He must have thought me completely mad. It was just that I loved Howard so much I didn't want another Wagner situation to spoil our wedding this time. Howard never made mention of the incident, but he did strike back by mentioning that he had seen Susan Hayward on several occasions while I was fooling around with the boys in Korea. He also threw up all the Eddie Fisher phone calls to me.

Later, when I was at the Beverly Hills Hotel, Rex, the maître d' of the Polo Lounge, informed me that Howard's first New Year's without me had been a jolly one. Evidently, he had three dates for dinner: Susan Hayward in one dining room, Jean Peters in another, and a young starlet named Merry Anderson in the Polo Lounge. Howard was jumping from room to room until Susan caught on. Her temper flared as hot as her bright red hair and she walked out on him. Susan had discovered Jean; Jean and Merry were completely in the dark, and I unfortunately learned of all three of them.

Naturally, I was hurt when Howard said he had seen Susan while I was gone, but I knew it could never become serious. Howard's only interest was her big-star status, and he had to add her to his list of superstars who desired him. I knew he could never take her to bed, because she had children. Like capped teeth or nose jobs, the marks of having carried and delivered children were something unacceptable, and Susan had given birth to twins. I seem to have been the exception, perhaps since it was Howard's child and I never showed any of the physical signs of giving birth because our baby had been so premature.

Jean's being there didn't bother me much either, because I knew their relationship had grown platonic and they hadn't had sex together for years.

I knew that Merry Anderson was finished too, when Rex said she lost a cap off a front tooth during dinner. Howard had Rex send her home in the hotel limousine.

Howard's boasts of his amorous exploits didn't work this time; I got the story in full detail before his innuendoes could gnaw at me. Howard was often amazed at my great ability for acquiring information and thought my network was better than his. He never caught on that I was using both his sources and mine.

Upon my return from Korea, I noticed that Howard was becoming increasingly preoccupied with the idea of his medical institute. He would mention how much needless suffering there was and sit staring into space for hours at a time. I couldn't help thinking that much of the suffering he referred to was his own. His five airplane crashes had to have caused considerable damage, and I could often sense him hiding his pain from me.

278

I was happy for myself and for Howard when on January 10, 1954, he released to the press the news that he was going to "provide millions of dollars for medical research to combat disease and human suffering." Howard's dream of twenty-five years was finally being realized. I felt it was my dream too, because it was the year we married on the boat that he decided to make the center a reality in his lifetime.

I wanted the world to know the warm, concerned, loving Howard. I was proud to be his wife and I wanted the world to know that, too. I tried to pin down Howard to a specific date for our public wedding; he said that would be impossible but he promised it would be soon.

One evening Howard took me out with Jack Fry, the former head of TWA, and his wife, Helen Vanderbilt. We planned a summer wedding at the Frys' ranch in Tucson, Arizona, and Howard flew us all to Las Vegas to celebrate. We went to a typical Vegas show. When the lights began to fade, the drums rolled, the curtains opened, and fifty gorgeous girls danced out, all of them wearing mink bikinis! I later learned that that part of the act was put in at Howard's suggestion.

Invitations for personal appearances were coming at me from all directions, but since Fox still didn't have a movie ready for me, I decided to go to the Argentina Film Festival. I also had an offer to headline the Flamingo Hotel in Las Vegas for an astronomical salary. Howard ignored the Vegas offer until I mentioned the film festival.

"How can you go off for another vacation when you just had one? How can you possibly leave when you've been offered this opportunity in Las Vegas? If you want a career, then you'd better settle down. You could give all that money to your parents. How selfish can you be?" On and on he preached until my head hung in shame.

Happily I remembered, "But, Howard, I can't sing and I haven't an act so how can I possibly play Vegas?"

"Look, if you stay here, I'll give you one of the greatest songwriters of all time, Mack Gordon. He's second in

279

ASCAP to Irving Berlin. I'll have him write original songs for you. I'll give you Bob Sydney [the famous choreographer] to stage your act. He's just finished the Debbie Reynolds picture, so he's still under contract to me. I'll have Michael Woolf design the most fantastic wardrobe ever seen in Las Vegas, and the RKO wardrobe department will make it.''

"But, Howard, I can't sing!"

"Yeah, but who's going to be listening? The men will be too busy looking at your body, and the women wouldn't like you if you could sing. Who the hell's going to know the difference? All your songs will be original, so if you go off key, the orchestra goes off key!"

Howard threw back his head in laughter. He thought this a great joke and besides, he had won the argument. I was going to Las Vegas.

Howard knew each person's Achilles' heel and used it to get his own way, regardless of time, effort, or cost. Unfortunately for him, I was his best student and was daily gaining on him.

One reason I secretly wanted to do the Vegas stint was revenge. One evening in New York, Eddie Fisher and I were riding in his limousine. He turned to me and said, "Sing something."

I told him I couldn't sing.

"Of course you can. Everyone can sing."

He sounded so encouraging that I felt momentary confidence and I belted out a few notes. Much to my surprise I thought I sounded pretty good.

Eddie laughed. He laughed! "Well, *almost* everyone. You have the *worst* voice I've ever heard."

His words stung, and I was determined he would eat them. Anyone who tells me I can't do something fires me to prove otherwise. Yes, I would show Eddie Fisher.

Mitzi Gaynor and Debbie Reynolds, who at that point hadn't yet gathered the nerve to try Vegas, felt that if I could do it anyone could. They later hired all the same people I had used, and Fun City has been graced with their talents ever since.

Five days a week for the next five months, I reported to a soundstage at Goldwyn Studios and was put through an eight-hour commando course. I was worked out, stretched out, was thrown through dancers' legs and over their heads, only to be caught at the last minute.

I had still been trying to tie Howard down to a specific date for our public wedding. I had to make my plans. One day Howard came to me with a suprise that quelled my insistence.

"We're going to be able to have the wedding sooner than I thought. I've finally got Jean taken care of. She's to be married at the end of May."

"Who is it Howard? Who's Jean marrying?"

"I've had the boy checked out thoroughly and he seems like a decent fellow. His name is Stuart Cramer. He comes from a well-respected family in North Carolina and he was an outstanding Marine ROTC student in college. The CIA selected him for duty in Korea and Istanbul. Jean's been in Europe shooting *Three Coins in a Fountain* and she met him on a plane coming home from Italy."

"It wasn't a TWA plane by any chance, was it, Howard?" I asked sarcastically.

"What is that supposed to mean?" he snapped.

"Nothing, dear. I just thought that maybe that's why you knew. Where will they be living?" I asked innocently.

"Washington, D. C.," he said gruffly.

"Where will we be living, Howard?"

"What do you mean?" he asked quickly.

"Well, Jean's taken care of. We can get married right away now."

"We'll live on the ranch like I said before, but you concentrate on your Las Vegas show. That's more important now. The wedding will come after that."

During my workouts for the show, Howard was always lurking somewhere in the background making note of my progress. One of my lead dancers, Tommy Mahoney, spotted Howard and said, "Does that man leering at you over there make you nervous? I'll throw him out if you like."

"Oh, no," I quickly lied. "He's some big shot with the press." That seemed to satisfy Tommy.

Sometimes Tommy would work me so hard that I'd ask him to let up for a few minutes. Then I'd throw myself on the floor and cry my heart out, assuring everyone beforehand not to worry, I wasn't unhappy; I just needed to release my exhaustion and tensions. Afterward, I'd jump up, and sing out, "Okay, you pikers, let's get back to work."

I found an eighteen-year-old pianist for rehearsals named Eddie Samuels. Later Eddie Fisher met him at my home and hired Samuels as his pianist; he was with him for many years. I also talked Howard into hiring a talented young musician named Jimmie Haskell to do my arrangements. It was the beginning of his illustrious career.

One afternoon after rehearsals, I stopped by my agent's office. He wasn't in, but there was a young boy sleeping on the window seat. I walked over and ever so lightly tickled his nose with the Venetian blind cord. The next thing I knew, I had been tackled and was rolling over and over on the floor with this exuberant youth.

Introductions seemed superfluous, but he pulled me to my feet and said, "Hi. I already know who you are. Elia Kazan told me all about you. I'm James Dean. That may not mean nothin' to you now, but wait, it will! I just finished a picture for Kazan called *East of Eden*.

Jimmy already seemed to sense his destiny while he hurried toward his untimely death. He had to do everything in the now. Heaven could wait. Only it didn't.

He had a devastating smile and a perky nose. His eyes, which peered out from behind thick glasses, sparkled when he laughed. In person, his head appeared a little too large for his body and was emphasized by his springy hair that waved in all directions. His clothes were unkempt, and he wore his scarred motorcycle boots with everything, even with his dark blue suit when he followed me to Sunday school.

I was eating dinner with my parents at their home that evening, as Howard was in Las Vegas, and asked this uncourtly waif to come along. He certainly wasn't the type my parents were used to seeing me bring home.

When I walked in the front door, I said, "Hi, Mom. Look what I found under a rock."

I think she believed me.

My father, who was always dignified and had great strength and patience, never recovered from the shock of watching Jimmy unzip his pants and let out a belch after dinner. I think that if my father hadn't been so stunned, he'd have thrown him out the window.

When I told Howard about the incident, he said, "That will teach you to take strays home with you."

As I came to know Jimmy better, I believed that his mannerisms were premeditated. In his eyes Brando was king, and Jimmy was out to steal his thunder. I think his behavior was an act, because he came from a very nice family in Indiana.

One day he asked me, "Have you ever met Marlon?"

I told him I'd seen him on two occasions and we had nodded at each other. Jimmy thought that was great and proceeded to tell me with great reverence about his one and only encounter with Brando.

"I was standing outside the Actors Studio and Marlon was just starting up his bike. He saw me starin' at him. He looked up at me from the curbside and he waved before he went speeding off. He never said nothin'; he just waved." That chance meeting burned forever in Jimmy's mind. Jimmy always felt there was a message and understanding in Marlon's look.

Jimmy went everywhere with me. Most of my life I've always had a shadow, a playmate, somebody who will go along with me to my lessons, my appointments, whatever I have to do. Not a romantic figure, just a buddy.

Howard met Jimmy and gave his okay for him to take me to a premiere of *The Red Garter*. The photographers were snapping our picture and asking a little disdainfully, "Who's that guy with you?" In fact, they kept trying to edge him out of the photos. I held him all the tighter. Jimmy was solemn in an almost defiant way. It was as if he were saying, "Just you wait. I'll be the greatest."

How well he knew. Less than a year later he was one of the biggest stars in Hollywood.

Daddy was so embarrassed when he went to his office. Everyone asked who the creep was with his daughter at the televised premiere. No one remembered a year later that "the creep" was superstar James Dean. The photographers who were breaking his door down later didn't remember either. When you're poor, you're a creep. When you're rich, you're eccentric.

When Jimmy met my favorite speech coach, Marie Stoddard, he cried with delight. "This is what I've been searching for." He made an appointment for himself the following day.

Marie loved telling the story of his first lesson. He arrived with a seedy-looking piano player. They both slumped down in their chairs.

Jimmy decided he would shock little old Marie. "Don't give me any of this shit that I remind you of Marlon Brando."

Marie pushed her glasses down on her nose, looked at him long and steadily, and said, "That's just what it is. Shit . . . *Shit!* And you're all wallowing in it."

Marie would laugh and tell how both those youngsters slowly starting easing up in their chairs until they grew taller and taller and were sitting at rapt attention. "Imagine those two whippersnappers thinking they could shock these old bones."

Jimmy started coming to the workouts at Goldwyn Studios with me. He loved to do the ballet stretches and barre work. He would sing along with me at the piano trying to help me stay on key.

Later, when he fell in love with Pier Angeli, we drifted apart. I became close with Pier shortly before she died, and most of our conversations were about Jimmy. She still loved him very much, and she told me that she had always regretted not marrying him. Her parents had encouraged her to marry Vic Damone because he was Italian and Catholic. Jimmy had stood across the street from the church and cried when she was married.

Howard flew Mother and me to San Diego, where I was going to try out my act at Topps before tackling Vegas. The rest of my troupe drove down or came on the airlines. Howard never understood why I didn't want them flying down with us, but I just couldn't let Tommy know that the man he'd seen leering in the background at the soundstage was Howard. He eventually found out when he saw the same man leering in the back of Topps and later at the Flamingo, but he never said another word.

Howard was my best critic; he loved the show and so did the audience. Mother cried as the audience brought me back for curtain call after curtain call. They yelled, "More! More!" but I couldn't give them any more. I had just sung them my entire repertoire so I did a scene from *Sheba*. That went over so well I left it in my act.

After San Diego, we were back home for a week before going to Vegas. Jimmie Haskell polished his arrangements while we were in San Diego and then his work was done. When he asked about being paid, he was given a Romaine Street address. The whole thing looked suspicious to him. He thought it was a very peculiar way to be collecting pay, but he was a newcomer to the Howard Hughes way.

Jimmie dubiously entered an unmarked door on the side of the Romaine Street building to find himself at the bottom of a steep dark stairwell. He climbed slowly and nervously up the stairs; at the top of the stairs was an old desk, and behind the desk sat a tall, impassive man (probably Bill Gay). When Jimmie told the man behind the desk who he was and why he had come, a drawer was opened, a large stack of cash was removed, and the bills were counted out.

When Jimmie asked if he had to sign anything for the money, his only reply was a slow, silent shake of the head.

As Jimmie headed back down the stairs toward the street, he felt as though he might be mugged at any second. He was carrying an enormous amount of cash; he had never seen or carried such a large amount before. Jimmie's knees were shaking as he left the building, and he didn't feel safe until the money had been deposited in the bank.

True to his word, Howard designed the sexiest dress ever seen in the showrooms. He wouldn't let me see it until the day we left for Vegas. It had taken thirteen women twenty-six days to appliqué the bugle beads. The dress appeared to be black, but every other bead was a steel gray which gave it an unearthly shimmer. The top was nude soufflé with a few beads strategically sprinkled over the bosom. From the stage and in photographs, which were retouched, you couldn't see the soufflé, so I appeared to be nude from the waist up.

I wore the gown opening night to please Howard; he mischievously sat back and glowed over the furor his dress caused. I was too embarrassed, after seeing the opening-night photographic coverage, to wear it again. It even appeared in the first issue of *Playboy* magazine. Later I had the top filled in solidly with beads, but Howard thought it was an insult to him that I wouldn't wear the dress he had so painstakingly designed for his big night.

After that first night, my act was so pert and clean that it was one of the few shows on the strip which parents could bring their children to see. I'm still delighted when I read *Variety*'s review of the show:

> Mack Gordon's original material is marvelous, but it doesn't give Miss Moore near enough chance to show off her lovely voice. This writer had no idea she was such an accomplished dancer. 20th is making a big mistake if they don't

make la Moore into their next musical star.

Determination and an uncomplimentary remark can often
make an ordinary gal succeed. The papers carried the story
that Marilyn Monroe had refused to do the musical *Pink
Tights* at Fox but that Frank Sinatra would prefer to do it
with Terry Moore anyway. The only night my determination almost failed me and I thought I might faint away with
stage fright was the night the boys came backstage and told
me Frank Sinatra was front row center. Somehow I managed to fool him too.

Howard kept a suite at the Flamingo for the duration of
the show. At first we thought we were going to be able to
spend a lot of time together, but by the time I finished my
third show it was 2:00 A.M. and the only show that stayed
open until the wee hours of the morning was the strip show
at the Silver Slipper casino, starring Sally Rand and a
couple of burlesque comics. It reminded me of the burlesque houses we had visited in the old part of downtown
Los Angeles while Howard was preparing me for his RKO
movie *High Heels*.

Sally Rand was around sixty then and still doing her
famous nude fan dance. The lights were low and she was so
clever with the fans that she continued that act until the day
she died. I felt I couldn't stand to see that show one more
time, but Howard guffawed over and over at the corny old
burlesque jokes. It was always the same, but he laughed as
heartily the last time as the first. I wasn't at all surprised
when later he purchased the Silver Slipper along with his
many other Las Vegas holdings.

Nicky Hilton seemed to always know the nights Howard
wouldn't be in Vegas and would come to my show, as did
Miguelito Alemán, the son of the president of Mexico. The
three-week run brought droves of friends and a constant
flow of suitors.

One night during a backstage party, I was surrounded by
a dozen handsome men. In the midst of all the commotion I

was handed an envelope; I automatically opened it expecting more goodwill and praise for my performance. To my surprise, it was a bill for my costumes coming to a total of fifteen thousand dollars.

The bill was from Howard. I wonder if he was punishing me in a jealous rage, or if that was just an effective reminder that he had played a large part in the success of the show. I don't think he expected me to pay the debt with money, but I was angry and proud; so I wrote out a check and marked the bill Paid in Full. He accepted the check and cashed it; I still have the canceled check.

I don't think I ever believed Howard would cash my check, but my father knew he would.

Daddy said, "Helen, you never wanted to do a nightclub act in the first place. Howard conned you into doing it by making all his big promises that he'd take care of everything. Let him! You fulfilled your part of the bargain."

"No, Daddy. If he cashes that check, then it's over."

"Hmph! How many times have your mother and I heard that before? You must be a masochist. What does it take for you to learn?"

"Money's not the issue here. You just don't understand because you've never been in love," I blurted out.

"Where do you get away with saying a thing like that?" Father snapped back angrily. "Your mother and I love each other very much. Twenty-six years together proves that."

"Never been in love? That's a terrible thing to say," Mother interjected.

"No, it's not," I said. "Oh, I know you love each other, but you've never been in love, so you can't understand." I ran to my room crying and threw myself on my bed. I had to give Howard the check; I wanted him to know that I cared nothing about his money, only about him. "The hell with him," I sobbed. "If he wants to take my money, let him. I'm young and talented. I can make more. I'll show you, Howard Hughes." I showed him all right. As I think back, I wonder how I could have ever been so dumb.

288

Chapter 28

My Vegas act closed on July 28. I was halfway through 1954, and financially I was just breaking even. The check I gave Howard represented all the profit I had made in Las Vegas after paying my company. Putting a new act together is extremely costly; you don't start making money unless you continue doing a show and playing the circuit. I had offers from the Chez Paree in Chicago, the top hotels in Florida, and the Copa in New York; but my nightclub act had been strictly geared for Las Vegas; so I couldn't continue unless I had new songs. I hated the saloon life anyway, and with Howard not allowing me to make any profit after six months of grueling, tortuous work, I decided to put an end to my nightclub career. I had already forgotten what I was trying to prove. Fox, still punishing me for the Korean debacle, hadn't come up with a picture for me.

I have always felt a terrible sense of guilt if I turned down work that was offered to me. So when the Drury Lane Theatre, outside of Chicago, asked me to do the play *Strictly Dishonorable*, I quickly accepted. I was furious at the way Howard had behaved and I wanted to be too busy to think about him. Learning and rehearsing a play in a week didn't leave much time for anxieties, and Heaven knows I was besieged by them.

I hadn't seen Howard since I wrote him the check for my costumes, but, as always, he knew my every step; he showed up while I was getting ready to leave for Chicago. I packed my bags as Howard begged me not to leave and tried to stuff a large stack of hundred-dollar bills in my hand.

"Keep it," I cried. "Believe me, you need it a lot more than I do. Someday, someday, you're going to be so sorry, Howard."

"I'm sorry already, baby," he replied.

"Oh, no you're not, but you will be. Just you wait."

Mother and I considered flying Pan American to Chicago, but TWA was free for us, so we boarded one of Howard's planes with the script for *Strictly Dishonorable,* under my arm.

We were met at the airport by Tony DeSantis, the theater owner and producer, and Paul Crabtree, the director. At the same time I was being paged to the phone. I started shaking all over as I put the receiver to my ear. What did Howard want now?

"Hello, baby," I said.

"This isn't baby, but I wish it were," a voice said. "This is Mr. Simmons from TWA. Mr. Hughes asked me to pick you and your mother up personally at the airport and take you to your hotel. However, with the rush hour, I'm going to be about fifteen minutes late."

"Thank you, Mr. Simmons." The disappointment and letdown were clearly evident in my voice. "But the theater has sent a limousine."

"But my orders are to—"

"I know," I interrupted. "But suppose I thank Mr. Hughes and tell him the car delivered me to the Ambassador East Hotel. That way, we haven't lied and you're off the hook."

Mr. Simmons thanked me profusely. I was about to hang up when the operator told me she had another call waiting.

"Put it through," I replied.

Howard came on the line bright and cheerful, "Honey, my top man is waiting for you there at the airport."

"Yes, Howard, the car is here and we're leaving for the hotel now," I said.

"Now, don't you and your mother take him gallivantin' all around. I want you to go directly to the hotel. He has orders to take you both to the Pump Room for dinner." He laughed warmly. "You'll like that because they serve everything on a flaming sword. It looks nice and it doesn't hurt the food too much."

Mother was motioning for me to hurry, but I thought I heard a weak alligator love call as I hung up.

"Don't tell me who it was," Mother said. "I can tell by the smile on your face. Honestly, Terry, that man can change your whole personality with just one phone call."

Looking back, I see how right Mother was. Howard *could* change my personality, but the intensity of my love for him could alter his personality, too, for better or for worse.

From the beginning of our relationship my strengths and weaknesses paralleled Howard's; we were engaged in a constant tug-of-war. Each of us protected ourselves from hurt by never trusting the other completely, but we suffered the repetitious hurt of mistrust. Each time he hurt me I could feel myself growing farther away from him. Each time I hurt him I could see it wearing on him physically.

Tony DeSantis and Paul Crabtree had met me at the airport because they wanted to change my mind about doing the play we had agreed upon. *Strictly Dishonorable* is a very innocently sweet play by Preston Sturges about the fortunes of a Mississippi girl who has a quarrel with her fiancé in an Italian speakeasy. She meets an opera singer who has an apartment upstairs and eagerly accepts an invitation to share his apartment for the night even though her host says his intentions are "strictly dishonorable." He does not seduce her, though; her childlike innocence both exasperates and fascinates him so much that he proposes to her. Her fiancé shows up and she has to choose between the two men.

Tony and Paul tactfully told me that this was the Bible Belt and they felt that after all the hoopla over the ermine swim suit that Terry Moore in *Strictly Dishonorable* might give the impression that it was a dirty play. They had done *The Little Hut*, which had sexual overtones, and it had bombed; they didn't want to repeat their mistake. After a great deal of persuasion, and a promise to pay for all our meals, I agreed to do *A Story for a Sunday Evening*, a boring play written and directed by Paul Crabtree. It had already failed on Broadway and everywhere else, but I didn't know that at the time. However, my notoriety, and the curiosity over the Korean affair, brought forth the audiences.

Howard called and said he was going to fly in, but I begged him to wait until after our opening. I had more lines to learn than in *Hamlet* and only six days to do it.

One night the theater arranged a publicity date with Jack Webb, who topped the TV ratings with his show "Dragnet." He sent a limousine to the theater to pick me up after rehearsals and we had a lavish dinner at the Pump Room. Jack was bright, handsome, and fun to be with; we had a fantastic evening, but unfortunately it hit all the papers. Howard was on the long-distance phone immediately telling me that Jack was a pseudo intellectual and a bore. When that didn't make an impression on me because I knew otherwise, he told me that Webb got his kicks out of tying up little girls. By now I knew enough not to believe him.

The play opened August 18, 1954, to a polite audience who seemed to find it amusing. Overall, the reviews of the play were poor, but I was relieved they were kind to me. The *Chicago Sun-Times* called me "the tastiest ingredient, managing to instill warmth, emotion and a pert charm into a rather thankless role." When I finished my week in Chicago, we packed up the play and moved to the Lakewood Playhouse in Barnesville, Pennsylvania.

Howard called me at the theater one night and told me he was flying to Florida to check out a possible site for his medical institute. He wanted to schedule his flight so he could stop in Pennsylvania and fly me to my next engagement in Fall River, Massachusetts. This was hurricane season, and two of the most devastating storms to ever come along, Carol and Edna, were wreaking havoc all through the southern and eastern states.

The night came for Howard to pick up Mother and me. It was at the peak of the hurricanes, and the flight conditions were treacherous. The airport did not have Civil Aeronautics Authority's approval to keep the lights on after dark, but, of course, Howard managed it. Even with Howard's flight expertise, however, he couldn't manage to land in these savage conditions; in fact, he just barely managed to make it to Florida.

There was another plane up there that night, a lost naval plane; piloted by Ensign J. G. Morse with a crew of three, it had been forced off course and desperately lost. They were out of fuel and had made their peace with God when, miraculously, Howard's lights appeared in the tempestuous night and guided them safely back down to Mother Earth.

The following day, Howard arranged a special flight to take Mother and me to the Somerset Playhouse in Fall River, Massachusetts. I took a week off to rehearse *Strictly Dishonorable,* the play I had originally planned to do.

During this time Howard remained Old Faithful on the phone, checking on me day and night. His calls were so frequent during rehearsals that the little boy whose job it was to raise the curtain asked the producer, "Will Miss Moore be taking phone calls during the performances?"

Though he had been faithful on the phone, a question arose as to how faithful he was with his time. In Earl Wilson's column out of New York, my photograph was featured as starring at the Somerset in *Strictly Dishonorable,* but the headline of the column was Howard's. It read: "Hughes Is on a Boat, Ava Reported on Deck."

I almost had a heart attack.

The article that followed said, "Howard Hughes is skippering a big chartered boat down around Miami and Havana and Ava Gardner's friends say she's often his first mate."

I was fuming with anger. Secret agent Howard had slipped up this time, ending up in the same gossip column as me without being mentioned with me. At the time I saw it as a blatant case of Howard having a final fling before the whole world would hear about our up-and-coming public wedding. I was jealous, but not as much as I would have been if I had known Howard had Jean Peters down there too. It seems that her marriage hadn't been so successful and she was already back on Howard's hands.

My information concerning Howard's activities while I was doing summer stock in 1954 comes from Glen Brewer, a handsome and faithful Mormon secretary who worked for Howard from 1950 to 1956. Glen was a go-between for certain of Howard's movie-star girlfriends like Jean Peters, Ava Gardner, and Susan Hayward, though not for me.

While I had been doing my nightclub act in Vegas, Howard had stashed both Jean and Ava in Lake Tahoe, Nevada. Jean was in a Glen Cove cottage and Ava was in a house on the lake less than two miles away. Both were there for their six-week waiting period in order to obtain Nevada divorces; Ava was divorcing Frank Sinatra, and Jean was divorcing Stuart Warren Cramer III, whom I later married on June 28, 1959. Stuart's divorce from Jean had been finalized in 1957. Stuart and I joked that he, Howard, and I had all had our Jeans/Genes.

Stuart and I were married for twelve years, and I had the children I yearned for: two beautiful sons, Stuart Warren Cramer IV, who was born in 1960, and Grant Lamar Cramer, who was born in 1961. We were divorced in 1971.

Glen's job was to baby-sit Jean during the day and Ava at night. He would arrive at Jean's house about noon and play cards with her; then around 5:00 P.M. he would take Jean and her mother or girlfriend to dinner. Around seven in the evening he'd hurry over to Ava's house and she'd fix dinner and then he'd take her out gambling.

Howard visited the girls only twice during their six-week stay, so Ava became bored and invited Luis Miguel Dominguin, the world's most famous bullfighter, from Spain to stay with her. Howard found out and offered Glen a reward if he could get rid of Luis Miguel. By this time Glen had grown fond of Ava and her friend.

Everything worked beautifully until one night, in the wee hours of the morning, when Ava invited the whole Duke Ellington band home for supper. Luis Miguel was tired of Ava's gambling and angry because she was drinking too much; she'd also lost all her money and they had to go home. When she arrived home with the whole band following, she whipped off one of her shoes and started rubbing the heel down the louvered door, which made a terrible racket. By this time Dominguin was so incensed he got up and smacked her in the jaw, knocking her over the railing and down a half flight of stairs. Glen rushed to Ava, who just lay there, apparently unconscious. He was terrified until she whispered without moving her lips, "Don't move me. I want him to think I'm dead."

Instead of coming down to see if she was hurt, Luis Miguel packed his bag and asked Glen to drive him to the Reno airport; an hour later he was on a plane bound for Spain. Glen was walking to his car when he heard a Dr. Moore, a code name given to Glen by Howard, being paged to the phone.

Howard's voice boomed over the long-distance wire, "Well, you did a damn good job, Glen. You got the S.O.B. out of there." There was a five-hundred-dollar bonus added to his next paycheck.

While I was playing my heart out in Barnesville, a near ghost town of a once-prosperous coal mining city, Ava's and Jean Peter's stay in Lake Tahoe was coming to an end. Glen Brewer said that when Howard made his two appearances in Tahoe he was never alone with either of them.

Glen said that Jean never gave Howard any trouble but Ava was always making waves so he gave her expensive jewelry to appease her. He'd only borrowed it from Tiffany's because he knew when Ava became angry she always threw it back at him or left it behind to show she wanted no part of him or his money. Howard, merrily, then returned it to Tiffany's.

Howard was never in love with Ava, but she was controversial and a challenge; she was always a playmate for him between her marriages and serious romances. Howard told me on more than one occasion, "The younger and more naive the girl, the more they fall in love with me. Lana [Turner], Ava [Gardner], and Rita [Hayworth] are the type who never fall for me. They pretend to; they tell me they love me, and I think they actually try. But it's come to my attention that none of them could make love to me unless they got drunk." His voice tapered off and his mind seemed elsewhere. Then he quietly shook his head. "No, none of them could ever love me."

I was curious because I thought Rita Hayworth the most alluring woman I'd ever seen. "I didn't know you'd gone with Rita," I gasped.

"Now, don't try to trick me. That was long before I knew you. I borrowed a home in Palm Springs and we stayed there for a while."

"Tell me about it," I begged.

"I just told you. For some reason that type of free-spirited woman finds me boring. They all want to get married, though, and they all want to give me a baby. They just like the idea of being Mrs. Howard Hughes. It's not my money; they have no respect for money. None of them. Why, if I married one of them, I'd be dead broke inside of a year." He submerged again deep into his thoughts, and I knew the conversation had come to a close.

Chapter 29

WHILE HOWARD WAS PLAYING IN FLORIDA, I SOMEHOW rehearsed and performed in my play with a limping heart. After the hurricanes hit, we were knee-deep in water and there was no electricity. I had to learn my script by candlelight, and we performed with the battery lights of cars shining on us. In the old tradition, the show had to go on; otherwise no one would have been paid. I couldn't wait to return to the beautiful fall weather of California. Howard was playing the injured party, but I wasn't buying it. I hadn't taken any calls from him since reading about Ava being on his chartered boat; but he was calling Mother, day and night, to try to get her to intercede and convince me that Ava Gardner had never been on the yacht. He even had Howard Strickling, the head of publicity at MGM, call to tell us that Ava was in South America promoting *The Barefoot Contessa* for United Artists at the time she was reported to be with Howard, but I knew if Howard wanted to collect on a favor, he could have called Louis B. Mayer to arrange for the head of MGM's publicity department to alibi for him.

As our plane was taking off, Howard's plane was

landing. Tears were streaming down my cheeks as I saw the familiar plane and visualized him at the controls.

Perhaps I was too exhausted to make rational decisions. The stock tour had been grueling and difficult. Howard Hughes was difficult enough to cope with when I was alert; now I wasn't up to his competitive games. There was no anger, no hurt, no fight left. I decided to accept Robert Evans's and Nicky Hilton's attentions; they never gave me any problems and they showered me with genuine affection. My heart wasn't involved, so they couldn't hurt me. Maybe if I gave them the opportunity they could even help me forget Howard.

I later learned from Howard's aide, Glen Brewer, that while I was seeing Robert Evans and Nicky Hilton, and had refused offer after offer to meet Howard in Florida, he had picked up Jean Peters in Lake Tahoe and flown her to Miami. Three days later he flew Ava from Tahoe to Florida with a stopoff in Los Angeles to see if he could change my mind. He couldn't.

Back in Miami again, Howard was busy interviewing doctors for the medical institute. Jean never gave him any trouble, so he paid little attention to her.

Ava was bored and ready to move on. Howard had promised her he would personally fly her all over South America to promote her new movie. Ava wised up immediately when she learned that neither Howard nor his airplane was licensed for flight in South America, and she took off like a shot for Papa Hemingway's home in Cuba. Howard sent Glen to bring her back, and he had a marvelous time with Ava and the Hemingways. Glen said that Papa stood looking out the window every day while he wrote *The Old Man and the Sea;* after his accident at Kilimanjaro, he always stood up as he typed.

After Glen had things patched up, Howard went to Cuba to pick Ava up and got rid of Ava's maid, Rene, and Glen in one swoop: Glen was left behind to escort Rene and her date to an all-black function that Ava had promised she would attend. After everyone returned to Florida, Glen was commissioned by Howard to escort Ava to the New York premiere of *Barefoot Contessa*. After the premiere, Glen ended up with Ava, Lena Horne, her husband, and a whole band of earringed gypsies at a little restaurant that stayed open all night just for Ava and her gang.

After a week in New York, Glen and Ava found themselves back in Florida. After a few days, Ava grew restless again, so Howard sent her to her sister's house in Palm Springs.

Jean Peters remained in Florida, where her now estranged husband, Stuart Cramer, visited her at Howard's suggestion. It has always seemed rather strange to me that Howard and Stuart became so friendly and that Stuart was working for the CIA at this time. Stuart told me that Jean was going through a difficult period.

Howard abhorred drinking. Rex, the maître d' at the Beverly Hills Hotel, later told me that he had strict orders not to serve Jean any liquor except for a half bottle of champagne on her birthday. Stuart told me that he and Howard had many discussions about Jean because they were both concerned about her welfare. Howard wanted Stuart in Florida with Jean because she had taken a boat way out in the ocean and nearly drowned; he took off for Las Vegas after he knew she was in good hands. Presumably, all he wanted was to see Jean and Stuart happily reunited.

I was back in California and not feeling too well, emotionally or physically. Howard, unknown to me, was planning a picture for Ava Gardner at Twentieth Century-Fox, where I was still under contract. By this time Howard had sold RKO, so he went to Darryl Zanuck and told him he could get Ava to play in a serious version of *Carmen* with Zanuck's help. Ava wanted a million dollars in cash before she'd even consider working for Hughes; Howard readily agreed. He and Zanuck set a meeting at the house Ava was staying in at Palm Springs and took Glen Brewer with them. Howard brought one million dollars in cash, which he carried in an ordinary brown paper bag. He told Glen that he was to sit on the couch all the way across the room from him and hold the money. Howard warned him over and over: "Under no circumstances is Ava to get her hands on that money. When I call you over, you are to show it to her, but I don't want you to say a word."

The meeting began with Darryl, Howard, and Ava sitting on one side of the room and Glen on the opposite side of the room with the million dollars. Howard's intention was to get Ava to sign without ever giving her the money. But Ava was too smart for them. She excused herself to go to the bathroom. After about twenty minutes, Zanuck said, "I wonder what's keeping Ava. Do you think she's fallen in?"

"What do you think, Glen?" Howard asked.

"I heard her little car pull away on the gravel driveway about twenty minutes ago, sir."

"I'll be a son of a bitch! Why the hell didn't you tell me?" Howard asked, bewildered.

"Because you told me ten times, sir, I wasn't to say a single word under any circumstances."

Ava was flying down the road toward Tijuana, Mexico. Meanwhile, back at the house in Palm Springs, the three dummies were left holding the bag.

Ironically, after Ava hired a mariachi band so she could dance all night, Howard had to send Glen down to Tijuana to bail her out. Ava hadn't taken any money with her.

Howard was quite tame by the time he returned to me. And it's a good thing he was, because I'd taken ill and Dr. Mason had admitted me to the Good Samaritan Hospital in Los Angeles for an examination and a rest. Ever caring and, as always, overly concerned, Howard was at my side the day I entered the hospital.

He spared no expense when it came to my medical care. He had to have the best doctors and nurses in the world for me and spent a great deal of time supervising them. I didn't even want him around me, but I didn't have the strength to throw him out, and he was so genuinely worried about my every complaint that I let him stay. Howard was a good listener, but even a better talker. After he heard me out, I had to listen to *him* complain.

Howard was forever complaining about the tremendous pressure on someone in his position. His favorite complaint was that he was being pulled from all different directions at the same time: TWA, Hughes Aircraft, Hughes Tool, movie projects, his operations in progress and *me*. He said we were "making a broken man out of him" or "tearing him apart." I felt that most of the pressure was on Noah Dietrich, but you couldn't say that to Howard. He felt he had to "watch them all like a hawk" or "they" would ruin him.

As I've said before, Howard could talk his way out of anything and make you feel guilty for ever doubting him. He set me to rest about any possibility of Ava's having been in Florida when he was there and convinced me that his sole purpose there was preliminary work on his medical institute. Although I now see how gullible I was, I still believe his reason for being down there was becoming increasingly more significant to him, and to me because I associated the medical institute with having a more normal life with Howard.

To cheer me up, Howard talked about how beautiful our wedding was going to be. In just a few minutes he was able to turn my numb disbelief into excited anticipation. When I wanted to set a date, though, Howard began to ramble on about how far behind he was in his work. He said it would be soon but some important decisions were past their deadline and everyone was breathing down his neck.

I wanted a better answer. "It's all so 'life and death' important because you make it that way, Howard. I'm what's important. Our love is important. Our life together is important. The medical institute is important. You don't need anything else. Why can't you see that? You don't have to work for the money; you've got plenty of that. You said you want to leave everything to medical research, so why not now, Howard? Why don't you sell everything and just concentrate on what's really important—us. I love you, baby. I'm not pushing you into the wedding. You're the one that keeps talking about it and telling me how much you love me. We're already married, but there's got to be a change in the way we live. The way you burden yourself with all this work is making me ill. Can't you see? I want you to be free to do what you want to do, what really means something to you!''

Howard took me in his arms. ''I love you, baby,'' he said. We held each other tightly. It was one of those long warm silent embraces of mutual need. Then I nearly fainted when Howard said he'd ''look into selling the whole works right away.''

A few days later I was released from the hospital. Fox had assigned me to play opposite Fred Astaire and Leslie Caron in *Daddy Long Legs*.

Out of the hospital, I was just about to settle back into my normal routine when Howard called with some startling news.

''I just spoke to Verne,'' Howard announced. ''You're pregnant!''

There was a long silence on the phone. I was too stunned to speak.

''Oh, no, not again! How can I have a baby when most of the world doesn't even know we're married? Look what happened with poor Ingrid Bergman in *Stromboli*. I just hate you, Howard Hughes. I hate you. I hate you!'' I screamed.

''Now don't get yourself excited—''

''Excited! That's easy for you to say. You're not the one who's pregnant,'' I sobbed.

''I thought you'd be happy because now I've put everything aside so we can be married. It's my baby too, you know. Do you think I'd allow another Germany? That hurt me more than it hurt you, but there was nothing I could do. The press thought you were still married to Davis.''

''Oh, Howard, you mean it?'' I exclaimed happily.

''Of course I mean it. I can't leave Las Vegas to come

after you, so I've arranged for John Seymore to pick up you and your family and fly you to McCarran Field tomorrow afternoon. I'll be waiting for you there and we'll fly to Tucson. I've already made the arrangements with Jack and Helen. You'll love the Frys' ranch.''

Mother was as excited as I was. We immediately went off to Beverly Hills to buy me an appropriate trousseau. We ended up at Magnin's, where I think I bought their whole supply of the shortie baby-doll nightgowns that Howard so dearly loved to see me in. I bought a beautiful powder blue Norell suit with bone accessories because I thought the weather would be warm in Arizona.

Daddy gasped at all the clothes when I modeled them for him late that afternoon; he thought I should wait till after the wedding before I started spending money. My father still had his doubts about Howard, though even he admitted this time he appeared sincere.

Nicky Hilton arrived. In all the excitement I had forgotten that I had a date with him that evening. He insisted on taking me to Trader Vic's at the Beverly Hilton Hotel. It was during dinner that I broke the news that I was flying to Arizona to marry Howard the following day. Nicky bravely wished me happiness. He always believed I would eventually marry him; it broke my heart when I watched him drive away that evening. Nicky was one of the best friends I ever had and I loved him dearly.

The following afternoon, Mother, Daddy and I flew to Las Vegas, where Howard, true to his word, was waiting for us. When we stepped off the plane I thought we would all blow away: Nevada was having one of the worst dust storms of its history. Howard, my father, Mother, and I all huddled together to keep from blowing over as we made our way to Howard's plane. He put my parents in the back and buckled me into the copilot's seat. Howard requested instructions for takeoff but was told all planes were grounded until the storm was over; the dust was so heavy we couldn't even see the runway lights. We decided the better part of valor was to spend the night in Las Vegas and try again in the morning. Even my father admitted that Howard couldn't have arranged the storm and it would be foolhardy to try. Howard was willing, but we were not. Howard was accustomed to breaking rules; he always thought rules were for other people, not him. Years earlier he had been told he would never get his flying boat off the water. He was forbidden to even try. While the world press watched, he lifted her off, circled around, and landed.

"Helen, if you think I'm pulling something we'll take off with a flashlight if we have to."

"No, Howard, it's a short flight. We'll be there in plenty of time. I prefer flying in the daytime anyway because I like to see the scenery. I've never been to Tucson."

Howard drove to the Desert Inn, where he checked us in. We went to the main dining room for dinner. Just as Howard's steak arrived, he was called to the telephone. He returned shortly, and I could tell he was angry.

"Why in God's name did you tell Nicky Hilton we were here?" he snapped. "I just got word he's in Las Vegas."

"Now, just wait a minute, Howard Hughes! Don't you go accusing me! How could I have possibly told Nicky I was here when I didn't even know I was going to be here myself? We were supposed to be in Tucson, remember?"

"Well, he's here, and I just hope he doesn't mess up the works. He'll probably make a last-ditch try to marry you. I'll be right back." Howard sped away toward the casino.

We went ahead and ate our dinner. When Howard still hadn't returned, I went into the casino looking for him. Who should I run into but Nicky Hilton. If Howard was mad, Nicky was livid—and drunk.

"If I get my hands on the son of a bitch Hughes, I'll kill him," Nicky roared, clenching his fists.

"Why, Nicky? What's happened?" I asked.

"I'll tell you what's happened. I flew up this afternoon and sat next to Debra Paget's mother on the plane. She told me that Howard has Debra at the Flamingo and she thinks she's going to marry him someday."

My mouth fell open.

"Wait a minute, that's not all. He's had Mitzi Gaynor here all weekend. She's at the Sands, and Jean Peters arrives tomorrow. Just let me get my hands on him. Nobody but nobody's going to hurt you. Nobody! I'll kill the S.O.B. I swear I'm going to kill him," Nicky said.

"Oh, no you're not. I am!"

By this time Mom and Dad were at my side and heard the story. Then . . . talk about timing. Evidently Howard hadn't noticed Nicky, or didn't recognize him, because he came merrily jaunting over big as life and happily announced it was clear for takeoff now.

Nicky announced, "It's Howard who is going to take off . . . right on the end of my foot."

Howard grabbed my hand and started walking toward the hallway off the casino, with Nicky and my parents in hot pursuit.

I was screaming for Howard to let me go as Nicky caught up to us. Nicky had Howard cornered, throwing rapid accusations at him to prove his point to me. Howard stood his ground, tall, straight, and very sure of himself. He appeared unconcerned and his sober eyes looked down on the unsteady defender of my honor.

"You're out of line, Hilton, and whatever your purpose is for this display, it's unwarranted. So calm down, sober up, and keep out of affairs that don't concern you."

Howard started to leave.

"Not so fast!" Nicky grabbed him. "If you want to talk about affairs, you owe Terry the truth. I want you to admit to having those other girls up here."

"This whole scene is ludicrous and I won't be a party to it. Who may or may not be in this town as my guest means little to me at present and should mean nothing to you. Helen and I were en route to be married until you interrupted. Now I suggest you leave."

Nicky started flailing wildly at Howard.

Howard was unshaken and threw up his arms to protect his face. Mom quickly hurled herself in front of Howard while Daddy and I tried to restrain Nicky.

305

Howard hadn't denied a thing. He did have women waiting, I thought. He always has and he always will have. I was furious and hurt. Why? Why? Why did he always have to ruin everything with his deceit?

"She's coming with me," Nicky said, and I did. As my parents and I were leaving with Nicky, Howard's last words were: "If you leave with Hilton, I'll see that you never work for a studio again."

His words were still ringing in my ears as we boarded for Los Angeles, and they haunt me to this day. That was 1954. Almost three decades have gone by without my participating in another feature-length film produced by a studio.

Thank God for Nicky Hilton. He showed me the understanding and kindness of a saint at one of the most catastrophic periods of my life. I thought my whole life was shattered. Nicky knew I was carrying Howard's child and he was willing to marry me and give the child his name.

On my return, Fox immediately put me into dance rehearsals for *Daddy Long Legs* with Fred Astaire, Leslie Caron, and the Roland Petit ballet troupe from France. Physical exercise and stretching are the best things in the world for me when I'm in a low period, so I decided to work out at the barre every day with the ballerinas. Luckily, Susan Zanuck stopped by one day when I was doubled up with cramps and insisted on taking me to her doctor. It turned out I was losing the baby. Even though I was only three months pregnant, the doctor insisted I stay overnight at the hospital.

I called Mother from the hospital to let her know what was happening, and she immediately called Dr. Mason, who had me transferred to Good Samaritan where he could keep careful watch over me. This time it wasn't Howard's flowers that arrived but Howard himself.

I begged Dr. Mason to do anything to save the baby; I felt it was my last tie to Howard. He explained that if the fetus had lived it would have grown into a malformed child; but I was so distressed at the time that I wanted that baby under any conditions. Later, when I was more rational, I realized it was nature's blessing.

When I awoke after losing the baby, Howard was sitting on my bed with tears in his eyes; his lips were trembling and he could barely speak. It was the first time I ever saw him visibly shaken. I believe he wanted that child and I believe he realized it was his last real hold on me. I believe Howard was ready for a more tranquil life and that our baby might have been the push that Howard needed to stop his reckless living.

I didn't know what I wanted. I felt a little empty, a little more numb to the pains of life, and weak in spirit. I was too weak to leave Howard, although I was under constant pressure from everyone to do so. Howard and I were too close. I depended on him too much, and that's the way he wanted it. It would have taken a major effort to break away from him. Staying with him required no effort at all.

I never returned to the workouts with the ballet troupe, but I did make the movie and had the opportunity to play and dance with one of the nicest actors I've ever known, Fred Astaire.

Thank heavens the studio kept me too busy to fall apart. The publicity department worked Bob Wagner and me overtime. I was a *Redbook* cover girl, and we were told we had to attend the *Redbook* awards, a huge party in honor of their editor, Wade Nickols. The party included every top star in Hollywood, so naturally R. J. and I had to be there. There is one thing that will always stand out in my mind about that evening. Mitzi Gaynor and I were both under contract to Fox, but we had never met. Sometime during the course of the evening I got up to go to the ladies' room. I noticed everyone from the press turn their heads and slowly get up; in fact, one columnist, Edyth Gwynn, followed me all the way to the door. I soon found out why: Mitzi Gaynor had gone in shortly before me. We bumped smack dab into each other. We were both unaware that the bathroom door was slightly ajar and eyes were watching our every move.

"Terry?"

"Mitzi?" I said with all the assurance I could muster, but it came out more like a gasp.

"Oh, Terry, I'm so happy to finally meet you. I was too scared to even go to the studio because Howard said you'd beat up on me."

I had to laugh, because Mitzi towered over me. She was adorable.

"I was in Las Vegas the same weekend as you and Debra Paget, but I had no idea either of you were there until I read it in the newspaper. I thought I was the only woman in Howard's life." She stopped to get her breath.

I was shaking my head laughing at the absurdity of it all. "Oh, Mitzi, not you, too. I can't believe it."

"Believe me, it will never happen again. I'm through . . . and I've you to thank for it," she said with real sincerity.

"Me?" I questioned.

"Yes, if it weren't for you I'd still be believing him. Let's have lunch tomorrow. We have so much to talk about, and I'd like to be your friend."

"I'd like to be your friend, too, Mitzi." As we exchanged phone numbers, everyone was running to their typewriters with the scoop.

Mitzi and I did have lunch. She was the smartest of us all: she never saw Howard again.

Faithful to his word, Howard had set the wheels in motion for the sale of his vast holdings. One day in October, a Mormon driver picked me up and drove me to the Beverly Hills Hotel where Howard was waiting for me. Instead of our normal bungalow, he had taken a room on the third floor at the end of the hall. It was dark as I entered the room, but my eyes soon adjusted. The hotel's front entrance could be viewed from the balcony's glass door and Howard stood watching it through a part in the curtain.

"What are you looking at, Howard?"

He motioned for me to sit down. "I've got something to tell you, Helen." He didn't turn to look at me.

308

"What's so important? You know I had a lot of shopping to do today."

"If you hadn't stayed out so late, then you wouldn't have gotten up so late, and you could have done your shopping this morning."

"Is that what you got me up here to tell me?"

"No. This is quite a bit more important than your shopping." He paused for a moment, evidently seeing who or what he wanted to see, then turned toward me with his hands in his pant pockets.

"Helen, I've done it." He showed a slight grin.

"What, Howard? Tell me."

"I've arranged to sell everything."

I flew across the room into his arms. Howard raised me off my feet and kissed me passionately.

"Who? When? Tell me!" I was so excited.

"The Rockefellers. We're having lunch here at the hotel." Then Howard grinned devilishly and picked me up in his arms.

"Only they're having theirs in the dining room and I'm having mine right here." He carried me across the room and laid me on the bed.

"Oh, Howard, never change your menu."

Slowly and ever so gently, he undressed me and melted into my body. We made love with a renewed passion. It seemed as thrilling for him as it did for me the first day he switched the *Constellation* on automatic pilot and carried me to the aft cabin. Each time I thought him spent, he wanted more. Selling his businesses was a tremendous sacrifice; he would be giving up a major part of what made him who he was. He knew the step he was taking was the right one for us and for his dream.

As he made love to me he seemed to be communicating what he was feeling. Although he was fearless in his decisions the uneasiness of this one had been building up inside him. He was venting some of the uneasiness through this intense physicality, and I was enjoying every movement. Howard was in no hurry to make his meeting with

Mr. Rockefeller. What seemed would be an endless ecstasy for both of us was interrupted by the phone. Howard let it ring a long while before making any effort to reach for it; he moved his meeting to some obscure address in a bad section of Los Angeles.

Howard got up and dressed. "Wait here. I won't be gone long."

A few hours later Howard returned to the room. I was on edge to see what kind of mood he would be in after giving up his companies.

He came in shaking his head. "The bastards wouldn't offer me what it's worth and I wasn't about to take a nickel less. I'm just going to have to think of another way."

I was afraid this would be a major postponement of the medical-research facility, although Howard assured me he'd come up with a quick solution.

I've always thought that what one dreams of is an indication of who the person really is. I so wanted Howard to fulfill his dreams. Howard has been accused by his enemies of using the Rockefellers to get an up-to-date assessment of his holdings, but I do not believe that; I know how many sleepless nights he went through and what he was striving for. He truly believed money came to him because he had a mission here on this earth. It was those around him who were to misuse his dreams for their own greed.

Chapter 30

DESPITE MY FEELINGS, MY FAMILY AND CLOSE FRIENDS were utterly disillusioned with Howard. Mother and Daddy resented him terribly after the second Vegas incident. Every time the phone rang or she heard the name Howard or Hughes, it made Mother's blood run cold. She was constantly trying to pull me away from Howard's influence; he had pushed her to the limit of her tolerance. I still loved Howard and depended on him heavily. I had always turned to him when there was a decision to be made. He solved everything from cramps to family crises; no decision was too small for him. I desperately wanted to believe what he repeated to me over and over: that I was special and different and his and he loved me more than anyone in the world. No matter what the people around me told me, I refused to heed their warnings that Howard was destroying me. Their persistent pressure was making it more and more difficult to be with this man I loved, and more and more painful to leave him. I often had to sneak and lie just to spend time with him, and Howard seemed to need me desperately, more deeply than he ever had.

Mother was happy and temporarily relieved when the

United States Air Force called to inform us that I had been voted their most popular actress. Bob Hope had put in a request for me to spend Christmas with him and the troops in Greenland but the air force said no. They offered me my own show, with my own DC-7 and a crew of eleven. They told me I could bring my parents and any entertainers of my choice. I readily accepted their offer to spend Christmas and New Year's entertaining our air force in Iceland, Scotland, the Azores, and Bermuda, even though Howard's sad eyes would haunt me all the way.

I discovered a beautiful brunette at that time who I felt had the potential of becoming a star. Her name was Angie Dickinson and I decided to take her with me. When the tour ended I knew I was right about her; she turned out to be a very special performer. The boys loved us, though neither of us could sing; believe me, no one ever noticed.

The air force show began with twenty-one appearances in fifteen days, covering over fourteen thousand miles, which were soon to be added to by many more. As the miles would burn behind me and the time would race by, Howard and I would grow further and further apart.

I was away from Howard on Christmas and New Year's, but he was on the phone to me. Fred Astaire had sent me a Christmas tree, and so Howard had it set up in his bungalow at the Beverly Hills Hotel. He said he'd leave it up until I returned home so we could have our Christmas together, just he and I, like a family. I was the only family Howard had.

It was 1955 and Mother and I were back in California in January for a brief wardrobe change before embarking on another trip. I had very little time to spend with Howard and I was beginning to believe what everyone was telling me: that I was better off away from him. He tried to act cheerful and make me laugh, but I could see through it to an inner depression. He had been very lonely while I was gone and pleaded with me not to leave again. I loved him, but I was scared; as long as I kept moving, I wasn't aware of it.

Howard's loneliness was rubbing off on me; I was feeling lonely being with him.

It wasn't long before Mother and I were off again. Our first stop was the Sombrero Playhouse in Scottsdale, Arizona, where I starred in *Oh Men, Oh Women*. While I was in Arizona, my old pals the air force checked me out as a jet pilot. I was thrilled to receive my papers because at the time I believe I was the first woman in the world to check out in a jet. Howard was very proud of me.

From there, Mother and I were off to Houston and then to New York City. We caught Morey Amsterdam's show at the Copacabana and then flew down to Florida, where I had a play to do in West Palm Beach. While I was there Howard decided he would fly down to Miami and spend some time on the medical institute and on me. Years later I learned that Jean Peters and Susan Hayward were down there, too, though their stories weren't so happy.

Stuart and Howard were still trying to straighten out Jean's drinking problem and depression. Howard was really concerned by this time; he was finally aware that his reentering her life was having a devastating effect on her. Stuart Cramer finally threw in the towel and said, "She's all yours. All I want is a divorce!" It would be well over a year before Stuart got his wish. Howard did everything he could to delay it.

Another tragic story was unfolding. In late February, Susan Hayward surprisingly agreed to help publicize her new movie, *Untamed*, though not surprisingly only in the Miami area. The studio's motivation for choosing Miami as the site of a premiere of a movie about South Africa and Zulu uprisings was never clear to anyone but Howard and Susan. Howard's scenario was already too complicated even for him by this time. Stuart Cramer and Jean Peters were still in Florida, and now I had arrived. All Howard was interested in was to get the medical institute on the road and to rekindle our marriage; he seemed to instinctively know it was now or never.

313

I stayed with Howard for a very short time in Florida. He got us a cheap hotel room off the beaten path where we could be together peacefully and openly and no one would know us from Adam and Eve. Howard soon got busy, and I became bored and lonely and sick of the shabby environment. We weren't even near the ocean. I had been invited to be Nicky Hilton's guest in Cuba, along with Eddie Arcaro and Rocky "The Champ" Marciano, so I teamed back up with Mother and we went to Havana to have some fun. I thought I was secretive enough about my destination, but Howard had me followed. At first I was angry but there was always that underlying safe feeling knowing Howard was watching over me, and I had nothing to hide or feel guilty or ashamed about. While I was in Cuba Nicky learned that I would be doing a film in England in May, so he invited me to the grand opening of the Istanbul Hilton in June. I accepted. What it represented to me was more travel, more fun, and more forgetting.

After Cuba, it was New Orleans, where Mother and I spent some time with Howard's friends, the Bob Mitchums. They found us hotel accommodations in the French Quarter and introduced us to the Montleone family, who invited us all to spend the weekend with them in Mississippi at their home on the bayou. My feet never touched the ground. Bob's and my picture hit every front page in Louisiana before we even had time to change clothes.

Then we flew back to New York en route to merry old England and a role in an independent film, *Portrait of Allison*. Howard kept up with my every move even though I usually told him where I had been, not where I was going.

Before making my plans to go to Europe I discussed them with Howard to receive his blessing and some assurance of his love and fidelity. Howard, in his ever-overprotective manner, had to call ahead and make sure that everything was on the up and up. The producer, Tony Owen, told Howard he needed me early for wardrobe fittings. Instead, I used my own clothes so I could go off for a lark in Spain.

On the plane, I had met a handsome bullfighter, Juan Posada, whom I hoped to see a lot more of. He didn't speak a word of English and I didn't speak any Spanish—yet. I discovered the greatest way to get along with a man is not to share the same language. Language is definitely a barrier.

Later, he met us at the feria in Seville and brought along a *dueña*, a chaperone, as was the custom in Spain. Howard would have liked that.

We flew to London to shoot *Portrait*. After three weeks of a grueling schedule, Tony Owen surprised me with a week off to attend the Cannes Film Festival because *Beneath the Twelve Mile Reef* was an entry.

The first person I met when I arrived in Cannes was Mike Todd, who asked me to go swimming. I told him the truth: that I hadn't brought a bathing suit with me. In true Mike Todd style, clothes started arriving from all the elite shops on the Riviera. I returned them all and kept refusing his subsequent invitations.

Howard had warned me over and over to stay away from Mike.

"Why Mike Todd's even older than I am." He chuckled. "But his reputation makes me look like a Boy Scout. He's in to Evelyn Keyes for a lot of money. He borrows from everyone and when he makes it again he never remembers to pay back."

"I just can't believe that, Howard." And I told him about the bathing suit incident.

"That's just what I'm talking about. That son of a bitch wouldn't know class if he fell on it."

He felt those remarks had taken care of Todd.

Mike kept calling, and Mother thought I should go out with him once so I wouldn't hurt his feelings. She was afraid his influence could hurt me in the industry.

Our evening started out badly. He insisted on telling me how irresistible he was and how many women were in love with him. He told me Grace Kelly wouldn't stop calling him, but "she was too tall." I doubted this because I had

315

seen Grace with handsome Jean-Pierre Aumont. From the dreamy look in her eyes, if she wasn't in love, she was certainly infatuated.

The following day in Monaco, she met her Prince Charming.

Mike told me he felt I was so good and pure that I was the only woman in all the world that he could sleep all night with and never touch me. He had too much respect for me.

I looked up at that "little dem, dese, and dose man" chewing on the huge cigar, and my heart went out to him. I thought that inside the rough exterior he was really very nice, and I told him so. He seemed so pleased that I actually hurt for him. I thought he must be a lonely, vulnerable man.

We spent the early evening with Sir Alexander Korda, Howard Hawks, Gary Cooper, and other show-business personalities. Later, Mike decided he wanted to gamble. He asked me to come with him to pick up some chips from his room right next to the casino. I waited in the living room while he disappeared into the bedroom. He soon reappeared in his pajamas and told me to get ready for bed.

My mouth literally fell open. "I'm not sleeping with you," I gasped.

Mike looked as startled as I was. "But—but you said earlier it would be very nice. You indicated that you wanted to."

"No! No, I didn't. I said it was very nice you thought so much of me that you could sleep all night without touching me." I hastily left and ran all the way back to the room, where I placed all the blame on poor Mother.

The following morning, Mother woke me at eleven and told me I had to hurry because she'd accepted a date for me to have lunch with Mike Todd, who had said the European royalty attending the festival would be there. Mother didn't understand what had transpired the night before; I was too embarrassed to tell her and it was too late to cancel.

During that elegant luncheon Mike was charming, and it was easy to see why Elizabeth Taylor later fell in love with him. Suddenly, out of the blue, he made a remark that stunned me. It was clearly intended to give the impression I *had* slept with him.

Everything blurred before my eyes. I was so humiliated I lost all control. I heard the other guests gasp as I picked up the butter plate and smeared it all over Mike Todd's face.

Before anyone could move, I was up and running. When I later returned to my hotel, Mother was waiting for me in the lobby. Mike had already told her about the whole incident. He said I was the worst child he'd ever encountered and that after the stunt I had pulled, no one would ever hire me again.

Just as I was about to join Mama Blue in repentant tears over my obvious disgrace, Raphael Hakim, one of those important people who had been present and who had overheard the whole incident, came over to us.

"Don't give it another thought," he laughed. "He can't do a thing to hurt you. As a matter of fact, everyone applauded after you left. They felt he'd had it coming for a long time."

It was a climactic ending to my one and only Cannes Film Festival. Howard phoned me as I was about to board a plane back to England and gave me a fifteen-minute I-told-you-so lecture. He had to hear the incident over and over until we nearly missed our plane back to London. There was no mistaking the amusement in his voice; I think he was relishing every moment what had happened to Mike Todd.

As *Portrait of Allison* drew toward completion, I was invited to attend a command performance by Queen Elizabeth, but my mind was drifting toward returning to Spain and my bullfighter. Suzie Zanuck, who was living in London at this time, warned me that I would live to regret not meeting the queen. Who knows such things at twenty-one? We left on the first plane for Spain.

Spain was even more enchanting on the second visit. We went to the bullfights and I was presented to President Francisco Franco and King Hussein of Jordan. Nearby sat glamorous Ava Gardner and rugged Ernest Hemingway.

But the sun also goes down, and I had to move on. I had

promised Nicky Hilton that I'd attend the grand opening of the Istanbul Hilton.

Mother and I went our separate ways after Spain. She flew back to New York with a puppy hidden in her mink coat that my bullfighter had given me, and I went on to Rome and then to Turkey.

The way I saw Istanbul was even more spectacular than the song that was popular at the time, "Istanbul-Constantinople." Conrad Hilton had his movie stars floating down the Bosphorus onto the longest red carpet I've ever seen that led to the entrance of a castle. Ann Miller, Irene Dunne, Sonja Henie, Joan Crawford, and a host of stars were each individually announced as we drifted down the winding staircase into the grand ballroom.

The following day Howard was on the phone fuming because a photograph had appeared on the front page of a Turkish newspaper that was not befitting Mrs. Howard Hughes. I've had many apologies from the Turkish press over that sneaky incident. I was posing, sitting on the grass, in a high-necked dress with my skirt pulled demurely over my knees. I was being photographed from the side, but one sneaky photographer, hidden in the bushes, took a picture straight on which showed a glimpse of my panties.

On the way back to the United States from Istanbul, the celebrity plane landed in Paris for fuel. Nicky and I and Sonja Henie, the famous movie and ice-skating star, jumped the plane and threw whoever Howard had following me at that time for a loop. Howard's calls stopped coming because he didn't know where I was. I decided to stay and have a little fun. Quite the adventuress, I even split up from Nicky and Sonja and went on with new friends. It wasn't long before I spoke French, dressed French, and completely immersed myself in Paris.

My new friends were all of different nationalities and they each taught me many things about their countries. They gave me new makeup tricks and took me to little out-of-the-way beauty parlors. One day I had the French look, another day an Egyptian appearance, and the next day the look of an Oriental. I was in Magicland, and I loved it. All good things seem to come to an end, though, and suddenly I couldn't return to Howard fast enough. I felt desolate without him. Oh please, dear God, I prayed, help me make it home safely to his arms and let everything be beautiful again, like it used to be.

The only problem was that I had spent all my money and hadn't even saved enough for the plane fare home. It would have been too humiliating for me to call Howard or my parents. I didn't want to hear that I was irresponsible and couldn't stand on my own two feet, so I called Abe Saperstein, who was in Germany with his Harlem Globetrotters. Good old Abe caught the first plane to Paris, packed me under his arm, and carried me home. For the first time I had been completely on my own, but everyone still treated me as though I were a baby.

On my return to the U.S. in July, Howard was busy in California and I was scheduled to do *Starlight, Starbright* at the Westport Theatre in Connecticut for the New York Theatre Guild.

Mother was back home preparing to make a move from a temporary apartment on Miller Drive off the Hollywood Strip to a new house in Coldwater Canyon.

In New York I had met a girl named Gloria Votsis who wrote for the fan magazines; we became close friends. While I was doing the play, Howard would call me every day using the name Charlie Grimes, and every day Gloria would answer the phone.

One day Howard called and I was unable to come to the phone because I'd broken out in a terrible rash and the local doctors didn't know what was causing it. Gloria said Charlie was frantic with worry and was going to fly a specialist in from Germany to see me. Gloria didn't know exactly who Charlie was then, but she figured he was somebody important. Before the specialist arrived, Gloria figured out what was causing the rash. In one scene of the play I walked onstage while wrapping a white fox fur around my neck and shoulders. I did this every night and Gloria noticed that where the fur touched my skin I was affected with the rash. When Mr. Grimes called her for a report on the status of my condition that night, Gloria made him a very happy man; Howard couldn't stand the thought of me suffering physically.

When the play closed I went home to California, and Gloria, who had never been away from her home before, accompanied me. I didn't have a real home to take her to because my parents were in the process of moving, so Howard put us up in the Bel Air Hotel. Of course, she didn't know who was taking care of it.

Southern California is an impossible place to live without a car, so I let Gloria use an old green Chevy that Charlie Grimes always left at my parents' house. It wasn't quite the style she was accustomed to at home, but it was transportation. One time she dented the old thing backing out of the driveway, and Mother and I caused such a commotion that we finally had to tell her that Charlie Grimes was Howard Hughes. I think Gloria (who later married and became Gloria Luchenbill) had a strong suspicion who Mr. Grimes was, especially when she heard that Texas accent.

The unpacking and organizing of moving into the new house seemed to drag on forever. Of course, after being gone on such a long and exciting trip, I had countless California friendships to renew; Howard was making me feel guilty for abandoning him all summer and was demanding my affections on his time schedule, and on top of everything else I had a film waiting, an independent production called *Shack Out On 101*. I had top billing and was the only woman; Frank Lovejoy, Lee Marvin, and Keenan Wynn also starred. I was made a producer and owned a percentage.

Our shooting schedule was only ten days long, so we had to work extralong hours. My beach scenes had Mother and me on location before dawn. Even though it was August, the early mornings were cold and windy.

320

In the hustle and bustle of the film, I had forgotten Mother's birthday. Afraid of upsetting any applecarts, she let it pass unmentioned. I felt so badly when I remembered, that I arranged a party on the set and told Howard a white lie about her birthdate so he would surprise her with a gift. It turned out to be a memorable birthday for Mother.

Chapter 31

In 1955, I was sitting in the Lanai Room of the Beverly Hills Hotel with one of my girlfriends, Yvonne Lohn. My mind was filled with memories of my recent trip through Spain. I still loved Howard, but our relationship was rapidly deteriorating. I no longer trusted him nor could I endure the whiplashes of remembering his previous betrayals.

Yvonne sat facing John Wayne and she proceeded to describe how devastatingly handsome his companion was. Soon our waiter handed me a note which simply read, "I'd like you to meet my good friend from Panama, Gene McGrath. Duke."

Within a few moments, Mr. McGrath was seated at our table. Gene was one of the most exhilarating and attractive men I had met, but I'd already had enough excitement for three lifetimes. My first impression was that I was being introduced to a con man. Perhaps I was being unfair, because I had no basis for my observation except his rapid speech. I added little to the conversation, but I did end up giving him my phone number even though I had no intention of going out with him.

I wasn't to see Gene for two weeks because he left that day for parts unknown, but from that moment he started a whirlwind courtship. Flowers and phone messages arrived from all over the world. Gene McGrath was hot on my trail, and nothing, nobody, not even Howard Hughes, was going to discourage him.

His charm and methods of wooing a girl were so like Howard's that at first I thought Howard was putting him up to it to keep me away from Nicky Hilton. My traveling in Cuba, Europe, and the Middle East with Nicky had really shaken Howard up, but when he caught wind of the mystery man after my heart, he began interrogating me with a jealous bite, as if it were a personal offense against him. His attitude angered me and I refused to even give out Gene's name.

Gene McGrath owned the Panama Insurance Company, which in turn owned shrimp boats, a coffee plantation, a flour mill, and more. He was the only private individual ever given an oil concession in Venezuela. McGrath, who had been awarded a Silver Star for his service in the U.S. Navy during World War II and attended the Georgetown School of Foreign Service, was sworn into the CIA because of his close personal and business ties to Central and South American leaders. He seemed like a good match for Howard but I didn't want to start anything between them.

I was still under contract to Twentieth Century-Fox and was being sent to several states to plug my latest movie, *Daddy Long Legs*. When I arrived in New York, two beautiful flower arrangements were in my suite. I could hardly wait to rip open the cards to find that one was from Gene and the other from Robert Evans.

Bob and I had dated each other since we were in our teens. At this time, Bob and his brother, Charles, jointly owned Evan-Picone, a manufacturer of well-tailored and expensive sport clothes. Bob always kept my wardrobe well stocked with handsome slacks and blouses. He later became an actor, the head of Paramount Studios, and the husband of four beautiful actresses, including Ali MacGraw.

Bob and I had a wonderful three days together dining at the finest restaurants and catching the latest Broadway shows. He was the perfect escort: always attentive, impeccably mannered, and stylishly dressed.

Howard phoned me daily, often several times a day. Each conversation was the same: Why was I mistreating him? Why was I cheating on him? Why was I allowing my mother and *parties unknown* to take me from him? Why couldn't I see that I was being railroaded out of his life? He'd never love anyone but me, and I'd never love anyone but him.

It became monotonous and depressing. I wanted to have fun. All I could think about as Howard repeated himself over and over was how many times he'd cheated on me and lied to me and the countless hours of pain and tears he'd caused me. I wasn't going to cry or fall for his sentimentality and go running back to him. Mother was right there with me, helping me to be strong, encouraging me to have fun and not let Howard use up my youth and ruin my life.

After my three-day whirlwind in New York (where I managed to do newspaper and television interviews and talk to Gene daily) I flew to Houston, Texas, where the same routine started all over again. This time, Gene flew in and whisked Mother and me off to his homes in Caracas, Venezuela, and in Panama.

At the airport we were waved through customs. There stood a handsome, distraught-looking Clark Gable, who had been held up for eight hours trying to get through customs. Gene helped him through in a matter of minutes, and he was extremely grateful. He was one of the last of the real he-men, I thought as we waved good-bye.

My knees were still weak from our encounter with Gable when we were met with a car equipped with sirens and machine guns which sped us into Caracas in record time. In Venezuela, the people were not allowed to use car horns, so when we went barreling down the street with horns blasting and sirens screaming, cars literally jumped off the roads to make way. Their newspapers, unlike ours, were not allowed to say anything derogatory about me. Their periodicals described me as the exquisite ballerina, *la bella* Terry Moore. There weren't enough superlatives to describe me. I couldn't believe what I was reading.

Once Gene had settled Mother and me in the beautiful Tomanaco Hotel, he sent an expensive gift to our room for every minute we were late. Each gift had a note attached: "You are now ten minutes late. You are now eleven minutes late," and so on.

That evening we attended a ball for President Marcos Pérez Jiménez and his lovely wife. Afterward they presented Mother and me with beautiful gold and pearl brooches.

I was the belle of the ball that night in the solid bugle-beaded dress that I had worn in Las Vegas. I wore my long blond hair streaming in waves down my back and no jewelry. I was in my element because South Americans love the three Bs: blondes, blue eyes, and big breasts.

We were famished by 11:00 P.M., the Venezuelan dinner hour. The cuisine was prepared by the finest Italian chefs, and we became lost in a deluge of delicacies and wines, none of which went untried. It seemed like an exquisite dream. I was quite certain that at the stroke of midnight I would turn into a pumpkin.

Gene held me tightly in his arms as the music swirled around us and would allow me to dance with no other man except the president. I was intoxicated with the joy of the evening. I was the fairy princess, actually living out my own fantasies, while my size-four feet seemed to float over the shimmering floor.

On our departure, they even held up the plane an hour and a half when we were late. Gene exhibited powers with Pan Am almost equal to Howard's with TWA.

The three of us whirled on to Panama, the permanent residence of the impermanent Mr. McGrath. The same royal treatment started anew: meeting the president of

Panama and all his eminent friends and associates, sightseeing, shopping, parties, and swimming and sunning at the El Panama Hotel.

There were romantic evenings under the stars when Gene held me close in his arms after the festivities had subsided. It was one of these star-fested magical nights when Eugene McGrath asked me to become his wife. I told him I needed more time to think it over and get to know him better.

Gene was an entrepreneur and knew all the ways to please a woman. In charm, intelligence and aggressive energy, Gene McGrath resembled Howard Hughes. He was younger and better looking, but, like Howard, he had a complete understanding of the value of power and money.

He was also a great lover, as I learned on one particularly romantic night in Panama. He led me to his music room and played me the symphonies of the ages. I felt my body melt under his touch while my head whirled with the intoxicating music. All my inhibitions and thoughts of Howard were swept away by his expertise in each and every part of the female body. I believed, at that moment, if I ever made love to another man I could never return to Howard. Every fiber of my being wanted this stranger. I wanted all of him . . . now. As our bodies discovered each other, I gasped, "The answer is yes. Yes, I'll marry you."

Afterward, I was paralyzed by fright. In my mind I was and would always be married only to Howard. But here was a man who could give me one thing I wanted most in all the world: children. Howard had had a vasectomy after the loss of our second child. He was now completely married to his idea of the medical institute and he didn't even want his own child to have a claim. I wanted children, but I was a coward: I was willing to risk bigamy rather than stand up with the courage that Ingrid Bergman displayed when she had children out of wedlock.

Our love affair was as much between Panama and me as between Gene and me. I liked everything about the country, the weather, and the people. I loved the Indian shops, the native dishes and the variety of fresh fish. I had another two-week-long vacation.

Mother and I returned to Los Angeles alone, and Gene followed a week or so later. A marvelous surprise awaited me: the award for the most promising newcomer of the year as a result of *Daddy Long Legs*. Imagine, I had starred in over twenty films in fifteen years, and I was being picked as a newcomer.

The award was really a good joke on Darryl Zanuck. He had put me in a supporting role as a punishment for the Korean fiasco. He had been upset by the unfavorable publicity for fear it might reflect on my home studio, Twentieth Century-Fox, and my independence infuriated him.

Marilyn Monroe refused to do *Pink Tights* but her costar, Frank Sinatra, said he'd like to do it with me. *Time* magazine wanted me for a cover story but decided to hold it until Zanuck made a move. He made none.

I suddenly remembered the threat Howard had made about my career when I walked away with Nicky Hilton. Was he keeping his promise?

Gene flew in from South America and I met him at the airport and buried him with my hugs and kisses. Our eyes devoured each other, and people all around us watched us happily.

"Did you mean it when you said you'd marry me, Mrs. McGrath?"

The "Mrs. McGrath" did it. It had the most beautiful ring I had ever heard and breathlessly I gasped. "Yes, yes, yes, of course I meant it."

I clung to him all the way to the car.

When we returned to my parents' new home, tucked into the side of Coldwater Canyon on a lovely little street called Noel, there was a houseful of people waiting for us. We had one of the first parties of the Christmas season. Walt Disney, Conrad Hilton and Nicky, Sidney Chaplin, John

Wayne, Joan Collins, Barry Sullivan, and a host of others were guests.

John Wayne hated to go to parties, but once there, he had more fun than anybody and he was usually the last to leave. He and his wife Pilar stayed late, and we confided our plans to be married and asked them to stand up with us. Duke had introduced us, and I hoped our marriage would be as happy as theirs.

I remember calling Gene Cutie Pie that night. Duke picked up on it and really gave Gene the raspberry. He started calling him Cutie Pie this and Cutie Pie that. Pilar merely turned to Duke and said, "Okay, Poopie Pie, let's go home."

Then Gene had his fun. Duke had the greatest sense of humor when it came to laughing at himself. He was my idea of pure masculinity. I was terrified at the thought of marrying again while I was still married to Howard, but somehow it seemed all right if Duke approved. In real life, John Wayne was bigger than any of the heroes he played; he and Howard were the only two men I really looked up to.

Howard pulled every ploy he knew to keep me from marrying Gene. His friends came to me one by one in his behalf. There were Walter Kane, Greg Bautzer, Pat DiCicco, and the employees who loved him and cared. They all told me the same story: that I was the only woman Howard ever loved, that he couldn't live without me.

My guard was doubled and detectives followed in droves wherever I went.

Gene was staying at the Beverly Hills Hotel. We stopped by his room one afternoon, and all of a sudden Gene exploded in outrage. He said someone had been through his room, though I could see no visible signs of it. He hurried to his briefcase; upon opening and examining it he became furious and exclaimed that Howard Hughes had been through his briefcase. I didn't get a peek at what was inside, but it must have been important because Gene never went anywhere without it and its contents always remained a secret, even to me. I did think it a little odd that Gene didn't call the police that day.

Flowers started arriving by the truckload, with messages like "Remember the measuring worm, don't forget our little brown owl and the alligator love call." He even sent me an owl pin of diamonds, sapphires, and rubies. I refused all his phone calls.

I got off one lovely parting shot at Howard the day before I was married. Gene and I were lunching at the Polo Lounge of the Beverly Hills Hotel. Rex, the maître d', told me that Howard had a tiny blonde living at the hotel who looked just like me. In fact, Rex had to deliver her food in half an hour and Howard was supposed to join her for dessert.

I quickly excused myself and went to a house phone. In my best Miss Nadine Henley voice, I said, "Hello, this is Mr. Howard Hughes's secretary, Miss Henley. I'm calling for Mr. Hughes. He wants you to be sure to smother Miss——'s steak with onions and garlic."

Then I went into great detail as to how the garlic was to be squeezed and the onion chopped so they'd have no suspicions. I repeated it over and over. Only one man in the world had such a penchant for details, and they knew it.

After my ten-minute dissertation on how to cook steak, I returned to our table with an enormous grin on my face. It was so wide it tickled my ears, and Gene kept wondering why I burst out in laughter every once in a while. I could hardly contain myself, but I told no one.

A few hours later, I was paged to the phone. It was Howard and this time *he* was laughing. If a woman smelled of onion or garlic, Howard *never* went near her for at least a month, and usually never again.

While I laughed, I cried silently. Somehow I knew I would never see him again.

He loved my one-upmanship, my mischievous pranks, and took them as meaning I still loved him and would come back.

He was right about the first part.

New Year's Eve 1955, the night before I married Gene, Howard called me.

"How can you marry this guy? You know you're still married to me and you know I'll always love you. This won't work any more than your marriage to Davis did. Your religion and your sense of decency are too deeply ingrained in you. You'll never feel good about yourself, and you don't even know anything about this guy."

"I know enough," I said. "He's kind and romantic and generous and handsome. People like him, and he's fun to be with. He's a war hero and respected by our government as well as other countries. I know enough, and there's nothing you can say that will change my mind."

"Please, Helen. I want you to reconsider this step you're taking. I know things about this guy. He's using you, and you're crawling right into his web."

"What do you know?" I snapped.

"Well, for one thing, he's tied up in something big, big and dirty. It looks like he's hooked up with a group that is out to get everything I've got, and you're part of their plan somehow."

"Howard, don't be ridiculous! I met him through John Wayne. Duke says he's the smartest man he knows."

"Hell's bells, Duke's as big a patsy as you," he exploded.

I thought that Howard was certainly becoming a more creative liar. It was so ridiculous that I terminated the conversation feeling sorry for him.

I had wanted a beautiful wedding, with all of my friends present. However, Gene's business in Central America was pressing him and he decided it must be on New Year's Day. Wilbur Clarke of the Desert Inn in Las Vegas was to make the arrangements.

I don't recall why, but Gene decided our marriage should be kept secret for a while. At the time, I thought it probably had something to do with my career or letting his family get used to the idea. Neither of us would ever really feel married, because he was a divorced Catholic and I a devout Mormon who still felt married to Howard.

Again, as with Howard, my life with Gene was cloaked in secrecy. New Year's Day started out ominously. We missed our plane and were late for our own wedding. I had wanted Duke and Pilar Wayne to go with us, but the only one allowed to know besides my family was Wilbur Clarke. He had even arranged for a Las Vegas city councilman to hold our license and not send it to the county courthouse until later so the press wouldn't get wind of our marriage until Gene was ready.

Wilbur was terribly nervous when we arrived, knowing that Gene wanted secrecy. He had Eddie Fisher and Debbie Reynolds, also newlyweds, as houseguests and had to keep our nuptials from them. I'm sure they wondered why we were herded off the moment we arrived.

I became Mrs. Eugene McGrath in one of those little Las Vegas chapels that all look alike.

The three years that followed were like a madcap dream and are unquestionably the most exciting years of my life.

In one year, we traveled over three hundred sixty-five thousand air miles. When I sat down at the dinner table, I would automatically reach for my seat belt. We had homes in Beverly Hills and Panama, and penthouse apartments in New York and Venezuela. We had racehorses and a yacht. I had clothes strewn all over the world so I could travel lightly. Gene bought me fabulous gifts: jewels, furs, clothes with matching accessories, and one of the first new Cadillac El Dorados.

I often thought that the precious briefcase that always traveled with him might be full of money, though I never knew it to be a fact. When we'd come into Beverly Hills from Panama, he'd drop me at my parents', charter a small plane, and make a quick round trip to Las Vegas, always leaving and returning with the briefcase. He never offered any information about his business in Vegas, and my parents and I never asked him about it.

He was a perfectionist and got upset if even my lipstick

331

was a little crooked. I had to carry a fresh change of clothes along so I was never wrinkled. I could never understand how he knew photographers would be waiting no matter what time of the day or night we arrived. Years later, I found out that he had always called ahead to alert them, and can't help but wonder if I wasn't the front for some worldwide operation he was conducting. Wherever we went I was the attraction and object of attention, giving him the perfect faithful-proud-husband-of-star excuse to travel.

He made me put every minute to good use. I had to make a list of everyone I should call with the phone number alongside to save time later. If he didn't feel someone could do me any good, he or she was crossed out. He would schedule just how many magazine layouts I should do and for whom. He completely organized me and equipped me with leather bound books from Mark Cross for every occasion. He even instructed me whom to be cordial to, what to say and when to say it. We would synchronize our watches before we went out to dinner with businesss associates, and then at a certain moment I had to say something that would lead him into saying whatever it was that he wanted said.

Gene's training turned me into the perfect hostess and taught me to entertain and handle almost any situation. Presidents of Central and South American countries were his friends and partners in business. I had the opportunity to know many of them and travel in their countries.

While we were living in Panama, the Central Intelligence Agency of the United States government came to see us and swore me to secrecy. I had to promise never to reveal my services for the agency while Juan Perón was alive. He was a fugitive from Argentina, living next door to us in both Panama and in Venezuela.

Bebe Rebozo was a very good friend of Gene's. After I also became his friend, he told me of his friendship with Joan Dixon, a Florida beauty who had gone to Hollywood to pursue a career. She was seen by Howard and subsequently was set up in a house with servants and bodyguard in the typical Hughes pattern. Of course, she had a contract with Hughes Productions.

Bebe was not favorably disposed toward the enigma called Howard and wanted to know if Joan was happy. I learned from the Mormon boys that she was content; she was ambitious to be an actress-singer and the situation was to her liking. From time to time I checked on Joan's progress and kept Bebe informed of Joan's life, for which he was grateful.

Once, when I mentioned to Bebe that I didn't have a godfather, he said he would like to be my godparent, which he became in 1956. Bebe would speak of his good friend Richard Nixon, who was then vice-president under President Eisenhower. He told us that Mr. Nixon would one day be president.

The cloak-and-dagger side of my new husband began a rapid increase in our third year together. Gene was spending more and more time away from me. I often suspected his secret-agent persona included the trail of beauties associated with 007 and others of his ilk.

Our extravagant marriage came to an end when I decided I had finally had enough. I consulted the bishop of my church and obtained a quick Panamanian divorce before the end of 1958, in order to survive. It broke my heart, and I never saw Eugene McGrath again. *C'est la vie*.

Chapter 32

Nineteen fifty-six is a year plagued with mysteries, pieces to the puzzle that would spell the destruction of Howard Robard Hughes.

"I am capable of accomplishing so much more," Howard once told me, "if these morons who are employed under me could just keep the crap cleared out of my way. There seems to be a new obstacle every minute. It's one crisis after another that Bill Gay or someone down the line has created or failed to solve, and the whole damn thing always ends up right on my back. I've lived my life for the advancement of my country. It's just ludicrous that every time I turn around, some goddamned government agency I've never even heard of is inventing some new tax or regulation that stops the progress of my organization. How can they be so blatantly stupid and fail to understand that they are stifling advancement? I've had the same problem as long as I remember, since I was a child."

I know Howard could and would have accomplished a great deal more in his life if his executioners hadn't built prison walls between the man and his goals.

One of his favorite childhood stories was of the time he lived in Houston, Texas, and owned a tricycle. His family had a straight driveway that had to be backed out of, but the little boy next door, who also had a tricycle, had a circular driveway and could pedal around and around. Howard yearned for a round driveway so he'd never have to stop or back up. He pleaded with his parents to build one, but they wouldn't listen. I believe this story of not being able to make the circle symbolized his feeling of unfulfillment, incompleteness. I believe Howard achieved completeness in flying, and in 1938 he finally got his circular flyway around the globe. Howard was only truly happy at the controls of an airplane where he was close to God and there were no restrictions, nothing to bind him. But in 1956 his wings were being clipped.

It was now that a major power struggle for control of the Hughes empire began from the inside; Howard was too strong, too sharp, and much too unpredictable for an outside business takeover to succeed. One by one everyone close enough to him who cared enough and had any influence was cut off from direct communication with Howard.

In January 1963, I ran into Dr. Verne Mason, who invited me to have lunch. He confided that he had talked to Howard the year before but that he had sounded ill and confused on the telephone.

"He isn't himself, and I don't think he ever will be again. I don't think this is *his* doing. He isn't running things now; he's being run."

"He's being run. . . . He's being run." These words stuck in my mind for the next seven years. They seemed to explain so much; the newspaper stories claiming the now eccentric billionare was being moved from city to city, state to state and finally country to country; nobody even claiming to have direct contact with the man, not even the friends who went back to his earliest days, the friends that I know he used to spend many hours on the phone with. There were even rumors that his alleged wife, Jean Peters, never saw him. The newspapers were now calling my Howard a recluse. A recluse! Can you imagine that?

This was not the Howard that I knew. This was not the

335

Howard that I spent so many good times with, so many frustrating times with, so many loving times with. Howard was not one to be run; Howard was the one who did the running. This wasn't *my* Howard that I was reading about.

I had an ominous feeling that Howard was being run to his grave.

In the middle of the night of March 7, 1970, the phone rang. It must have rung seven or eight times before I finally forced my hand to reach for it.

"Hello."

"Hello, Helen."

"What? Who?"

"Hello, Helen?"

My body started to tremble, and I felt the adrenaline rushing inside of me. In an instant every fiber of my body was fully alert. I was now more awake than any other time of my life.

"Howard?" I was almost too afraid to ask.

"Yes, baby, it's me."

The tears started to well up in my eyes. My throat went dry and I started sobbing uncontrollably. "Howard, Howard, is it really you?"

On the other end of the line I heard a "Yonk."

There was a click on the line. Howard was gone. I'll never know if we were cut off or if he hung up.

Though I cried myself to sleep, I felt an inner comfort and warmth in the understanding that Howard hadn't forgotten me. Wherever he was and whatever was happening, he still cared.

On January 7, 1972, Howard Hughes had his famous telephone news conference in answer to the Clifford Irving book scandal. Howard chose my birthday for the interview. I felt he was trying to tell me something.

In June of 1972, Perry Leiber, Summa's public relations man, told me that Howard was well and getting ready to fly again. I rejoiced in this news, hoping the impossible was possible, and reported this on "The Merv Griffin Show" in

August 1972, a show dedicated to Howard: but Howard didn't come out of seclusion.

In September of 1973, I went to London to try to see Howard. I made repeated efforts to gain access to the Hughes suites on the ninth floor of the Inn on the Park. All the approaches were blocked by people I had never seen. With a small group of friends, I succeeded in having the elevator stop at his floor but we were promptly thrown out. Even so I hoped that maybe the news of this attempt to get through to Howard would somehow reach him.

In April of 1975, I wrote Howard the following letter. Roy Crawford, one of the boys that I liked, tried to get the letter through for me.

April 6, 1975

Dear Howard,

I am now the same age as you were when we met. It enables me to look back and understand many things I was incapable of knowing then. You were absolutely right when you told me I'd never find what we had together again. I have loved you consciously and unconsciously my whole life. My only regret is we've spent all these years apart.

You always said we were alike. I don't put much credence in astrology but we even have similar horoscopes.

I feel you raised me and the only marriage I've ever believed in is ours—and I know now I'd like to spend the rest of my life with you.

By now we both realize how short a lifetime really is, I'd like to share eternity with you. It's too lengthy to explain my meaning in this letter so please ask one of the Mormon boys around you about eternal marriage. It can even be done posthumously.

Oh, Howard, I've had to fight it so hard alone. Romantics like us with a lot of imagination will always be called crazy. I've had my own flying boats through the years, but like you I swear I'll get it off the ground.

*How many times I've wished I could talk with you
and have the benefit of your advice.*

*I always knew it would be my love that would outlast
everyone else's.*

> *All my love,*
> *Helen*

Roy returned my letter, unopened, with this note.

> P. O. Box 2500
> Encino, CA 91316
> September 30, 1975

Ms. Helen Koford
Los Angeles, CA 90049

Dear Helen:

I have not talked with Johnny Holmes about this but
mailed it to him with a note of explanation. I sent
another note when you requested that it be returned
to you in case it had not been delivered, so I am
returning it to you without its being opened.

I do not know the reasons why Johnny would not make
the delivery, but I am sure it was a matter of judge-
ment on his part. I'm sorry I could not accomplish it.

> Best regards,
>
> *Roy*

RC:kn

Attachment

In 1976, while Howard was in the Bahamas, two FBI men came to see me. None of us knew if Howard was alive. It was impossible to get through to him.

I told them I was leaving to make a movie in the Bahamas. The FBI promised to put me in touch with the Bahamian head of security, who would help me in my efforts to see Howard.

The day before I left Los Angeles, I called Johnny Holmes, the longtime Hughes aide who had refused to give Howard my letter. His wife said, "Johnny is on his way to Mexico. I just got back from the Bahamas today. He stayed with the boss."

On April 5, 1976, I was in Kentucky visiting friends. It was there that I received the news that I had been dreading all my life. Howard was dead!

In an instant all the wonderful times Howard and I spent together flashed through my mind.

Overcome with a grief that could only have a special meaning to me, I went to my room by myself and with a shaking hand and tear-soaked eyes I wrote the following:

The Wise Brown Owl

You gave me a wise brown owl to wrap around my heart,
You said it would protect me whenever we're apart;
You took me in your arms and promised to be loyal,
For you said we had something you didn't want to spoil.
Then I watched your tall, rangy body as you walked away
And climbed into your plane for the last time that clear April
* day.*
You threw me a kiss and waved a fond farewell;
When I would see you again, only time could tell.
No matter how many messages I would ever send
Once you disappeared, they said I'd never see you again.
Even though it's years since we've been apart,
My love is still raging in my heart.
Oh, now I know that you could never never die,
Because I still hear your plane circling in our sky.
I just wait for the day God gives you permission to land.

I know the first thing you'll do is kiss my trembling hand.
Then you'll take me in your arms and put me in your plane,
And I'll copilot beside you to the place from where you came.
Then our plane will spread its wings like an eagle and bid the
    world goodbye,
And we'll climb to the edge of heaven, higher and higher into
    the sky.
We'll float toward forever, where all is peaceful and still,
Leaving behind the people still hunting for the will.
At last we're together flying among the stars.
When I looked out the window, we were gliding by Mars.
We flew past the pale blue moon and headed for the sun.
Our love was victorious, we had won, we had won!
At last we were free to love and just be . . . together.
Then Howard pulled out the throttle while we continued to
rise,
Laughing at the world behind us with its gray smoggy skies.
       Howard be thy name!

Epilogue

IT IS NOW EIGHT YEARS SINCE MY BELOVED DIED. WHILE
the living, breathing, physical body of Howard Hughes
died, his spirit lives on. His will for life lives; his love lives;
his love for me lives.

I now understand why this book had to be written. I was
in Lexington, Kentucky, on May 5, 1976, when several
hours after awakening, I remembered that I had dreamt
about Howard during the night. I was entering our bedroom
in bungalow nineteen at the Beverly Hills Hotel from an
outside entrance. Howard was lying in bed with a uniformed guard at his side. The moment Howard saw me, he
sat up and swung his long legs over the side of the bed,
smiling warmly at me. As he rose from the bed, I could see

341

another Howard sitting in exactly the same position. But this Howard, though he was also smiling, was transparent, ghostlike. As the two Howards reached out their hands and encouraged me to come to them, the dream faded.

My good friend and famous author, psychic Jess Stern interpreted the dream for me. He told me the double Howards represented Howard leaving his earthly body to rise up healed and whole again. "You are loved by both the earthly and the spiritual Howard. His spirit is with you and protecting you."

I never would have been able to bear the loneliness or had the patience to write this book if I had not believed that Howard wanted it to be written. I have sometimes felt that he pushed me to the typewriter; at times I thought the keys traveled faster than my fingers. Sometimes I would relate a particular conversation and felt Howard saying, "No, I said such and such." Then I would remember correctly; Howard was always right.

Now I have been legally recognized as Mrs. Howard Hughes and my career is flourishing again. Along with Joanne Toadvine and others, I have founded Help Them Walk Again, an organization that aids victims of spinal and brain trauma. We have opened our first clinic in Las Vegas, Nevada, and will continue to grow until all those condemned to wheelchairs can throw them away and walk again. I am beginning to realize Howard's lifelong dream.

How do I feel . . . ? Grateful.

Thank you, Mom. Thank you, Jerry. Thank you, Mr. Lazar. Thank you, Howard, for our years together and a love that has survived death and time.

Thank you, God.

Amen.